IN MY MOTHER'S WOMB

IN MY MOTHER'S WOMB
The Catholic Church's Defense of Natural Life

Donald DeMarco

TRINITY COMMUNICATIONS
MANASSAS, VIRGINIA

© Trinity Communications 1987

ISBN   0-937495-15-8, paper
          0-937495-17-4, cloth

Cover design by Jeanette O'Connor,
featuring Raphael's *The Holy Family*.

To Fr. Alphonse de Valk, C.S.B.
a priest for life

I am grateful to Malcolm Muggeridge and William May for their personal encouragement, intellectual inspiration, and Christian example; and for graciously introducing the reader to the ensuing defense of the Church's teaching on natural life.

May 9, 1987
St. Gregory Nazianzen
Bishop, Confessor, and Doctor

Acknowledgements

The chapters of this book have appeared in a variety of periodicals. I wish to thank the editors of these periodicals for permitting their re-appearance, though in variously revised and updated forms, in the present volume.

Part I

1. *Homiletic & Pastoral Review*, July and August-September 1984.
2. *Faith & Reason*, Vol. XI, Nos. 3, 4, 1985.
3. *Homiletic & Pastoral Review*, January 1986.
4. *The Human Life Review*, Fall, 1982.
5. *Life Ethics Centre*, St. Joseph's Univ. College, Univ. of Alberta, 1982.
6. *Fidelity* (206 Marquette Ave., South Bend, IN 46617), August 1984.
7. *Social Justice Review*, May-June, 1987.

Part II

1. *Linacre*, August 1987.
2. *Conrad Grebel Review*, Winter 1984.
3. *Homiletic & Pastoral Review*, November 1983.
4. *The Human Life Review*, Fall 1983.
5. *Faith & Reason*, Vol. X, No. 1, 1984.
6. *International Review of Natural Family Planning*, Spring 1985.
7. *Fidelity*, April 1987.

"Him whom the heavens cannot contain, the womb of one woman bore. She ruled our Ruler; she carried Him in Whom we are; she gave milk to our Bread."

St. Augustine

TABLE OF CONTENTS

Preface	*xiii*
Foreword	*xvii*
Introduction	*1*
PART I	*5*
1. Abortion and Church Teaching	*7*
2. Abortion and Language	*26*
3. Abortion and the Unborn	*46*
4. Abortion and the Family	*55*
5. Abortion and Contraception	*67*
6. Abortion and Bio-engineering	*82*
7. Abortion and Compassion	*89*
PART II	*101*
1. Bioethics and Church Teaching	*103*
2. Bioethics and Theology	*112*
3. Genetic Engineering	*122*
4. Fetal Experimentation	*131*
5. In Vitro Fertilization	*143*
6. Sex-Preselection	*160*
7. Surrogate Motherhood	*173*
Conclusion: Technologized Parenthood	*183*
Appendix: Vatican Instruction on Life in its Origin	*205*
Index	*229*

Preface

I learned from Mother Teresa the difference between a materialistic society seeking to acquire wealth and power in order to "raise the standard of living" for materialistic purposes, and her insistence on thinking of all life as sacred. So you have the "sanctity of life," on the one hand, and what is called the "quality of life," on the other. But of these two concepts, that which is central and the one on which depends our civilization, religion and everything that is wonderful in the record of Western Civilization, is the "sanctity of life."

When I went out to Calcutta with a camera crew and a producer to make a program about Mother Teresa I walked with her through the clinic into which babies are brought who have been picked up in dustbins and other unlikely places, yet the clinic rightly boasts that they have never refused a baby. I said to Mother Teresa, purely to carry on a conversation for television, "But Mother Teresa, everybody seems to think that there are too many people in India. Is it really worthwhile going on with all this trouble to bring up a few more?" She did not say anything, but she picked up one of these babies, and it was the tiniest baby I have ever seen, absolutely minute! Holding it up and with a look of extraordinary exultation she proclaimed, "Look, there's life in her!" Here at last, I thought, we know what the sacredness of life is.

There is one other episode with Mother Teresa that I want to mention. Like so many things she did, this episode had a vague theme of comedy in it. It happened in Canada, in Toronto. She was put on a program with a French geneticist, Jacques Monod, to discuss his attitude toward life, which was that the whole of our destiny is written in our genes (g-e-n-e-s, if you don't mind, not j-e-a-n-s; it is rather important to keep that distinction clear). Mother Teresa simply sat in the set apparently bending her head in meditation. She was in fact praying, which is what she always does when there seems nothing better to be done. Finally, the host of the show turned to her and said, "Mother Teresa, have you nothing to say?" She looked up from her prayers and simply said, "I believe in love and compassion," and resumed her prayers, and that was that. What was interesting is that, as Dr. Jacques Monod was leaving the studio, he was heard to say, "If I see much more of that woman, I shall be in very bad trouble." And I know perfectly well what sort of trouble he would have been in! So much for that diversion.

I did, as a matter of fact, think I ought to have a look at the famous oath that doctors used to take when they became doctors, the Hippocratic Oath. I had noticed that no one seems to be taking it now, and when I read it, I could understand why. These are two of the essential features of the oath that physicians all used to swear: "I will give no deadly medicine to anyone if asked, nor suggest any such command, and in like manner, I will not give a woman a pessary to produce abortion." Well, obviously, as I read it I realized that it was no good going on with that.

In the field of transplant surgery there is another problem: the growing traffic in organs. Putting them on the market is becoming an extraordinarily lucrative occupation. There was a newspaper report recently telling us that you could get a lot of dollars for a kidney in good condition. That is going to be a very big trade and, furthermore, of course, you could carry it further and go in for mass commerce of various parts of the body.

There is, no doubt, a big demand for organs for transplantation, but to an old fellow like me, it all has an unsavory feeling about it: you are taking from cadavers or from living human beings, organs they are prepared to get rid of, or, as is tragically the case, from people in the world who are so poor, so without the necessities of life, that they are prepared to offer their own organs for sale in order to be able to satisfy themselves in other directions. Now to me, at any rate, this is a sort of very sad thing. One cannot actually nail down why it seems horrible that a kidney should be sold for a large sum of money, or that there are people so desperately in need of kidneys that they are prepared to pay large sums for them, but to me these contracts have something very creepy and unpleasant about them. This may be just prejudice, and it may be that when I have departed this world, which will be quite soon, and had some rest in a better place (I hope), I shall see that it's all to the good. But I feel in my bones that there is something terrible in it.

We are in danger, it seems to me, of losing the respect for the dead which has prevailed through the centuries, not just of Christendom but of other civilizations as well. The practice has been to cover dead bodies respectfully, recognizing that, with the departure of the soul, the remainder is just a carcass to be disposed of by burial or cremation. Now, however, there is the possibility of financial deals with dead bodies; the cadaver has come to have a market value, leaving no place for requiems, prayers, or mourning with kidneys, hearts, eyeballs and other such items up for sale.

You can speak of strict controls, but when it comes to the point in matters of this kind, controls go by the board. When the abortion Bill was being canvassed, the argument all the time was, "Of course we don't want people to have abortions, of course we're going to have the best possible means of dealing with that, but it must be available for us." And yet, within a matter of months or even weeks, those who had brought in the Bill were complaining that they had no idea it would result in the current absolute holocaust. At the present moment, it is believed with reason that in England a human fetus is being disposed of every three minutes. These things are happening, and they are happening not because those concerned in the mechanism of the Bill are heartless or brutal, but because it places us on a slippery slope. In the case of abortion, one can see that, once you accept its validity, then the slippery slope works. So, in the end, you finish up with the strange, and, I think, terrifying situation which you have today of abortion being done incessantly, on the one hand, and of underage children being encouraged to receive contraceptives, on the other.

All these things, which will be in the history books, are marking the total decadence, the breakdown, of what is called Western Civilization. I believe that the people who are working even in the field of transplantation, in the most respectful way, and believing that what they are doing is good, should think very carefully about what the consequences of that sort of thing can be if it gets out of control.

I want to conclude my remarks with just a few words about myself. I have reached the stage in life when any kind of thought of being ambitious or wanting to distinguish myself or something like that is all a thing of the past. You are living in the shadow of death, which is not a bad shadow at all. I have found this and I thought I would like to tell you just because it might perhaps mean something to you as you grow older.

The feeling you have as you approach this inevitable end is not one of sadness or despair. It is one which has in it a considerable joy. Perhaps I can explain it better if I give a sort of image of it. You wake up in the middle of the night, perhaps at about three o'clock in the morning, and you wonder whether you are really in your body. You look beneath the blankets and there is this shriveled old body, but you are not there. Somehow or other this is a splendid thing! This makes you realize as never before what a marvelous privilege, what a terrific thing it is, to have been born into this world, to have lived out your life with its infinite mistakes and sins and all sorts of things in it, and then to come to this realization that at the end it is not just curtains! All that is most wonderful because it seems to burgeon. Grandchildren, however mischievous they may be, have a sort of halo about them because they represent life continuing, and not quality of life. Not, "Has he been a success or failure? Is he rich or poor? Is he stupid or clever?" Nothing of that. Not even, "Is he a mongoloid or non-mongoloid?" but he has *life*.

My life is moving towards its close, but that is not the end. What the end is who can say? Or what, specifically, does it matter? In that mood at the end of a life, you have as never before, a sense of how beautiful it is to have been privileged to live. How enchanting it is to have had loving relationships with your fellow human beings. How even joyful it is to have had a command of language and to have found in that use of words a special joy and satisfaction which perhaps even partakes of that most wonderful of all sentences: "In the beginning was the Word . . . and the Word was made flesh and dwelt amongst us, full of grace and truth."

Malcolm Muggeridge

Foreword

Strong loves unite the parts of this intelligent and important book. There is first the love that Professor DeMarco has for the Church. He loves the Church because he believes that it is the light of the world and the guardian of precious truths about the meaning of human existence. Thus he is mightily concerned, throughout the volume, to present the teaching of the Church in all its depth and richness and at the same time to combat vigorously the grotesque distortions of Church teaching so frequently popularized today, particularly in the abortion controversy. He wants the teaching of the Church to be known for what it is, a liberating message of the wondrous, awesome dignity of human beings, of the destiny to which they are summoned, of the mission that has been given them. The positive, liberating character of the Church's teaching is set forth throughout the book, but in particular the chapter devoted to the positive quality of the Church's teaching on bioethics develops this theme, and does so magnificently.

A second strong love manifested in this volume is a love for human beings. DeMarco views human beings as the Church does, namely, as beings made in the image and likeness of God and summoned to a life of union with Him. In addition, with the Church, his love is for the integral human being of flesh and blood. That is, his love is for each individual man and woman, boy and girl, boy-baby and girl-baby (whether born or preborn), not for an abstract humanity. Each individual human being is, precisely by reason of being a human being to begin with, a being of transcendent and surpassing dignity. For the human being is the kind of being that God Himself became and is. God could not become incarnate in a dog or cat or chimp, because in creating these animals He did not make them inwardly receptive of the divine. But He could and did become incarnate as a human being, and He could become so because He had made the human being the sort of being inwardly capable of receiving a share in His own life. This sublime truth about human persons is the central theme of many chapters.

In developing the truth about human beings, DeMarco also provides devastating critiques of the reductionist philosophies of our day, including the pseudo-personalism that equates the personal with what is consciously experienced. On this view, human beings in whom the capacity consciously to experience interpersonal relations has not yet developed are not regarded as persons—nor are those in whom this capacity has been irretrievably damaged. DeMarco is superb in showing the superficial shallowness of this phenomenalistic view of human existence. Likewise incisive are his criticisms of the Promethean view of human beings, with its rejection of God and of objective moral norms. DeMarco clearly unveils the materialistic, deterministic, and dehumanizing presuppositions of this philosophy of human existence and exposes it for the sham that it is.

A final love revealed in this book is DeMarco's love for language and for truth. With realistic philosophers of all ages and with the Church he regards words as insights into reality. As such, they can fulfill their proper function only when they are subordinated to and measured by the things they name. But words, DeMarco shows, can be debased and abused, manipulated and devalued. When this happens, reality itself is distorted and a proper grasp of the truth is made most difficult. The devaluing, devitalizing, and debasing of language has, in our day, been most eloquently revealed in the abortion controversy. Thus several chapters in this remarkable volume show, in detail, how language has been twisted to serve ideological ends in talking about abortion, control over conception, and relieving the human estate. The humanity of unborn human life has been denied and concealed by talk about "fetal tissue," "products of conception," etc., while the ugliness of fornication and adultery has been masked by talk about "creative interpersonal relationships," "creative adultery," etc.

Reverence for the word of God entrusted to His Church, reverence for the "created words" that human beings are, created words that God's Uncreated Word became and is, and reverence for the words human beings use to communicate truth to one another are the hallmarks of this important work. Readers will find it well written, urbane and erudite. But above all, they will find it a work of an intelligent Catholic layman who loves his faith and is gifted with uncommon wisdom and the ability to express it in a way that everyone can grasp. It is a pleasure to recommend it warmly.

William E. May
Professor of Moral Theology
The Catholic University of America
August 12, 1986

Introduction

"One of the most ominous features of the present epoch," wrote Dietrich von Hildebrand, "is undoubtedly the dethronement of truth." Yet truth is so elementary and ultimate that its conscious denial is as self-contradictory as the actions of a man who thanks God every morning for making him an atheist. But an age that rejects truth is one that deprives itself of the awareness it needs even to realize that it is engulfed in darkness. Ours is not a philosophical age. Truth, nonetheless, is irredeemably stubborn and is affirmed even when it is denied, for even the most hardened sceptic believes his scepticism to be true.

Truth is immensely unfashionable in our time and anyone who makes any claim to truth is judged guilty of unpardonable arrogance. Nonetheless, truth provides the most natural way of avoiding arrogance. It is truth, not private opinion, convenience, or force, that is the ultimate arbiter of disputes. And it is truth, not the desire to avoid arrogance, that allows discussion to proceed independently of any taint of egoism. St. Thomas Aquinas, with characteristic simplicity and directness, explains why this is so: "The human intellect is measured by things so that man's thought is not true on its own account but is called true in virtue of its conformity with things." Therefore, the man who has grasped the truth about anything has a good reason for remaining humble, because the truth of his thought is determined by how well it conforms to something outside of himself. Man cannot take credit for the truth he is privileged to know. What truth he knows should inspire in him a deep-felt sense of gratitude.

The Church is a protector of truth. In this regard, she is faithful to the Gospel message. "The Spirit is the Truth," exclaims John the Evangelist (1 John 5:6), and "We are of the Truth" (1 John 3:19). St. Paul adds that God "desires all men to be saved and to come to the knowledge of the Truth (1 Tim. 2:4) and St. James writes: "Of his own he

1

brought us forth by the word of truth (James 1:18).

At the same time, the Church is divinely commissioned to love. Truth has to do with ideas and the reality attained through them. Love has to do with persons. Love for persons and fidelity to truth are not only compatible, but they need each other. The deeper one's love is, the more he is bound to speak what he holds to be true. If a man truly loves his neighbor, it is painful for him to see him deprived of truth. "No greater joy can I have that this, to hear that my children follow the truth" (3 John 4). Truth and love do not exclude one another any more than do mind and heart; for when we love, we admire with the heart, and when we admire, we love with the mind.

It has been said that tact is a way of making a point without making an enemy. The Church has a far more formidable task in proclaiming truth—unpalatable as that truth may appear to some people—while expressing love. This requires something much rarer than tact; it requires wisdom, courage, and patience.

The Church counsels us to be patient with sinners, tolerant with unbelievers, compassionate toward the poor, and forgiving to our enemies. But she also asks us to be faithful to the truth. As Pope John Paul II said to an international prolife audience in Rome:

> What is needed is the courage to speak the truth clearly, candidly, and boldly, but never with hatred or disrespect for persons. We must be firmly convinced that the truth sets people free (John 8:32). It is not our own persuasive argument or personal eloquence, however helpful these may be, but the truth itself, which is the primary source of freedom and justice.

In today's complex, technological world, there is much confusion concerning bioethical issues. Even within the Church, many people in leadership positions reflect a fundamental inappreciation of both the Church's competence to teach and the wisdom of her message. They often try to resolve complicated life issues in terms of "compassion" or "conscience." Compassion, however, is seldom, if ever, the dividing line for moral disagreements. It is erroneous, as well as unjust, to believe that pro-abortion advocates, for example, have compassion and their pro-life counterparts do not. Compassion may express love, but it does not provide light. And love is more effectively expressed when one is better enlightened. Neither is "conscience" alone an adequate substitute for truth. Many people form their conscience by the Media, or on ignorance or misinformation. Conscience may excuse a person of moral culpability, but it offers no assurance that an action consistent with conscience is objectively correct or practically helpful. In this context, the words of Mahatma Gandhi are worth citing: "It is because we have, at the present moment, everyone claiming the right of conscience without going through any discipline whatsoever that there is so much untruth being delivered to a bewildered world."

Those Catholics who openly dissent from Church teaching and proclaim that truth is somehow incompatible with "compassion" and "conscience," fail to understand how the Church embraces all three. Thus, "exclusion" becomes the cause of division within the Church, and even of heresy. As a consequence, we find bitter disagreement and widespread confusion within a Church that should be offering a unified hope and a healing light to all mankind. And much of this turmoil and confusion springs from a rejection of truth. Examples abound: A Catholic college publishes a journal which promotes abortion in the name of "compassion." Contraception is commonly taught *merely* as a matter of "conscience;" the chairman of a Catholic University's theology department teaches that contraception is a "moral imperative." The Austrian bishops approve *in vitro* fertilization for married couples. A Philadelphia Catholic newspaper sees nothing wrong with IVF apart from masturbation and abortion. A Canadian priest, sponsored by the bishops, delacres that IVF is a valid treatment of infertility for married people. A Catholic nun proposes at a teachers' convention an apostolate of female religious who would serve as surrogate mothers for infertile women. Another Catholic nun appears on the Phil Donahue Show to promote abortion, and dismisses the unborn child as merely a "mass."

If the intellect is in darkness, it is not long before the whole body is plunged into darkness. "If your eye is worthless, your whole body will be in darkness" (Matt. 6:23; Luke 11:34). The Catholics who oppose Church teaching act out a kind of Galileo trial in reverse. The Church, confident that the mind can know truth, encourages man to use the resources fetology places at his disposal to determine the nature of the fetus; to use sociological data to analyze the concomitant increases of contraception and abortion; to use his medical knowledge to examine the adverse effects on human subjects of IVF, fetal experimentation, and other modes of bio-engineering. But the dissident will not look! He prefers to believe that "looking" is a waste of time since his "conscience" and "compassion" are all the enlightenment he needs. He then accuses the Church of being presumptuous, arrogant, and out of step with the modern times. But the Church gently advises him again—to look.

"Man's unhappiness," wrote Carlyle, "comes of his greatness: it is because there is an Infinite in him, which with all his cunning he cannot quite bury under the Finite." The Infinite in man is the image of God. The Church knows this and has proclaimed it clearly and forcefully throughout her history. It is a truth, but it is also that point which marks the clearest and most dramatic intersection of truth and love. The Church declares that every human life contains something of the divine. Consequently, no matter how weak and humble, however disadvantaged or socially outcast, every human life is worthy of love. In his Exhortation on the family (*Familiaris Consortio*), the Pope eloquently expresses the Church's mind on this matter when he writes:

> The Church firmly believes that human life, even if weak and suffering, is always a splendid gift of God's goodness. Against the pessimism and selfishness which cast a shadow over the world, the Church stands for life: in each human life she sees the splendor of that 'Yes,' that 'Amen,' who is Christ Himself. To the 'No' which assails and afflicts the world, she replies with this living 'Yes,' thus defending the human person and the world from all who plot against and harm life.

PART I

Abortion and Church Teaching

A carefully developed, historically accurate treatment of the Roman Catholic Church's teaching on abortion is valid and desirable in its own right, that is, for scholarly reasons alone. The moral teaching of the Church throughout history on abortion is obviously pertinent to the Church historian, the moral theologian, and the Catholic philosopher. The manner in which the current abortion debate is being conducted, however, provides an additional reason for such a treatment. Pro-abortion polemicists, after having sought to identify the anti-abortion movement with the Catholic Church, have now attempted to discredit Church authority by arguing that its teaching on abortion has been, throughout history, inconsistent, self-contradictory, unscientific, and politically inspired.

Two rather salient facts make it apparent that the anti-abortion movement is not identifiable with the Catholic Church: 1) the presence of hundreds of thousands of non-Catholic individuals who actively oppose abortion, together with the existence of many anti-abortion groups who are affiliated with non-Catholic agencies and institutions; 2) the fact that the underlying reasons for the Catholic Church's condemnation of abortion are philosophical and humanitarian, based on the right to life of innocent human beings, and therefore are not peculiarly Catholic.

The assertion that Catholic Church teaching throughout history on abortion is confused and inconsistent is historically indefensible. The historical record shows beyond any doubt that the Church's teaching, namely that abortion is a grave moral evil, has been *clear, emphatic,* and *unwavering*. Therefore, an historically accurate treatment of the Church's teaching on abortion shows that the pro-abortionist's claims against the Church are without foundation. At the same time, such a treatment shows the Church to be not only a reliable and consistent teaching authority on the subject of abortion, but also a compassionate and balanced one, fully sensitive to the rights of everyone involved—including the pregnant woman—and deeply aware of abortion's psychological and social implications. It is with these considerations in mind that the following presentation has been prepared.

The Church's teaching that direct, induced abortion is always a grave evil has been clear, emphatic, and unwavering. Nonetheless, surrounding this core of consistent teaching, and entirely extrinsic to it, have been other matters that people have often confused with Church teaching. It is important, therefore, to distinguish between what is and what is not Church teaching.

The first distinction to be made is between moral law (as conceived in the Catholic tradition) and canonical penalty. Whereas the Church's moral law has always classified every destruction of the unborn as gravely sinful, its canonical penalties have varied throughout history and were sometimes modified either by the cultural attitudes and scientific opinions of the day, or because of their lack of effectiveness. Rev. R. J. Huser's careful study of the development of canon law with regard to abortion provides extensive amplification of this point.[1] In 1588, for example, Pope Sixtus V tried to discourage abortion by issuing severe penalties, such as reserving absolution from excommunication for all those who procured abortions to the Holy See. A few years of experience showed that the severity of this penalty was not only ineffective, but occasioned much spiritual harm inasmuch as it discouraged people from going to confession. Accordingly, in 1591, Pope Gregory XIV rescinded some of the harsher penalties of his predecessor and returned absolution to the local ordinary.[2]

Canon law does not determine the morality of abortion. It always assumes this and proceeds to determine how the Church, as a community, should deal with members who are guilty of abortion. The very fact that there have always been canonical penalties for abortion is a reflection of the Church's position that abortion is a grave evil; for canon law never prescribes penalties for venial sins—prayers and good works

---

[1]Roger J. Huser, *The Crime of Abortion in Canon Law* (Washington D.C.: Catholic University Press, 1942)."The Church has always held in regard to the morality of abortion that it is a serious sin to destroy a foetus at any stage of development. However, as a *juridical norm* in the determination of penalties against abortion, the Church at various times did accept the distinction between a *formed* and a *non-formed*, an *animated* and a *non-animated* foetus." Preliminary Note.

[2]Lucius Farraris, *Bibliotheca iuridica moralis theologica* (Roma: 1885) I, 36-38.

have always been regarded as sufficient for their remission.

A second distinction separates official Church teaching from the expressed opinions of individual ecclesiastical writers. The Church may consider various opinions without adopting them as her official teaching. For example, in 1679 a decree of the Holy Office, under the authority of Innocent XI, condemned the positions of two important writers of that century: Thomas Sanchez and Joannis Marcus. Sanchez, a Jesuit theologian, held that abortion is lawful if the fetus is not yet animated when the intention is to prevent a girl, detected as pregnant, from being killed or defamed. Marcus, the Proto-physician of Bohemia, claimed that the fetus lacks a rational soul until birth.[3]

If Church teaching is to remain clear and consistent, it is necessary to exclude confusing and contradictory opinions. At the same time, if Church teaching is to develop, it is necessary that there be research and debate. No one familiar with the development of the Church's teaching on abortion throughout history could fail to recognize that it is indeed clear and consistent and has, in fact, developed in an atmosphere of meticulous research and lively debate.

A third important distinction divides essential Church teaching on abortion from the prevailing opinions of contemporary scientists. This distinction is of particular historical importance with regard to the question of ensoulment. But this question, concerning the age or stage of the fetus when the rational soul in infused, was always extrinsic to the church's fundamental teaching that abortion is a grave evil. The ensoulment (or animation) question never deflected the Church from her contention that abortion is always a grave evil. Thus, scholar John A. Hardon, S.J. can write:

> The exact time when the fetus becomes 'animated' has no practical significance as far as the morality of abortion is concerned. By any theory of 'animation,' abortion is gravely wrong. Why so? Because every direct abortion is a sin of murder by intent. It is, to say the least, probable that every developing fetus is a human being. To deliberately kill what is probably human is murder.[4]

John Connery, S. J., who spent several years carefully researching the Roman Catholic Church's treatment of abortion in history, comes to the same conclusion:

---

[3]Denzinger-Schoenmetzer, *Enchiridion symbolorum* (Rome: Herder, 1965), 2134-2135.

[4]John A. Hardon, S.J., "A Catholic View," *The Human Life Review*, Fall 1975, p. 46.

Whatever one would want to hold about the time of animation, or when the fetus became a human being in the strict sense of the term, abortion from the time of conception was considered wrong, and the time of animation was never looked upon as a moral dividing line between permissible and immoral abortion.[5]

Given these three important distinctions, it becomes easier to understand how the Church's teaching on the immorality of abortion remained constant throughout its history. A constant teaching prevailed despite the fact that it was accompanied by a variety of extrinsic factors that did change: canonical penalties, the opinions of individual ecclesiastical writers, and the speculations of contemporary scientists. There is consensus on this point by all scholars who have studiously investigated the Church's teaching on abortion. Some representative examples:

Germain Grisez writes:

The Roman Catholic tradition is marked by clear, consistent, comprehensive, and firm teaching against abortion in general.[6]

According to John Hardon, S. J.:

On the level of morality, Roman Catholicism has always held that the direct attack on an unborn fetus, at any time after conception, is a grave sin. The history of this teaching has been consistent and continuous, beginning with the earliest times and up to the present.[7]

Finally, in the words of scholar David Granfield:

To summarize, throughout its history, the Catholic Church has resolutely opposed the practice of abortion. From the first recorded condemnation in ecclesiastical writings in the *Didache* . . . to the most authoritative recent pronouncements . . . we find no authoritative deviation from the doctrine that abortion, at any stage, is a serious sin against God, the Creator of all human life.[8]

One of the key sources of the ensoulment or animation debate, which proved to have a long and controversial history, is a most im-

---

[5]John Connery, S. J., *Abortion: The Development of the Roman Catholic Perspective* (Chicago: Loyola University Press, 1977), p. 304.

[6]Germain Grisez, *Abortion: the Myths, the Realities, and the Arguments* (New York: Corpus Books, 1970), p. 165.

[7]Hardon, p. 93.

[8]David Granfield, *The Abortion Decision* (Garden City, N.Y.: Doubleday, 1971), p. 66.

probable one—the Septuagint translation of a passage in Exodus. The Septuagint is the Greek translation of the Old Testament, made in the third century before Christ. Ptolemy II of Egypt is supposed to have brought seventy (or seventy-two) scholars to Alexandria, and in seventy (or seventy-two) days they are supposed to have completed the translation from Hebrew to Greek.

The passage in Exodus (21:22-25), an ordinance of Moses, prescribes the appropriate punishment for causing an accidental miscarriage. The Hebrew text clearly states that a man who causes a miscarriage must pay a fine if the woman does not die, but if the woman dies, he must be put to death according to the more general law: "Whoever strikes another so that he dies, must be put to death" (Exodus 21:12).

But an incorrect translation (intended or untended) in the Septuagint version gives a totally different meaning to this Mosaic Law. The word "zurah" or "surah," which means "form," is erroneously used for the word "ason," which means "harm."[9] Thus, the Septuagint version conveys the meaning of the fetus "not being further formed" rather than the woman "not being further harmed." The penalty, therefore, was now understood to be a fine if the fetus was not formed, but death if the fetus was formed. Thus, through a mistranslation by Hebrew scholars who were conversant with Greek thought, the distinction between the "formed" and "unformed" or "pre-formed" fetus was given moral significance and Biblical authority. Hebrew thought had never divided man into body and soul. The notion that the fetus could be unformed was more compatible with contemporary Greek thought which had already believed that human life begins at some stage in fetal development when "ensoulment" or "animation" takes place. Aristotle had identified this time of animation with observable movement and believed it differed according to sex:

> In the case of male children the first movement usually occurs on the right-hand side of the womb and about the fortieth day, but if the child be a female then on the left-hand side and about the ninetieth day.[10]

---

[9]*Ibid.*, p. 44. It is likely that the Septuagint translators deliberately introduced a variant translation because it was more in agreement with current practice in their own community or with their own conception of justice. See Immanuel Jakobovits, *Jewish Medical Ethics* (New York: Bloch Publishing Co., 1959). See also Sidney Jellicoe, *The Septuagint and Modern Study* (London: Oxford at the Clarendon Press, 1968).

[10]Aristotle, "History of Animals," *The Works of Aristotle, Vol. II* (Chicago: Encyclopedia Britannica, 1952), Bk. 7, Ch. 3, 583b, p. 109. Felinus Sandaeus of Ferrara (d. 1503) calculated that animation took place on the for-

This erroneous statement of fact, with its curious numerical pinpointing of the time of animation for male and female, was to have a long life in biological and legal circles. The authority of Aristotle, which was based on his genius for observation and systematic thought, influenced the uncritical acceptance of this error.

The Septuagint mistranslation of the Exodus passage had allowed Greek thinking in biological matters to gain a theological respectability it did not deserve. Nonetheless, this thinking, involving the distinction between the pre-formed and formed fetus, provided the basis for a lively debate that continued for several centuries. In one sense the Septuagint text provides a strong argument against abortion by implying that killing a fetus already formed—which would exact the death penalty for the assailant—is equivalent to homicide. At the same time, it provides a basis for the claim that aborting a fetus not yet formed is neither immoral or unlawful.

Tertullian (240 A.D.) is the first Christian to use the distinction between the pre-formed and formed fetus in the early Christian era. Cyril of Alexandria (d. 444), commenting on the Septuagint text from Exodus, states that the fetus does not belong to the human species until after forty days, that is, until it is formed. Theodoret (c. 393-457), Bishop of Cyrus (near Antioch), also following the Septuagint text, reasoned that God did not infuse the human soul until the body was formed. Accordingly, he taught that Moses had decreed that abortion of a formed fetus is homicide, but it is not homicide if the fetus is not formed.[11]

Augustine, in his commentary on the Septuagint passage, argues that the Mosaic Law did not want to treat the accidental abortion of an unformed fetus as homicide. Nonetheless, Augustine speculates that in some way the unformed fetus might be animated, that is, human, even before it is fully formed or recognizably human.[12] In another context, Augustine conjectures that all who have begun life will rise again, even those who have not been "formed."

Early Christian writers consistently classified abortion as a grave evil even though they did not uniformly agree that all abortion (particularly of the unformed fetus) is equivalent to homicide. St. Basil the Great, however (374-5), found the distinction between formed and unformed too subtle to be morally relevant:

---

tieth day for the female and on the eightieth day for the male fetus.

[11]Migne, "Quaestiones in Exodum," *Patrologia Graeca*, 48, 80: 271-74.

[12]Augustine, "Quaestionum in Heptateuchum," ii, 80; *Patrologia Latina*, XXXIV, 626.

> A woman who deliberately destroys a fetus is answerable for murder. And any fine distinction as to its being completely formed or unformed is not admissible among us.[13]

The notion that the fetus passed through distinct stages of formation was used as a basis for determining private penances during the following centuries. The Penitential of Theodore, Archbishop of Canterbury (668-690), for example, exacts a penance of one year or less if the aborted fetus has not yet reached forty days of development, but three years after that time.[14] The Old Irish Penitential (c. 800) required three and one-half years of penance if a conceptus is aborted, seven if it is "formed," and fourteen if the "soul" has entered.[15]

The first time the distinction between the formed and unformed fetus became legally operative in Church history is in Gratian's *Decretum* of 1140. This monumental work is the first fully systematic attempt to compile ecclesiastical legislation and earned Gratian the name "Father of the Science of Canon Law." Basing his position on writers such as Ivo of Chartres, Augustine, and Jerome, Gratian states: "He is not a murderer who brings about abortion before the soul is in the body."[16] He did not, however, indicate when the fetus is formed.

The Decretals of Pope Gregory IX in 1234, which formally legislated for the whole Church, sustained Gratian's distinction concerning the formed and unformed fetus, though in an ambiguous fashion. Commentators on the *Decretals* drew the conclusion that while all abortion is gravely sinful, the abortion of an unformed fetus should be considered as quasi-murder, that is, murder in some qualified sense.

The distinction between the formed and unformed fetus (animated and unanimated), though recognized and accepted by many jurists, philosophers, and theologians, was used only for purposes of classification and distinguishing penalties. The first person in the Christian tradition to suggest that the distinction might be used as a basis to justify abortion in special cases is a Dominican, John of Naples (c. 1450). In an unpublished work, the *Quodlibeta*, John argues that a doctor may and should give the mother an abortifacient medicine if it is necessary to save her life, provided he is certain that the fetus is not

---

[13]St. Basil the Great, "Three Canonical Letters," *Loeb Classical Library*, III, 20-23.

[14]*Medieval Handbooks of Penance*, transl. J. T. McNeill and Helena Gamer (New York: Columbia University Press, 1938), p. 197.

[15]*Ibid.*, p. 166.

[16]Gratian, *Concordia discordantium canonum*, Decretum, Ad. c8, C. XXXII, q. 2.

animated. This opinion was brought to light by another Dominican, Antoninus, Archbishop of Florence.[17] Discussion of this exception occupied the attention of theologians for the next three or four centuries, until theories of delayed animation—on which it was based—became obsolete.

The exception introduced for discussion by John of Naples met with considerable opposition, although it did claim some followers, particularly the Jesuit theologian Thomas Sanchez. Sanchez' argumentation to justify abortion in certain instances (and when it was determined that ensoulment had not yet taken place) was eventually condemned in 1679 by Pope Innocent XI. A French Jesuit, Theophile Raynaud (1582-1663) was the first author to argue in favor of aborting an animated fetus to save the mother's life. Raynaud's position was unique for his time and had no adherents for the next two centuries.

In the seventeenth century, two scientists—Thomas Fienus and Paolo Zacchia—who rejected the Aristotelian theory of delayed animation, made important historical contributions that led ultimately to the Church's abandoning the speculation that there is such a thing as an unanimated (or non-human) fetus.

Fienus, a professor of medicine at Louvain, published a bio-medical treatise in 1620 on the formation of the fetus (*De formatrice fetus liber*). He concluded that the soul is infused on the third day. The Aristotelian notion of a succession of souls or "functions" of one soul (first vegetative, then sentient, and finally rational) made no sense to him. He developed nine lines of argumentation to support his thesis. In general, Fienus argues that the soul must be present at the beginning in order to organize the body. Moreover, in order to avoid an unnecessary multiplicity of explanatory factors, there must be one soul from the beginning that establishes the specific unity and individual continuity of the developing embryo.[18]

Concerning the Septuagint passage in Exodus, Fienus stated that it does not oblige one to believe that the unformed fetus has no rational soul, but only that it is an incomplete man. He also points out that the Latin (Vulgate) text, which is authoritative in the Church, makes no distinction between the formed and unformed fetus. St. Jerome had translated the Bible into Latin directly from Hebrew and therefore avoided the erroneous Septuagint version of the celebrated Exodus

---

[17]See Connery, pp. 114-116. Some authors have questioned whether John of Naples really advocated induced abortion or merely allowed treatment aimed at curing some maternal ailment.

[18]Thomas Fienus (Feynes), *De formatrice fetus liber* (Antwerp: 1620), pp. 157-181.

passage.

Zacchia, physician general of the Vatican state, published a book, also in the year 1620 (*Quaestiones medico-legales*), in which he argues a position remarkably similar to that of Fienus. He concludes that the rational soul is created and infused at conception. He also maintains that the development of the fetus is a continuum, rather than a series of distinct stages. Like Fienus, he reasons that the soul must always organize the body if development is to be determined from within.[19]

Concerning the Septuagint passage, Zacchia argues that it is commentary and not inspired text. The dichotomy between animated and non-animated fetuses, he contended, is maintained by lawyers because they want to distinguish the punishments for abortion. Besides, early pregnancy is an uncertain fact and the law takes the less strict possibility.

In 1644, Pope Innocent X conferred upon Paolo Zacchia the title of "General Proto-Physician of the Entire Roman Ecclesiastical State."

The rejection of the theory of delayed animation by these two scientists was met with considerable opposition. Nonetheless, the reasonableness of their arguments—which received added confirmation from the scientific research of Harvey, who discovered the circulation of the blood, Gassendi, DeGraaf, and others—gradually found acceptance. By the end of the seventeenth century important theologians such as Caramuel of Prague and the Spanish Jesuit, Juan Cardenas, found the distinction between the animated and unanimated fetus to be of no practical significance. Cardenas argued that abortion to save the life of the mother is impermissible if there is any reason to suspect the presence of a rational soul. But, Cardenas added, this suspicion is always present. It took another century, however, before immediate animation was generally accepted.

In 1869, Pope Pius IX officially removed the distinction between the animated and unanimated fetus from the penal legislation of the Church. This was, of course, disciplinary and in no way involved Church teaching on abortion.[20] Henceforward, every direct killing of human life after conception would be treated in the same way, that is, the penalty of excommunication applied to all abortions.

The *Code of Canon Law* promulgated in 1917 states that all who procure abortion ("not excepting the mother") incur an automatic excommunication.[21] It further advises that all aborted fetuses, if delivered

---

[19]Paolo Zacchia, *Quaestiones medico-legales* (Lyons: 1701), lib. 6, tit. 1, qu. 7, 16.

[20]*Codicus Iuris Canonici Fontes*, 9 vols. (Rome, 1923-39), n. 552.

[21]Canon 2350, paragraph 1.

alive, should certainly be baptized and, if doubtfully alive, should be baptized conditionally.[22] In addition, it directs the baptism of a child in its mother's womb if there is no hope that it will be born in a normal manner.[23] These canons make it clear that the Church recognizes the personhood of the unborn child at every stage of its development. The 1984 Code of Canon Law (Canon 1398) reaffirms automatic excommunication for anyone who procures an abortion.

The earliest explicit teaching against abortion is found in the *Didache* (*The Lord's Instruction to the Gentiles through the Twelve Apostles*). This work (c. 80) is the oldest source of ecclesiastical law and, after the New Testament, the first Christian catechism. The pertinent passage reads: "You shall not slay the child by abortion."[24]

The second reference to abortion appears in a theological tract known as the Epistle of the pseudo-Barnabas, written about 138. This work was highly regarded for centuries, especially by the theologians of Alexandria. The author treats abortion as a corollary to the law of fraternal charity: "you shall love your neighbor more than your own life. You shall not slay the child by abortion."[25]

Athenagoras, an Athenian philosopher, states in a letter to Marcus Aurelius (177) that: "All who use abortifacients are homicides and will account to God for their abortions as for the killing of men."[26] Clement of Alexandria, the "Father of Theologians," wrote in 215 that abortions "destroy utterly the embryo and, with it, the love of man."[27]

Two early Church councils—of Elvira in Granada, Spain (c. 305) and of Ancyra in Galatia, Asia Minor (314)—condemned abortion. These councils established a firm historical precedent on the matter of abortion which later councils—the Council of Chalcedon (451) and *Consillium Quinisextum* (692)—ratified and strengthened.

During the early period of Christianity many important writers clearly and emphatically condemned abortion as a grave evil. Among these writers are Hippolytus (235), Cyprian (258), St. Ambrose, Bishop of Milan (375), St. Jerome (d. 420), St. Augustine (d. 430), Caesarius, Bishop of Arles (d. 543) and St. Martin of Braga (580). The Christian respect for all human life during the early Christian era, exemplified in part by its opposition to abortion, contrasted markedly with the pagan

---

[22]Canon 747.

[23]Canon 746.

[24]Didache, II, 2, tr. J. A. Kleist, S.J., *Ancient Christian Writers*, 6 (Westminster, 1948), 16.

[25]*Epistle of Barnabas*, II, 19.

[26]*Legatio pro Christianis*, c. 35.

[27]*Octavius*, c. 30, nn. 2-3.

world in which abortion and infanticide were common practices. This Christian attitude toward the unborn was all the more striking since it resisted the prevailing Stoic view that associated life with breath, holding that the fetus was not alive until it could breathe and because it maintained its opposition to all abortion despite Septuagint teaching and Aristotelian thinking, both of which made distinctions between the formed and unformed fetus.

In summarizing the teaching and historical contribution of the early Church on the subject of abortion, John Noonan, Jr. writes:

> The monks had transmitted the apostolic and patristic prohibition of abortion. The canon law set it out as a universal requirement of Christian behavior. The theologians explored the relation of the law to the theory of ensoulment, but on one basis or another condemned abortion at any point in the existence of the fetus. The prohibition was still absolute.[28]

The early period of Christianity established a firm and consistent opposition to abortion. Later periods were faithful to this tradition despite continuing attempts on the part of various ecclesiastical writers to find an exception to the Church's condemnation of direct abortion in every instance. The Church did not always regard all abortion as simple homicide, however, although it regarded the abortion of an unformed or unanimated fetus (if there were such a thing) as anticipated homicide or homicide by intent because it always involved the destruction of a future human being. The distinctions between true homicide and *quasi*-homicide, and formed and unformed fetus had practical significance only with respect to legal classification and the grading of penances relative to the reconciliation of sinners.

The pronouncements by modern popes on the subject of abortion omit these obsolete distinctions. Hence, their opposition to abortion may appear more definitive and unqualified than statements made by earlier popes. Nonetheless, the Church's moral teaching that abortion is always a grave evil has remained intact throughout history.

One of the reasons cited for imposing a more severe penalty on late term abortions is that it represents a greater danger to the woman. But the danger to the woman of early abortion was also noted. Juan de Lugo, a Spanish Jesuit whom Alphonsus Liguori called the greatest moralist after Thomas Aquinas, drew attention to the fact that an abortion even in the earliest period of pregnancy is more dangerous to the

---

[28]John T. Noonan, Jr., "Abortion in the Catholic Church: A Summary History," *Natural Law Forum*, 12 (1967), p. 104.

woman than carrying the pregnancy to term. This was unarguably true given the state of medicine in the year 1642 when de Lugo wrote *Justice and Right*, a work that earned him his cardinal's hat.

The Church was also, and at all times, concerned about the woman's spiritual welfare. Since it regarded abortion as a grave sin, it believed that it posed a serious danger to the woman's immortal soul. Naturally, it wanted to discourage women from having an abortion since it regarded this violation of the commandment to love one's neighbor as a form of spiritual suicide.

In the thirteenth century Thomas Aquinas dealt with the questions of whether it is permissible to section the uterus of a pregnant woman if this were the only way to baptize the fetus that is in danger of dying. The argument in favor of doing this is that the eternal life of the fetus is more important than the temporal life of its mother. Aquinas refuses to allow this and quotes St. Paul (Rom. 3:8) who says: "We should not do evil that there may come good." It is an impermissible evil, according to Aquinas, to impose direct physical harm on a pregnant woman (in all probability causing her death) even when the good that is intended—the eternal salvation of the fetus—might be construed in a particularly theological sense to be a greater good than continuing the temporal life of the mother.[29] Aquinas does not believe that an unbaptized fetus is necessarily deprived of salvation; but the logic of his argument reveals his conviction that even if the fetus stood to suffer a greater loss than the loss of its mother's temporal life, the mother's right to be protected from assault remains inviolable.

The three-century theological discussion between 1450-1750 centered on whether a woman ever had a right to abort. The factor that sustained the discussion was a genuine and abiding concern that, in certain circumstances, continued pregnancy would endanger a woman's health, marriage, or reputation. No exception was found that would permit direct abortion, however, because no exception could be found that did not logically extend to other exceptions that were not prudent to make or failed to uphold the principle that all innocent human life warrants equal protection. But the debate continued in an effort to protect the pregnant woman as much as possible without violating more general principles that protected everyone.

The pregnant woman had a right to life and a right to be protected from assault. This was never questioned. But these rights implied other rights, particularly, a right to medical treatment in the event of illness. An important distinction was introduced in the sixteenth century by Antonius de Corduba, a Franciscan theologian, between medicine

---

[29]St. Thomas Aquinas, *Summa Theologica*, III, q. 68, a. 11, ad. 3.

for the health of the mother (*de se salutifera*) and medicine for what would directly cause the death of the fetus (*de se mortifera*). Corduba reasoned that since the mother has a greater or prior right to life (*ius potius*), she has a right to therapeutic treatment even if that treatment results in the accidental death of the fetus.[30]

Corduba's contributions concerning the pregnant woman's right to therapeutic treatment united with those of many other writers. Eventually a rationale was developed which permitted indirect abortion in the interest of the mother's health. Pope Pius XII added his approval to this rationale when he said:

> Deliberately we have always used the expression 'direct attempt on the life of an innocent person,' 'direct killing.' Because if, for example, the saving of the life of the future mother, independently of her pregnant condition, should urgently require a surgical act or other therapeutic treatment which would have as an accessory consequence, in no way desired or intended, but inevitable, the death of the fetus, such an act could no longer be called a direct attempt on an innocent life. Under these conditions the operation can be lawful, like other similar medical interventions—granted always that a good of high worth is concerned, such as life, and that it is not possible to postpone the operation until after the birth of the child, nor to have recourse to other efficacious remedies.[31]

Thus, it is morally permissible to remove the Fallopian tube in the instance of an ectopic pregnancy or to remove a cancerous uterus since the primary purpose of these therapeutic procedures is to save the life of the mother, not to destroy the fetus, a consequence that happens indirectly or accidentally. The acceptance of indirect abortion, as Noonan remarks, indicates that Church teaching is something less than an "absolute valuation of fetal life."[32]

The Church has always upheld the principle that all innocent human life is deserving of protection. In trying to find exceptions to the abortion prohibition in the interest of providing better care for the pregnant woman, the Church never treated one form of human life as more important than another. Pope Pius XII makes this point clear when he states:

> Never and in no case has the Church taught that the life of the child must be preferred to that of the mother. It is erroneous to put the

---

[30]Antoninus de Corduba, *Quaestionarium theologicum*, q. 38, dub. 3 (Venice, 1604).

[31]*Acta Apostolicae Sedis*, 43 (1951), p. 855.

[32]Noonan, p. 125.

question with this alternative: either the life of the child or that of the mother. No, neither the life of the mother nor that of the child can be subjected to an act of direct suppression. In the one case as in the other, there can be but one obligation: to make every effort to save the lives of both, of the mother and the child.[33]

Although the Church's prohibition of all direct abortion has been clear and consistent throughout history, its overall treatment of abortion is highly comprehensive and extraordinarily complex owing to the many subtleties involved in its theological and philosophical discussions together with the intricate secondary issues of animation, formation, and the grading of penalties. This fact may help to explain why so many contemporary writers are either ignorant or confused about what the Church has actually taught on the subject of abortion. At the same time, there can be little doubt that in some instances the reason for misrepresenting Church teaching is rooted in anti-Catholic prejudice. Roger Wertheimer, himself an advocate of abortion, is as correct as he is candid when he declares:

> I think it undeniable that some of the liberals' bungling can be dismissed as the unseemly sputterings and stutterings of a transparently camouflaged anti-Catholic bias . . . [34]

In Chandrasekhar's *Abortion in a Crowded World*, the presence of an anti-Catholic bias is both obvious and disturbing. Catholic doctrine on abortion is "rigid, irrational, and cast-iron;"[35] it is also "changeless and monolithic."[36] In relation to the plight of modern man in an "overpopulated" world, the Church, in opposing abortion, is guilty of "sickly sentimentalism" and "foolish wickedness."[37]

Chandrasekhar does not understand the meaning and limitation of law. A law should be just. And if it is just, it should not change to become unjust simply to avoid the criticism of being "rigid." But inasmuch as it is just, it is not compassionate. Justice is supposed to be non-partisan; it is not supposed to feel differently toward one than toward an-

---

[33]*Acta Apostolicae Sedis*, p. 43. Pope Pius XI had said in *Casti Conubii* that "The lives of both [the woman and her unborn child] are equally sacred and no one, not even public authority can ever have the right to destroy them."

[34]Roger Wertheimer, "Understanding the Abortion Argument," *The Rights and Wrongs of Abortion*, ed. Cohen, Nagel & Scanlon (Princeton, New Jersey: Princeton University Press, 1974), p. 29, f. n. 6.

[35]S. Chandrasekhar, *Abortion in a Crowded World* (Seattle: University of Washington Press, 1974), p. 26.

[36]*Ibid.*, p. 36.

[37]*Ibid.*, p. 37.

other. Justice is "blind." Moreover, only human beings, not laws, are capable of expressing compassion. It is the combination of just laws and compassionate people that is needed. If people lack compassion it is folly to expect that compassion can be expressed by the law. The Catholic law which forbids abortion is an expression of a higher law which obliges everyone to love his neighbor without prejudice.

Protestant theologian Harold O. J. Brown, in his book *Death Before Birth*, contends that the early Christian church "consistently taught" that "abortion is permissible" (though an evil) to "save the mother's life."[38] The only reference he offers to support this historically incorrect claim is from Tertullian, a Christian heretic of the third century. It is not at all clear that even Tertullian approved abortion under these circumstances. "But even if Tertullian were speaking with approval of the procedure," writes John Connery, "it would be the only explicit approval of an exception to the condemnation of abortion to be found in the first millenium."[39]

Linda Bird Francke, in her popular book on abortion, makes the following assertion, though without giving any supporting references:

> In terms of canon law, for centuries the Catholic church accepted the abortion in a woman until the "quickening" of the fetus—that time when the woman first feels it moving in her womb. It was then, the church reasoned, that the "animate soul" entered the fetus, changing it from an "inanimate soul" to a person. Though the quickening usually occurs between the sixteenth and eighteenth weeks of gestation, the Catholic church moved the date up to forty days.[40]

Wendell Watters, a Canadian psychiatrist, makes the unsupported claim that prior to 1869 and except for three years during the reign of Sixtus V (1588-1591) "the Church had officially accepted the theory of delayed animation for 500 years."[41] This, of course is completely untrue. The Church had never at any time "officially" accepted the theory of delayed animation. It did, however, mitigate punishment if the abortion was of an unanimated fetus. But it never taught that there was such a thing as an unanimated fetus; it gave the benefit of the doubt to the penitent that this might be the case in an early abortion.

---

[38]Harold O. J. Brown, *Death Before Birth* (Nashville: Thomas Nelson, 1977), p. 22.

[39]Connery, p. 42.

[40]Linda Bird Francke, *The Ambivalence of Abortion* (N. Y.: Random House, 1978), p. 13.

[41]Wendell W. Watters, *Compulsory Pregnancy: The Truth About Abortion* (Toronto: McLelland & Steward, 1976), p. 90.

The only *official* Church teaching on the subject of animation is that of Pope Innocent XI which condemned the position that ensoulment took place at birth.[42]

Whether the fetus ever was unanimated, when it might have been animated, and how such a diagnosis might be made were all speculative questions that were wholly extrinsic to the fundamental teaching that abortion was wrong at any time. In fact, there never existed an empirical method by which a judgment could be made that the fetus is indeed "not animate."

On the basis of this misunderstanding, Watters then concludes that the elimination of the distinction between the animated and unanimated fetus in 1869 "was a pivotal one in the history of abortion." Prior to 1869, according to Watters, "abortion before ensoulment was tolerated by the Catholic Church."[43] Watters also fails to recognize the difference between opposing abortion because it is homicide and opposing it because it is homicide by intent. He illogically assumes that if the Church, at certain times and in certain circumstances, regarded abortion as less than homicide it probably "tolerated" or even "sanctioned" abortion. This is roughly equivalent to arguing that it must be all right to kill a privately owned race horse because such an act does not constitute homicide. At any rate, Watters insists that the real reason the Church opposed abortion was not moral or religious but political.[44]

Watters's book, promoted as one destined to become the "definitive book about abortion," has the appearance of scholarship. This makes it all the more dangerous because uncritical reviewers repeat as Gospel the distortions Watters claims to be facts. Thus, one reviewer can blithely announce in a woman's magazine, concerning Watters' treatment of Church history:

> Readers may be surprised to discover that the Catholic Church's position on abortion has varied widely over the years. Until just over 100 years ago, the Vatican's attitude towards abortion was relatively tolerant.[45]

Eugene C. Bianchi, a former Catholic priest, expresses the complaint that: "Other voices need to be heard from the Catholic tradition

---

[42]See Connery, p. 308: "The only opinion the Church has ever condemned was that which identified animation with the time of birth. It has never taught immediate animation."

[43]Watters, pp. 90-1.

[44]Watters, pp. 92-3.

[45]Penney Kome, "Woman's Place," *Homemaker's Magazine*, 1976.

that argue for openings on the yes side of the abortion issue."[46] Bianchi seems unaware of Church history on the subject in which every conceivable rationale for justifying abortion was brought forward, heard, and thoroughly scrutinized before being dismissed. But his "yes" to abortion is rhetoric at its emptiest. The Catholic tradition is in continuity with the Jewish tradition on the matter of saying "yes," but a saying "yes" not to death but to *life*. The Old Testament is a continuous affirmation of the goodness of life. A striking example of this attitude occurs in Deuteronomy. After summarizing the entire code, the lawgiver calls attention to the fundamental moral choice that must be made: "See, today I set before you life and prosperity, death and disaster."[47] To love and serve God is to choose life; to reject God and depart from Him is to choose death.

> Choose life, then, so that you and your descendants may live, in the love of Yahweh your God, obeying his voice, clinging to him; for in this your life consists, and on this depends your long stay in the land which Yahweh swore to our fathers . . . [48]

Books, reviews, magazines, pro-abortion leaflets, and newspapers commonly misrepresent the Church's teaching on abortion. Newspapers are especially notorious in this regard. A typical example of newspaper distortion is the following:

> Abortion was only declared illegal and condemned by the Roman Catholic Church in the 1800's, the Catholic church condoned abortion until the fetus "quickened," meaning the time when a pregnant woman first feels the unborn child moving.[49]

Nor are Catholics excepted from gross misrepresentations of Church teaching. One author, who identifies himself as a Catholic, has written a book which purports to tell the *facts* about matters pertaining to human sexuality. In this rather lengthy work, he summarizes the Catholic teaching on abortion in the following way:

> *Catholicism.* Although Catholic teaching on abortion has shifted through the centuries, the current position is clear: abortion is murder. This position has been fixed since 1869, when Pope Pius IX reinstituted

---

[46]Eugene C. Bianchi, "Compassion is Needed," *National Catholic Reporter,* June 8, 1973.

[47]Deuteronomy 30:15.

[48]Deuteronomy 30:19-20

[49]Ann Lukits, "The Agony of Abortion," Kingston, Ont. *Whig Standard,* Sat. Sept. 24, 1983, p. 1.

the doctrine that the soul enters the body at the moment of conception; from that moment on, the fetus is therefore a person. Furthermore, because the fetus has a soul it must be baptized in order to remove original sin. Catholics therefore believe that not only is abortion murder, but it also condemns the unborn person to hell.[50]

This passage, stated gratuitously with no supporting references, is particularly remarkable because it contains nine major errors in the space of four sentences, and fails to make a single correct point concerning the Catholic Church's teaching on abortion. It provides an unusually concentrated example of academic incompetence, demonstrating in embarrassing detail the author's poor diction, faulty logic, bad theology, and ignorance of history.

Catholic teaching, of course has not "shifted" through the centuries. Although the word "murder" has been used by some ecclesiastical writers, the Church does not identify abortion with murder. "Murder" is a legal term and involves a judgment about the disposition, knowledge, and intention of the alleged murderer. Murder and homicide (the killing of a human being) are not the same thing. Immediate animation is not a doctrine, and Pope Pius IX did not "reinstate" any doctrine concerning abortion in 1869.

The assertion that the fetus must be baptized in order to remove original sin is theologically indefensible. Aquinas maintains that children in the womb can "be subject to the action of God, in Whose sight they live, so as, by a kind of privilege, to receive the grace of sanctification; as was the case with those who were sanctified in the womb."[51] The most celebrated instance of this form of sanctification is John the Baptist who, as a six-month-old fetus in the womb of Elizabeth, "leapt for joy" at the salutation of Mary who was "with child of the Holy Spirit."[52] Furthermore, the Church teaches that, in addition to water, there is baptism by blood and desire.

There is no clear doctrine of the Church concerning what happens to unbaptized infants after they die. Since the twelfth century, the opinion of the majority of theologians has been that these unbaptized infants, because they are innocent of any *actual* sin, are immune from all pain of sense. This was taught by St. Thomas Aquinas, Scotus, St. Bonaventure, Peter Lombard and others, and is now the common teaching in the Church. St. Thomas says: "Although unbaptized infants

---

[50]Michael Carrera, *Sex: The Facts, The Acts, and Your Feelings* (New York: Crown, 1981), p. 290.

[51]*S.T.* III, q. 68, a. 11, ad. 1.

[52]Luke, Chap. I.

are separated from God as far as glory is concerned, yet they are not separated from Him entirely. Rather are they joined to Him by a participation of natural goods; and so they may even rejoice in Him by natural consideration and love."[53] Again, he says: "They will rejoice in this, that they will share largely in the divine goodness and in natural perfections."[54]

The claim that Catholics believe abortion condemns the unborn to Hell is baseless and invidious. There is not a shred of evidence that the Church has ever taught this or that Catholics do indeed believe it.

The so called "information explosion," which is greatly facilitated by the mass media and its pressing day-to-day needs, has created a wide gap between information and scholarship. Although there is more print available to the general public today than ever before, people have less time and, perhaps more importantly, less inclination to discuss, digest, criticize, and challenge what they read. The gross misrepresentations that frequently appear on so important a matter as the Church's teaching on abortion should inspire a renewed interest in scholarship and, one may hope, a renaissance in critical thinking.

---

[53]St. Thomas Aquinas, *In II Sent.*, dist. XXXIII, Q. ii, a. 5.
[54]*Ibid.* a. 2.

Abortion and Language

Words (*Les mots*) is the title of Jean-Paul Sartre's autobiography. It could just as well be the countersignature of our present age. Just as Sartre's "words" present an image of alienation from the flesh and blood existence of their author, so too, much of the verbiage that floods our civilized landscape exists without bearing any discernible connection with the substantial world it is meant to signify. Words have lost their link with the world. They have become little more than momentary stimulants for the unthinking masses whose apparent need for stimulation is limitless. Words are processed, circulated, consumed, absorbed, and then forgotten—a pattern whose endless repetition is best typified by the daily press and commercial advertising. Words influence, but fail to nourish; they arouse but do not enlighten.

Thus, when a major moral controversy arises, such as abortion, a numbing war between words prevents any discussion concerning which view is more moral or realistic. A formidable impasse has existed for some time now precisely because words no longer direct us toward a common reality or a common moral vision, but lock us in a futile verbal struggle which prohibits understanding and perpetuates division.

On one side of the abortion issue is the organization that identifies itself as "pro-life." This identification label rankles the opposition for two fundamental reasons: 1) because it insinuates that the opposition is not fully sensitive to the value of life, an insinuation the opposition vehemently rejects; 2) because it suggests that "pro-lifers" are in full support of all life, an unconvincing claim in the light of what is perceived to be their less than pure attitudes on issues involving war, capital punishment, and the rights of animals.

The "pro-life" group identifies the opposition as "pro-abortion," a label which the opposition also rejects, maintaining that it does not promote abortion in individual cases, but merely its availability. Once the availability of abortion is secured, individual women are then free to choose abortion for themselves.

Those labelled as "pro-abortionists" are understandably emphatic in identifying their position as "pro-choice," and strongly disavow the "pro-life" charge that they are "anti-life." "Pro-choice" advocates take pride in their rhetoric of choice, for it conveys a liberal frame of mind which is neither dogmatic nor judgmental, and suggests a compassionate and humanitarian disposition that is fully accepting of the pregnant woman and whatever choice she makes concerning her pregnancy. Moreover, it allows them to intensify their negative portrayal of their opposition from "anti-abortion" (a source of annoyance to the opposition which prefers to be viewed by the more positive sounding expression, "pro-life") to "anti-choice" which carries the rhetorically strategic implications of being anti-freedom and virtually anti-human.

Both sides have adopted a rhetoric that casts themselves as being in favor of something good and their opposition as being against something good. This verbal stand-off is confusing to people who are not committed to either side. Such a stalemate, however, plays into the hands of the "pro-choice" allegiance, for, if it is impossible to determine which side has the superior moral vision, the only fair thing to do seems to be to allow women to choose for themselves. When there is genuine doubt in a moral issue, moralizing or legislating takes on the appearance of authoritarianism. If it cannot be decided what is moral, then it must be moral not to decide. This victory by default for the "pro-choice" side effectively makes irrelevant any discussion of real issues such as the nature of the unborn, the physical and psychological sequelae to induced abortion, the trivialization of sex and procreation, and the effect abortion has on the integrity of the family.

A purely rhetorical debate, which does not get beyond words, is a victory for "pro-choice" because "pro-choice" seems more neutral than either "pro-" or "anti-abortion." But a "pro-choice" position is not really neutral. As a matter of fact, it is decidedly inclined toward abortion. Whenever a pregnant woman makes her "conscientious" choice which is also said to be "anguished" or "agonizing," it is invariably for abortion. Although "pro-choice" rhetoric logically implies that a woman's conscience or her anguished or agonizing choice is equally disposed toward birth as well as abortion—the myth of neutrality—in actual practice it is not, André Hellegers makes the point that "any such 'agonizing decision' which results so consistently in the death of the fetus should not be described as an 'agonizing choice'."[1] And Joseph Sobran asks

---

[1] André Hellegers, "Abortion and Birth Control," *The Human Life Review*. Winter, 1975, p. 22.

the question that he says "never gets answered": "Why it should be the decision to kill the child, rather than the decision to let it live, that is represented as the triumph of conscience?"[2] The answer, of course, is that "pro-choice" is a rhetorical ploy that covers the reality of "pro-abortion." And this is precisely why "pro-choice" advocates want to keep the discussion away from reality and permanently on the level of verbal rhetoric.

By insisting that the discussion remain on a purely verbal plane, "pro-choice" enthusiasts adopt the curious position that reality actually interferes with moral decision-making. Their belief that a position of "moral neutrality" is really morally neutral and does not affect their decision betrays an ignorance of the most fundamental law of the cosmos, namely, that nothing stands still. Existence abhors neutrality more firmly than nature abhors a vacuum. A log in the water is carried downstream. Untreated silver tarnishes, unprotected iron rusts. Muscles that are not exercised atrophy. Moral indifference is not a virtue but a vice. Indecision and ignorance are liabilities. Nowhere in the physical world or in the moral sphere are there any points of neutrality. Everything is either developing or decaying; nothing is at rest. In the absence of a positive effort there is a negative slide. The Law of Entropy describes a cosmic fact and offers a parable by which we gain insight into the dynamics of our own moral condition. Without grace, gravity reigns. If one takes a neutral stand on the abortion issue, he becomes—by force of gravity—drawn toward abortion. That is the reality of it. And as long as words are kept disconnected from reality, this fundamental axiom, which describes the inherent dynamism of all things, remains ignored.

Physicians have called attention to the fact that showing a pregnant woman the image of her fetus on an ultrasound screen, even before quickening, can help complete the bonding process between that mother and her child, and influence her against abortion.[3] In such cases, the real image of the fetus is like grace acting against the gravity toward abortion that sets in when such forms of grace are withheld. Nonetheless, the question has arisen as to whether ultrasound viewing would give an unfair advantage to those who represented the interests of the fetus. Ultrasound would seem an unfair maneuver since it violates a context of "neutrality." As doctors have reasoned: "Ultrasound examination may thus result in fewer abortions and more desired pregnan-

---

[2]M. J. Sobran, "The Abortion Ethos," *The Human Life Review*, Winter, 1977, p. 16.

[3]J. C. Fletcher, Ph. D. and M. I. Evans, M. D., "Maternal Bonding in Early Fetal Ultrasound Examination," *The New England Journal of Medicine*, Feb. 17, 1983, p. 392.

cies."[4] The truth of the matter, of course, is that ultrasound provides what words should ordinarily provide, that is, an insight into reality. And the more one knows about the reality of the issue, the better able he is to make the right decision. Reality does not interfere with moral decision-making, it is merely indispensable if the moral decision is going to be a wise one. The criticism that ultrasound is unfair because it violates neutrality is made by those who try to conceal their pro-abortion bias under a camouflage of "pro-choice" neutrality, realizing that if all positive realities are withheld, abortion will eventuate just as surely as the release of one's supporting grip will cause a ball to drop to the ground. By keeping the abortion debate on a verbal level and thereby excluding the pertinent realities, "pro-choice" rhetoric—under the guise of neutrality—effectively promotes abortion.

But abortion is more than a verbal issue that is to be fought the way sales wars are waged between competing brands of soft drinks and laundry detergents. Abortion is a *real* issue that involves flesh-and-blood people and has far reaching consequences. Tradition knew this well and its prohibitions and restrictions of abortion reflected a stubborn realism. "Pro-life" people evidence their sensitivity to this tradition in their fondness of citing Edmund Burke's remark that in order for evil to triumph all that is necessary is that good people do nothing.

The "pro-choice" insistence on severing rhetoric from realism reveals the inherent weakness in its position, but it also reveals culture's woeful lack of respect for the real, truth-communicating function of the word. And the "pro-choice" movement is taking full advantage of this lamentable state the word has reached. Words fulfill their proper function when they are subordinated to and measured by the things they name. "All education," writes Richard Weaver, "is learning to name rightly, as Adam named the animals."[5] When words are no longer measured by the truth of things, they become instruments of deception. "The rectification of names," said Confucius, is perhaps the main business of government: "If names are not correct, language will not be in accordance with the truth of things."[6] The sentiment is by no means uncommon and we find it echoed throughout Western history from Heraclitus to Hammarskjold. Heraclitus, anticipating John the Evangelist's lofty use of the Word, stated: "One ought to follow the lead of that which is common to all men. But although the Word is common to all,

---

[4]*Ibid.*

[5]Richard Weaver, "The Power of the Word," *Ideas Have Consequences* (Chicago: University of Chicago Press, 1948), p. 149.

[6]Quoted by Henry Fairlie in "The Language of Politics," *The Atlantic*, Jan. 1975, p. 25.

yet most men live as if each had a private wisdom of his own."[7] And Dag Hammarskjöld, former Secretary-General of the United Nations, remarked:

> *Respect for the word* is the first commandment in the discipline by which a man can be educated to maturity—intellectual, emotional, and moral.
>
> Respect for the word—to employ it with scrupulous care and an incorruptible heartfelt love of truth—is essential if there is to be any growth in a society or in the human race.
>
> To misuse the word is to show contempt for man. It undermines the bridges and poisons the wells. It causes Man to regress down the long path of his evolution.[8]

For Hammarskjöld, words, when properly employed, represent avenues to grace; when they are misused, they serve the cause of gravity. The first responsibility of the writer involves an uncompromisable integrity in his use of words, an insistence that there must always be a fidelity between the word and the reality it signifies. This is why Alexander Solzhenitsyn, who knows a great deal about the misuse of the word in the hands of a totalitarian regime, says that he studies the words in his Russian dictionary "as if they were precious stones, each so precious that I would not exchange one for another."

The function of the word is to mediate the world. Language is a bridge that connects the mind of man with the extra-mental world that lies beyond words. The fact that man does not always use his words in a way that is commensurate with what they signify is only too evident. Blasphemy is a case in point. As Chesterton has remarked:

> Blasphemy is not wild; blasphemy is in its nature prosaic. It consists in regarding in a commonplace manner something which other and happier people regard in a rapturous and imaginative manner.[9]

Blasphemy is a lie inasmuch as it speaks of grace in terms of gravity. The public may have come to associate blasphemy with excitement, but that is because they have lost their sense of proportion between the word and the reality it represents. "Our words have wings," George Eliot reminds us, "But fly not where they would." Chesterton's intention in asserting that blasphemy is not wild—when everyone knows it

---

[7]Heraclitus, Fragment 2.

[8]Dag Hammarsjöld, *Markings*, tr. Leif Sjöberg and W. H. Auden (New York: Knopf, 1964), p. 112.

[9]G. K. Chesterton, *William Blake* (London: Duckworth, 1910), p. 178.

is—is to startle people in the hope that they might rectify their use of words and better align them with reality.

The ideologue offers another example of trying to give the word more importance than the reality it is supposed to mediate. His aim is to substitute the word for the world and his strategy is an expression of faith in verbal magic: "I want the world to be a different way than it is. I will insist that people speak as if it is that way—this will bring it about." For the ideologue, the word does not mediate the created world; rather, the world is created by the word.

When the late Dr. Alan Guttmacher, former president of the American Planned Parenthood Association, was involved in preparing a series of television programs on physical and mental health for teenagers, he urged that in at least sixteen of these programs the word abortion be employed in such a way as to "detoxify the viewing audiences from cultural shock at the word."[10]

Similarly, a moral theologian once complained that "adultery" is a "negative" word that should be replaced by the more positive sounding "flexible monogamy" in order to invest marital infidelity with a more positive reality. Man's belief in the magical properties of words notwithstanding, Limberger has the same disagreeable odor no matter what appellation it receives.

In general, the dissociation of the word from the world follows a diversified pattern. Of particular interest among these forms of dissociation include the following: 1) Deification, 2) Devaluation, 3) Devitalization, 4) Deterioration, 5) Deception, and 6) Doublethink. In each of these forms there is a failure of the word to unite the mind with the truth. To the extent that these forms are prevalent in culture, a fruitful debate on abortion, or any other moral issue, becomes increasingly unlikely. Fruitful debate presupposes a link between word and world.

The story is told of a woman from Siam who decided to abort when she learned that she was carrying twins; she could not face the prospect of giving birth to Siamese twins. The woman, needless to say, was reacting to the word rather than the reality. Another story centers around a Canadian farmer who lived close to the American border. When authorities surveyed his property for legal purposes, they discovered that the actual site of the farm was in the United States. Upon learning this, the farmer was greatly relieved, commenting that he didn't think he could take another one of those Canadian winters! The winters, naturally, would be no different because of the change in the word which describes their geographical location. Nonetheless, as the

---

[10]Quoted in *Alliance for Life National Newsletter*, Vol. 10, April 1974, p. 4.

word becomes mightier than the reality it signifies, it becomes increasingly difficult to separate fact from fiction. A television weatherman solemnly predicts "rain tonight in some official areas."[11] An anxious mother decides to bed her infant in a play-pen in order to avert "crib death." A youngster stitches a Levi label on his Brand-X jeans so that he can be accepted by his peers.

The folly of mistaking words for things, of abandoning the world for the word is perfectly exemplified in commercial advertising, an enterprise whose annual budget in the United States alone is estimated at $50 billion. Advertising can be, as George Orwell has remarked, "the rattling of a stick inside the swill bucket," but the rattling itself is often hypnotic. "Sell the sizzle, not the steak," is a sacrosanct first principle in the advertising industry. When admen identify a certain shade of lipstick as "Pizzicato Pink," they are banking on verbal magic to sell their product. "Pizzicato" has nothing to do with the plucking of string instruments; it is exotica, pizzazz, intoxication, romance, sensuousness, frivolity, and pseudo-elegance. Likewise, "Apricot Shimmer", is not a lipstick color but the lushness of tropical fruit or surrender to sexual passion. Advertising uses words not to convey meanings but to create illusions.

The philosopher Usener, alluding to the capacity words have to overwhelm people, speaks of them as "momentary deities." Literary critic George Steiner has pointed out in his book, *Extraterritorial*, that eleventh century theologian Peter Damian believed man fell into paganism through a grammatical flaw: "Because heathen speech has a plural for the word 'deity,' wretched humankind came to conceive of many gods." The very existence of the word "deities," for Peter Damian, was enough to convince people that it must denote a reality. Words can be as large, if not larger, than reality itself. The United States government plays on the assumption that the word itself is the reality when it recruits comic strip character Snoopy to exhort the public to "savEnergy."[12] By allying the two words together, an entire "e" is saved. Presumably, we can savEven morEnergy if we bind more words together.

The modern writer who is perhaps best identified with dissociating words from the world in order to make them into "deities" unto themselves, is Gertrude Stein. A brief excerpt from her book, *Tender Buttons*, is sufficient to illustrate the point:

The care with which the rain is wrong and the green is wrong and the

---

[11]*Time*, August 25, 1975, p. 57.
[12]Edwin Newman, *Strictly Speaking* (New York: Warner, 1974), p. 2.

white is wrong, the care with which there is a chair and plenty of
breathing. The care with which there is incredible justice and likeness,
all this makes a magnificent asparagus, and also a fountain.

Stein uses words not as windows that open to the world, but as
walls that exclude the outer landscape. Her experiment in separating
words from the world strips words of meaning and leaves her reader
with a profound sense of alienation—between author and language,
language and reality, author and reader. Stein's deified language de-
composes into a loose assortment of atomic units—reminiscent of the
cubism of her close friend, Picasso—that no longer has the capacity to
convey an integrated meaning.

"Pro-choice" rhetoric continues this modern penchant for deify-
ing words and abandoning reality. "Pro-choice" is like "Pizzicato Pink";
it sounds good. And there it rests its case. In addition, it is consistent
with the modern process of fragmentation which reduces organic struc-
tures to collections of discontinuous bits and pieces. In the world of
abortion, society reduces to a collection of private and isolated individuals.

It is fatal in art as well as in thinking to abandon the world for the
word; but it can also be fatal in life. Some "pro-choice" supporters have
proposed the deification of words as a "possible solution to the abortion situation." This "solution" consists in substituting the letters "MR"
(for "menstrual regulation") for the more problematic word
"abortion." Professor Luke Lee and John Paxman write: "MR can be
performed with or without confirmaton of pregnancy, an important difference between MR and conventional abortion. . . . For many women,
not knowing whether amenorrhea is a result of conception may be of
great psychological value."[13] The reality of abortion can be conveniently
obscured by calling it MR. But the fact remains that a blanket of words
is not an adequate protection against the force of reality. Words should
reflect reality. If they are to have psychological value, that value should
be grounded in the truth they convey. Psychological value uprooted
from truth is fraudulent and, at best, can confer only temporary and superficial benefits. We are not just to people if we are concerned about
their psychological comfort and nothing more. The deification of words
makes the preposterous claim that the word is more important than the
world and that ideology is more real than reality.

The deification of words elevates them to a greater importance

---

[13]L. T. Lee and J. M. Paxman, "The Population Council," *Studies in
Family Planning*, Vol. 8, No. 10 (Quoted in *Lifelines National*, Fall 1978, Vol.
7, No. 3, p. 8.8

than reality itself. The devaluation of words, on the other hand, reduces them to less importance than what they are naturally as conveyors of meaning. Nonetheless, the two processes are closely related. It is axiomatic that whenever something is elevated above its nature, it is, in the final analysis, degraded. For, in trying to make something fulfill a function for which it has no aptitude, one makes a mockery of it—like the horse who tried to sing like a nightingale and lost its ability to whinny like a horse. People invariably lose faith in what appears ridiculous. Hence the deification of words leads to their devaluation.

The facile use of superlatives to advertise mediocre commercial products, illustrates the point. Not only does such a practice empty the language of words to express true excellence, but it devalues the superlative. If all movies are "great," the word "great" loses its credibility, becomes devalued, and finally means nothing. If every experience is "fantastic," the word soon becomes bankrupt.

News reporting is often as irresponsible as commercial advertising in its use of words. In 1979 the media created a sensation out of a malfunction that occurred at a nuclear power plant at Three Mile Island in Pennsylvania. No one was killed and public-health damage, if any, was unmeasured. The New York *Post*, however, ran banner headlines on its front page: one day it was NUKE LEAK GOES OUT OF CONTROL; the next day, RACE WITH NUCLEAR DISASTER.[14] Even after the hydrogen bubble began to dissolve, one network referred to the incident at Three Mile Island as a "calamity," a description which prompted George Will to ask the question: "What language does the network reserve for events that kill people?"[15] Recently, a group of people held a candlelight vigil on the site of the "calamity" to commemorate its fifth anniversary.

When the cry of "wolf" is made too often, it ceases to alarm people. In becoming devalued, words lose their capacity to arouse. As our faith in language diminishes, our faith in more graphic means of making a point increases. Since we are a technological society, we inevitably put additional faith in technology. According to one writer: "Part of the devaluation of language results from a feeling that somehow it is no longer effective. Samuel Johnson's society pinned its faith on language; Americans attach theirs to technology. . . . Man does not ascent to heaven by prayer, the aspiration of language, but by the complex rockets and computer codes of NASA."[16] But our loss of faith in language is also, and out of desperation, an invitation to violence. The poet W. H.

---

[14]"Covering Three Mile Island," *Newsweek*, April 16, 1979, p. 93.

[15]George Will, "As I Was Saying," *Newsweek*, April 16, 1979, p. 100.

[16] "Can't Anyone Here Speak English?" *Time*, April 25, 1975, p. 56.

Auden has warned us that when language is "corrupted, people lose faith in what they hear, and this leads to violence." Words, once believed to be grace that counteracts the human gravitational pull toward violence, seem impotent against the impressive weight of technology and violence. Abortion, needless, to say, is one of many points where technology and violence intersect.

Given the current devaluation of words, it is easy for many to dismiss "pro-life" expressions such as "Stop the Killing," "Abortion Kills," "Save a Human Life . . . Fight Abortion," "Death Before Birth," and so on, as just another wave of irresponsible rhetoric. The cry of "wolf" falls on deaf ears.

British literary critic David Holbrook has observed that ours is a time when "the capacities of English-speaking people to contemplate the mysterious and metaphysical through the word are weakened and unexercised."[17] His observation warrants thoughtful attention. As words are devitalized to accommodate bureaucratic, ideological, or political needs for more neutral expressions, language begins to lose its capacity to evoke feelings of awe, wonder, or reverence. "Awesome" is currently the antithesis to "gross" in the two-word vocabulary of today's teenager. "Wonder" is routinely applied to brassieres and anti-biotics. And to call someone "irreverent" is not to suggest impiety, but to confer praise.

One enterprising hospital has translated and tranquilized the word "death" into "negative patient care outcome." And California Governor Edmund Brown, Jr. has established a council on "wellness." The combination of these two instances of newspeak has inspired language ombudsman Edwin Newman to quip that couples may soon be marrying each other "for better or for worse, in sickness and in wellness, until negative patient care outcome do us part."

"Vanity of vanities, saith the Preacher . . ." But in one new translation the words become, "A vapor of vapors! Thinnest of vapors! All is vapor!"—moving one critic to decry the "turning of the most passionate cry in the literature of nihilism into a spiritual weather report."[18]

In order to devitalize the word "recession," the United States government, according to William Safire, has experimented with more tepid alternatives such as "a mild downturn" and a "soft landing."

The poet, on the other hand, being more attuned to the pulse of truth and tragedy, assumes the important task of preserving language's vitality. In his hands, words evoke a presence, make their subject live in

---

[17]David Holbrook, "Letters to the Editor," *Spectator* (London, 24 March 1961), p. 400.

[18]Melvin Maddocks, "The Limitations of Language," *Time*, March 8, 1971, p. 20.

the listener's imagination. His contribution in restoring life to language becomes all the more urgent as the subordination of words to various political and practical needs continues to erode their power. American poet Robert Penn Warren sees the poet as a sublime gadfly, an ever vigilant ombudsman who keeps what Santayana called "the prestige of the infinite," the boast of technology, from overshadowing the prestige of the intimate, which is the business of poetry."[19]

In the abortion discussion, however, "pro-choice" defenders regard the neutralization of language as an ideal. A child that is developing in its mother's womb, therefore, becomes a "fetus," or a "product of conception," or simply a "conceptus." Even Bernard Nathanson, now an apologist for the right to life of the unborn, prefers the word "alpha," in the interest of what he calls "neutralizing the discussion." In addition, "life" becomes "potential life," and abortion becomes the "termination of pregnancy" (which is also what birth is) or the "interruption of pregnancy" (as if the pregnancy were to be resumed after a brief pause). "VIP" is a canonized code word for "Voluntary Interruption of Pregnancy."

When words are devitalized, bled of their life substance, their power to elicit an awareness of the value they signify weakens. The neutralization of words in the abortion debate, therefore, is a capitulation to the "pro-choice" position. For words that no longer convey objective values present the image of a world without values that can be altered according to one's own values. A neutral discussion is tantamount to an inducement to interpose one's own values. M. J. Sobran writes:

> To say that a woman is "with child" is to affirm that what she carries in her womb is a member of the human family, akin to all of us: it is to speak not with the forceps of analysis, but with the embrace of metaphor. But to call the child a "fetus" is to pickle it in a kind of rhetorical formaldehyde, and to accept the burden of proving what cannot be proved by empirical methodology: that the pickled thing had a right to live.[20]

A dead language cannot evoke live values. Words ought not to be devitalized—in the interest of fairness—because reality itself is vitalized. Martin Heidegger spoke repeatedly of language as "the house of Being." We cannot get to Being, to the reality of things, through a language whose relationship with Being has been dissolved. Philoso-

---

[19]Robert Penn Warren, *Democracy and Poetry* (Cambridge: Harvard University Press, 1975).

[20]M. J. Sobran, "Rhetorical and Cultural War," *The Human Life Review*, Vol. 1, No. 1, Winter 1975, p. 93.

pher Ludwig Wittgenstein alluded to the same dilemma when he remarked that "The limits of my language are the limits of my world."

The word "life" itself loses at least some of its objective meaning
in a mental climate which accepts that it is a popular soft-drink which
"adds life,"[21] or makes one "come alive." And what tragic implication
can the word "murder" have for Magda Denes who says that "Abortion
is murder of a most necessary sort?"[22] If there is more "life" in a soft
drink than in a developing fetus, and if murder is "a necessity" whereas
protection for the unborn is a "violation of a woman's rights," it is only
because words have undergone a process of devitalization whereby they
have lost their capacity to direct the mind to a world of objective values
that transcend one's arbitrary will or private dispositions, a truth Shake-
speare expressed when he stated that "Value dwells not in particular
will."[23]

Since there is nothing neutral in reality, neutrality should not be
an ideal when it comes to using language in order to discuss real moral
values. There can be no poetry that defends or celebrates abortion because poetry, in respecting the vitality of words, unites us with the vitality inherent in existing things. To treat something which is vital as if it
were neutral is to relinquish care for it and allow it to be overtaken by
the force of gravity—a neutral language must ultimately become a dead
language. And a dead language cannot inspire moral action.

Writers for newspaper headlines have contributed to the deterioration of language by sacrificing style and syntax in order to catch the
reader's eye and, at the same time, save valuable space. One celebrated
headline in *Variety*—"STIX NIX HIX PIX"—represents quintessential
newspaper-speak. The elusiveness of this cyrptogram's meaning is born
out by the difficulty it posed for French translators. The original meaning expresses the fact that the inhabitants of rural districts (STIX) dis-
liked (NIX) certain movies (PIX) dealing with bucolic themes (HIX).
French readers may have been even more startled when they read the
translated version as: "*Morceaux de bois nient paysans au cinéma.*"
Translated back into English, the phrase becomes: "Pieces of wood dis-
own farmers in the cinema."

Public advertising, such as the proliferation of signs customarily
found in a city's shopping district, also attests to the commercial need
for truncating and sensationalizing language. Traffic signs, product la-

---

[21]See Karl G. Schmude, "Redeeming the Word," *Communio*, Summer
1980, p. 159.

[22]Magda Denes, *In Necessity and Sorrow: Life and Death in an Abortion
Hospital* (New York: Basic Books, 1976).

[23]*Troilus and Cressida*, I, iii, 52.

bels, thirty-second TV commercials, billboards, sky-written messages, T-shirts, postal meter slogans, and bumper-stickers are a few more of the many instances in which language must be severely altered in order to fit space, time, novelty, and attention needs.

The factors that contribute to the deterioration of language are limitless. The binary language of the computer forces upon us its own dipolar rhythm: feed-back, in-put, out-put, work-out, leg-work, sit-in, love-in, and so on. Police prose offers an amusing burlesque of administration jargon: "I apprehended the alleged perpetrator." "A number of shots were fired at the deceased person, mortally wounding him." The "officialese" of a United States handbook refers to a shovel as a "combat emplacement evacuator," and the CIA uses the expression "non-discernable micro-bio-innoculator" to describe a poison dart. Finally, "a bucket of sunshine" is an official military euphamism describing an exploding nuclear missile.

We are all familiar with political blather, bureaucratic gobbledygook, the surreal boobspeak of commercial advertising, the sludge of academic writing, sledgehammer slogans, medical jargon, and the yahoo erudition of Howard Cosell ("I am impressed by the continuity of his physical presence."). These exemplify practices that contribute to the growing deterioration of words, rendering language dense and confusing, robbing it of its artistry and grace. Much of what passes for education, complains one educator, takes on the rhetorical form of "para-sense"[24]—verbal constructions that sound like sense but are devoid of sense as well as reference. "The English language is dying," moans another educator, because it is not being taught."[25]

In J. M. G. Le Clézio's novel *The Flood*, the anti-hero succumbs to the deluge of words he encounters in his daily life. Even while strolling down the street minding his own business, words assault him from every direction: instructions (Walk—Don't Walk), threats (Trespassers Will Be Prosecuted), and newsstand alarms (Plane Crash at Tel Aviv). All words blur together and become a meaningless buzz in his ears. Finally, in self defense he suffers what might be called semantic aphasia—a numbness to the meaning of words. His malady is symbolic of a cultural epidemic of semantic aphasia that results from a prolonged and ubiquitous deterioration of words.

Semantic aphasia may be best associated with the use of acronyms, word initials that do not even hint at what they conceal. At

---

[24]J. M. Cameron, *On the Idea of a University* (Toronto: University of Toronto Press, 1978), p. 33.

[25]Leon Botstein, president of New York's Bard College, quoted in *Time*, August 25, 1975, p. 56.

some abortion clinics, aborted fetuses are routinely called P.O.C.s (standing for "products of conception"). In some hospitals, the term for patients believed to have no hope of recovery is "GORKs," the acronym for God Only Really Knows.[26]

Neuro-surgeon Harley Smyth decries the use of medical officialese to justify abortion, such as "therapeutic," which treats no disease and cures no symptom or "reactive depression in pregnancy" which he says "must represent one of the most serious of all prostitutions of psychiatric diagnostic language."[27]

One of the most inventive expressions of medical officialese is related to an abortion performed in 1981 at New York's Mt. Sinai Hospital. In this case, an expectant mother was carrying twins, one of whom was diagnosed to have Down's syndrome. Doctors offered her the unusual option of destroying the Down's syndrome fetus in the womb by drawing out its blood through a needle. The prenatal procedure was performed and the mother delivered one healthy baby and one papery vestige of the fetus that had been.[28] The expression coined to obscure the purpose of the procedure was "selective delivery of discordant twins," an expression that omits reference to the selective killing, and fabricates a "discordant" relationship between twins who are merely different from each other.

The deterioration of words represents a linguistic counterpart to Newton's Second Law of Thermodynamics—a Second Law of Verbaldynamics according to which words drift downward toward a sea of incomprehension. The character in LeClézio's novel is a victim of this downward drift and represents the predicament of many others who suffer from the same phenomenon.

"Pro-life" writers consistently complain about the deterioration of words and many ardently seek to restore them to a condition of grace. "Pro-choice" writers have a different complaint: not that words are deteriorating, but that "pro-life" people are trying to impose their own values on others. The "pro-life" position recognizes clearly that the values they uphold are not "their values," but objective values that extend

---

[26]A former nurse on trial in the death of a patient allegedly confessed she had discontinued the respirator of several patients but only if they were 'gorks'—hospital slang for patients who showed no signs of life except breathing and heartbeat. See *Pro-Life News/Canada*, Vol. 4, No. 2, April 1979, p. 7.

[27]Harley S. Smyth, M.D., D. Phil. (Oxon.), F.R.C.S.(c), "Motive and Meaning in Medical Morals," Alliance for Life Annual Conference University of Toronto, June 1976, p. 6.

[28]Kerenyi and Chitkara, "Selective Birth in Twin Pregnancy with Discordancy for Down's Syndrome, 304 New England Journal of Medicine 1525 (1981).

to all human beings. To make this point in a cogent and convincing way, however, demands a language that is healthy. At a certain point in the deterioration of words, it is no longer possible for language to communicate values that are universal and objective. At this stage, the only values that language can communicate are those of the individual. The deterioration of words, then, is necessary in order to allow the "pro-choice" position to survive as a cultural force, for a deteriorated language provides an effective barrier against all moral values that transcend those of the mere individual.

The process of deification, devaluation, devitalization, and deterioration by which words are dissociated from their proper meanings facilitates deception. Although deception involves an intent to mislead, it is relatively easy to conceal such an intent when using words whose popular usage is already misleading. While "pro-life" writers and speakers are trying to restore language to health, their adversaries are taking advantage of the weakness of language in order to deceive the public even further. And because language is currently in so weakened a state, there seems to be no limit to the amount of deception that is possible.

American abortionist William Baird, in a documentary produced for close-circuit television and shown to thousands of college students, explains in reassuring tones to a young woman who is nine weeks pregnant how her "pre-fetus" will be removed and how she will feel strong enough by that evening to dine with her boyfriend.[29] Canadian abortionist Henry Morgentaler complains to a news reporter that, "People who say the heart starts beating 18 days after conception are crazy. At 10 weeks, the embryo still only weighs one ounce, so how could it have a fully formed heart?"[30] It is a matter of scientific fact that at four weeks the embryo's skin is so transparent that one can observe blood pumping through its heart. At eight weeks the heartbeat is sufficiently strong and clear that it can be taped and played on an inexpensive cassette recorder. Can Baird, Morgentaler, and others be as ignorant about their career specialty as they claim?

The abortionist is sometimes called a "health care provider" and the clinic where he works is a "health care facility." Such appellations suggest that pregnancy is *unhealthy* when, in actuality, the pregnancy is merely *undesired*. Dr. Elizabeth Connell, president-elect of the Association of Planned Parenthood Physicians and associate director of

---

[29]Edwin A. Roberts, Jr., "What others say: About destruction called 'abortion'," *The National Observer*, n.d.

[30]Lynda Hurst, "Pro-Abortionist: Decision is woman's abortion doctor says," *The Toronto Star*, Thursday, November 29, 1973, E1.

the Rockefeller Foundation, told her audience at an APPP conference that "pregnancy is a kind of nasty communicable disease, too."[31] Her remark had been buttressed by the opening paper at the conference—prepared by three employees of the United States Department of Health, Education, and Welfare at the Center for Disease Control in Atlanta—entitled, "Unwanted pregnancy: a sexually transmitted disease." To blur the distinction between pregnancy and the developing fetus, and then associate the fetus with venereal disease is nothing less than willful deception. (Presumably the male has the venereal disease, or pregnancy, first and then transmits it to the woman.)

Some victims of "pro-choice" rhetoric discover the deception, but too late. In July of 1977, *Good Housekeeping* did a feature called "Are You Sorry You Had an Abortion?" The fact that emerges most clearly from the article is how women were deceived. One woman recalls her experience in these words: "Oh, my God, I thought, I've just killed my baby and *all it was supposed to be was some bloody tissue.*" Another woman, who had been told that her three-month child was "a clump of cells," exclaimed: "When I saw that a three-month old 'clump of cells' had fingers and toes and was a tiny perfectly formed baby, I became really hysterical."

Bernard Nathanson has amply documented the pattern of "pro-choice" deception in his two books: *Aborting America* and *The Abortion Papers*. On the other hand, no one realistically accuses "pro-life" supporters of deception. The great task of "pro-life" writers and speakers is to use words already weakened through misuse to describe accurately what any honest and competent fetologist describes when referring to the developing human fetus.

Sir William Liley, the father of modern fetology, found it a bitter irony that just when scientific observation greatly enlarged our appreciation of the importance of human intra-uterine life, there should arrive such sustained pressure to reduce it to a biological triviality and a social non-entity. "In this Orwellian situation," wrote the late Dr. Liley, "where so much semantic effort and logical gymnastics are expended in making a developing human life into an 'un-person,' modern anatomical, genetic, immunilogical, endocrinological and physiological facts are a persistent embarrassment."[32]

The Orwellian situation to which Dr. Liley refers is "doublethink," an ultimate state in the degeneration of language and thinking where people annunciate bald contradictions without the

---

[31]*Love, Life, Death, Issues*, Vol. 2, No. 4, Dec. 15, 1976.
[32]Sir William Liley, "The Development of Life," *Quality of Life* ed. D. K. Bonisch (Dunedin, N.Z.: The Guild of St. Luke, 1975), p. 80.

slightest suspicion that what they are saying makes no sense whatsoever. Orwell defined "doublethink" in *1984*, his immensely successful description of a totalitarian anti-utopia, as "the power of holding two contradictory beliefs in one's mind simultaneously, and accepting both of them."[33] It was the hope of Orwell's Party intellectuals that eventually all people would speak directly from the larynx without thinking at all.

Orwellian doublethink has been a normal strategy for "prochoice" rhetoricians since the earliest days of the debate when they sought to identify abortion with contraception. Surgeon General C. Everett Koop has alluded to the terms "postconceptive contraception" and "postconceptive fertility control"—promulgated as synonyms for abortion—as "doublethink of the highest magnitude."[34] As abortion became more accepted in society, the attempt was made to identify infanticide with abortion. A physician and member of the University of Virginia Medical School, asserted three times in a brief article in *The New York Times Magazine* that parental refusal to allow a life-saving operation on a Down's Syndrome baby is "a woman's second chance to have an abortion."[35]

Once the human fetus had been dehumanized through an assortment of "verbal abominations,"[36] to use Gordon Zahn's expression, "test tube" babies and fetal experimentation provided new reasons to re-humanize him. If a human being was conceived in a woman and subsequently aborted, even as late as the third trimester, it was described in a variety of ways ranging from "an inch of tissue" to "garbage." But if a human being was conceived in a petri dish and spent no more than six days there, it metamorphosed into a human being—a "test tube" baby! The need for experimentation on human fetuses because knowledge so gained would have direct applicability to other human beings, also required the verbal re-humanization of the fetus. The subject that *was* and then *was not* human became human once again, perhaps outdoing doublethink with a new violation of thought and language—triplethink!

By using the word "doublethink," Orwell's characters were admitting that they were tampering with reality. But by a fresh act of dou-

---

[33]George Orwell, 1984 (Middlesex, England: Penguin, 1954), p. 171.

[34]C. Everett Koop, M. D., "A Physician Looks at Abortion," *Thou Shalt Not Kill* (New Rochelle, N. Y.: Arlington House, 1978), p. 9.

[35]Paul Ramsey, "Abortion: A Review Article," *The Thomist*, Vol. XXXVII, No. 1, January 1973, p. 201.

[36]Gordon Zahn, "Abortion and the Corruption of Mind," *New Perspectives on Human Abortion*, ed. Hilgers, Moran, and Mall (Frederick, Md.: University Publications of America), p. 335.

blethink, they could erase this recognition, the lie always being one step ahead of the truth. Although Orwell has aroused people to oppose doublethink in theory, he has not been nearly so successful in helping them to recognize it when it appears. Thus, many instances of double-think, particularly in the case of "pro-choice" rhetoric, go unnoticed while statements that are not contradictory are taken as prime examples of doublethink. From the file of a university language professor comes this presumed paragon of doublethink: "The U. S. navy has a warship, the Corpus Christi." The name, however, was taken from the town in Texas and not from its Latin signification. In this instance, political ideology is one step behind the truth, the very verbal imprisonment which Orwell warned against. A similar victim to political myopia is a U. S. group called the Committee on Public Doublespeak of the National Council of the Teachers of English. Its annual Doublespeak award for 1983 went to President Reagan for his quote: "A vote against MX production today is a vote against arms reduction tomorrow."[37] The award could have been conferred posthumously to America's first president who said: "To be prepared for war is one of the most effectual means of preserving the peace." Of course, Washington was merely echoing a maxim that is at least as old as the Roman Empire—*Si vis pacem, para bellum.*

Reagan is hardly guilty of authoring that year's most perfect example of double-think. He was simply reiterating an ancient belief that an arms build-up can be a deterrent to war, and couching that belief in modern terminology. The belief may be paradoxical, but it is not illogical. Opponents may disagree on political or tactical grounds, but the remark, innocent as it is of logical or semantic contradiction, is no example at all of double-think, let alone the best example of its kind for the year.

The English Committee's official Doublespeak Award for 1984 went again (as did its first award in 1974) to the U. S. state department, this time for its replacement of the word "killing" in its official reports on the status of human rights in countries around the world by the phrase "unlawful or arbitrary deprivation of life." The state department, however, is merely clarifying the meaning of "killing" in a specific context by saying that it is unlawful or arbitrary (not all killing is unlawful or arbitrary). What results is a clarification, not a contradiction.

Consider a few other references to killing which were passed up by the Committee. The head of the crisis-intervention unit at Toronto

---

[37]"1984, Newspeak doesn't call a spade a spade," *Kitchener-Waterloo Record*, Saturday, December 31, 1983, E1.

East General Hospital has gone on record as saying that "If someone is confronted with certain knowledge that he or she is going to die a painful, undignified death through terminal illness, then suicide can be a viable option."[38] Canadian abortionist Henry Morgentaler has argued that "abortion is necessary to protect the integrity of the family." On a more recent occasion, he admonished Cardinal Carter for objecting to "the killing of innocents" by describing the Cardinal's words as "the rhetoric of violence."

Also, consider University of Alberta law professor Ellen Picard's assertion that parents who interfere with their minor daughter's (under the age of sixteen) attempt to obtain an abortion, would run the risk of being charged with "child neglect" and face the possibility of losing custody of the child to provincial child care authorities.

It may be impossible to imagine a better candidate for the 1984 doublethink award than the brain-child of Drs. Chervanak *et al.* which appeared in the prestigious *New England Journal of Medicine*.[39] In buttressing their "argument" for third trimester abortions, the doctors state: "prenatal death does not constitute a harm, nor does the prenatal termination of the fetus' life through induced abortion constitute an injury." Could someone in any other field than medicine get away with such undiluted double-think? Imagine a scout carrying the following message back to his company: "We are happy to report that neither General Custer nor any of his men were either injured or harmed at the Battle of Little Big Horn. Incidentally, they were all killed."

When words are dissociated from the world and from truth in order to provide a neutral discussion, or to promote a particular ideology, or to further some private interest, genuine communication between opposing parties becomes impossible. In the abortion discussion, this communication stalemate represents an advantage to the "pro-choice" position and abortion, since failure to communicate a world of objective values leaves people unaided and without the inspiration that is needed to choose the more difficult path of protecting life. "Man is born broken," writes the playwright Eugene O'Neill, "He lives by mending. The grace of life is glue." Words are a mending grace, providing life with the possibility of higher levels of integration; but only when their connection with the world of truth and value is preserved.

The proper use of words is indispensable for the proper function-

---

[38] William Safire, *William Safire on Language* (New York: Avon, 1981), p. 288, quoted from Toronto's *Globe and Mail*.

[39] Frank Chernak *et al.*, "When is Termination of Pregnancy During the Third Trimester Morally Justified?" *New England Journal of Medicine*, Vol. 310, No. 8, p. 502.

ing of society, a truth well understood by the ancients. A Confucian maxim states with unarguable simplicity: "If language is incorrect, then what is said is not meant. If what is said is not meant, then what ought to be done remains undone."

The use of words constitutes a moral action, and a person is as accountable for his words as he is for his deeds. The Bible offers stern warnings against the abuse and careless use of language, such as in *Matthew* 12:36: "Every idle word that men shall speak, they shall give account thereof in the day of judgment." Recalling his days as a journalist with the *Manchester Guardian*, a now chastened Malcolm Muggeridge confesses:

> It is painful to me now to reflect the ease with which I got into the way of using this non-language; these drooling non-sentences conveying non-thoughts, propounding non-fears and offering non-hopes. Words are as beautiful as love, and as easily betrayed. I am more penitent for my false words—for the most part, mercifully lost forever in the Media's great slag-heaps—than for false deeds.[40]

The way we use words reveals our concern for truth as well as our concern for our fellow man. The abortion debate provides what appears to be an ideal opportunity—for anyone who can be objective about the matter—to assess which side of the debate is more faithful to these concerns. We cannot but be judged by our words, for they make all too clear, as much as do our actions, the kind of people we are.

---

[40]Malcolm Muggeridge, *Chronicles of Wasted Time*, Vol. I (London: Collins, 1972), p. 171.

Abortion and the Unborn

In Somerset Maugham's autobiography, *The Summing Up*, we find the following confession of the author's frustration at trying to find the perspective in which his proper worth as a human being might be found:

> To myself I am the most important person in the world; though I do not forget that not even taking into consideration so grand a conception as the Absolute, but from the standpoint of common sense, I am of no consequence whatever. It would have made small difference to the universe if I had never existed.

This is a simple and candid remark, but one that has application for all of us. If we look out at the world exclusively from the viewpoint of our own subjective centers of consciousness, we see ourselves as unique and supremely important beings, while regarding all others as more or less external objects of secondary significance. This is the subjective perspective in which we consider ourselves to be of more interest, importance, and worth than anyone or anything else in the universe. But this perspective is contrary to common sense and clashes with a more objective perspective. It could hardly matter, from the objective perspective of the cosmos, whether or not we were ever born. We are just another crest of foam on the vast ocean of humanity; here one moment and gone the next, no better or worse than any of the other evanescent members of our species. But here, the objective perspective is false to our uniqueness, contrary to our inner experience of ourselves we gain in consciousness.

These two perspectives are perfectly disjunctive. Each is partly true and partly false, but they have nothing in common with each other to allow coincidence or complementarity. According to the subjective perspective, one exaggerates his sense of worth beyond all reasonable bounds; according to the objective perspective, he underestimates his worth to the same unreasonable degree. The former views man as all-important; the latter regards him as having no importance whatsoever.

If we are to locate the worth of the human being, we must find it in the context of his truth. The truth of man, however, is not to be found in either the subjective or objective perspectives, which are both fragmentary and extreme. This chapter will argue that the truth of the human being—and particularly the human being not yet born—and consequently his worth, is to be found in an organic perspective in which the human being is understood as a person who is both a subject and simultaneously a member of the human family, one whose destiny is inseparable from the destinies of others.

Because the organic perspective is taken as normative, we will use a term that denotes the defective or privative quality of the subjective and objective perspectives. This word is "disorganic," which logically contrasts with "organic," as its privative opposite (the way "disorganize" is related to "organize," or disarray" is related to "array"). The word "disaster" originally had an astrological meaning, referring to being on the "wrong" side of the stars. "Disorganic" means being on the "wrong" side of the organic.

Pope John Paul II, as the philosopher Karol Wojtyla, sought to understand the human person in a way that encompassed the cosmological involvement of the person in the world without reducing him to the objective status of the world. Accordingly, he views the objective perspective as a way of explaining human reality in terms of man's reducibilty to the world:

> The whole scientific tradition of the complexity of human nature, of the spiritual and bodily *compositum humanum*, which through scholasticism passed from the Greeks to Descartes, moves within the limits of this definition, that is, on the basis of the conviction as to the essential reducibility to the level of the world of that which is essentially human.[1]

The objective perspective robs man of both his uniqueness and transcendence. We find extreme formulations of this reduction of man to the world among the mechanists of the modern world who accepted the materialism that was inherent in the philosophy of Descartes. La Mettrie, who authored *Man a Machine* (1768), praised Descartes for being "the first to prove that animals are true machines." Later Du

---

[1] Karol Wojtyla, "Subjectivity and the Irreducible in Man," *Analectica Husserliana*, 7, 1978, p. 109.

Marsais asserted that all men are machines, and noted that the only difference between a philosopher and other men is that the former is a machine which, "owing to its mechanism, reflects on its own movements."

Psychiatrist Viktor Frankl has reported the following definition of man which appears in a biology textbook: "Man is nothing but a complex biochemical mechanism powered by a combustion system which energizes computers with prodigious storage capacities for retaining encoded information." Such an objectivized caricature of the human person could hardly be uttered as insight were it not for two forces that dominate modern culture: scientific-analytic thought and technological achievement.

C. S. Lewis has pointed out in *The Abolition of Man* that as man reduces everything to "mere nature" for the sake of scientific conquest, he reduces himself to "mere nature" in the process and thus ceases to be man. It has been the irresistible temptation in the modern age for man to allow himself to become indistinguishable from objects he seeks to understand. E. M. Forster articulated the predicament of modern man's loss of uniqueness sharply and succinctly when he stated in his 1925 novel, *A Passage to India*: "Everything exists, nothing has value."

The process by which modern man has objectivized his own nature has objectivized even more so the nature of his own unborn progeny. For objectivized man, his children in the womb are merely discardable objects. Thus, he commonly thinks of them as property rather than as persons, as burdens more than blessings.

In a strictly objective frame of reference, the unborn are without distinction, rights or even humanity. They are merely part of the world process, commonly looked upon as factors that swell an already allegedly overpopulated planet. Thus sociologist Margaret Mead can confidently and casually criticize pro-life advocates for discerning in the offspring of mankind a value that transcends the world:

> The Right to Life people, it seems to me, are tied to a past when, because women died so young their reproductive period was very short (only about 15 years in the late Middle Ages) and because so many children could not survive, there was always the danger that there might not be enough people to carry on the world's work.[2]

Such a view of the unborn is commonplace. By assigning them a subordinate role in the world process, they are regarded as mere func-

---

[2]Margaret Mead, "The Many Rights to Life," *Redbook*, July 1978, p. 174.

tionaries. Their permission to live is contingent upon their fitting into the plans and purposes of their parents or of society in general.

There is little exaggeration in the remark that, "Today a woman has not conceived a child until she has decided not to abort it."[3] This remark, of course, alludes to the subjectivization of the nature of the unborn. Today's liberated woman assumes full dominion over that which moves and grows within her uterus. Her unborn is what she wishes it to be and its own substantial reality is defenseless against the awesome power of her will. She has not conceived a child if the idea is repellent to her. She has conceived a child only when her will asserts to the fact. Objective reality is not the determining factor.

A woman asks, "What really is the difference between having an abortion and giving a child up for adoption?"[4] Her interlocutor proclaims the obvious: "fundamentally the difference between a dead and a live baby. . . ." "I still don't see the difference," the questioner replies. She was, of course, referring to the difference it made *to her*; in either case she would be without the child. Her life, supposedly, would be no different if the child were aborted or adopted. She was speaking from a reference point that is purely subjective. A more objectively realistic perspective—which would include the child himself, for whom the difference between his being alive and being dead would indeed be crucial—is simply irrelevant. The subjective perspective of the woman is all that matters.

A woman's "right" to privacy inevitably extends her "right" to occupy a private world, that is, to be free from any association with objective value. Not only may a woman abort because she considers her pregnancy to be inconvenient, but she may even deny that it matters to her child whether he lives or dies, is human or not human, is adopted or aborted. The assertion of secular feminists that a woman may resolve her pregnancy solely in accord with her own wishes is quite evidently mounted on a premise that is subjective in the narrowest sense.

But the narrowing dynamism of feminist subjectivization tightens to strangle even women themselves. One influential feminist claims that no woman who is, in principle, opposed to aborting her own child can consider herself a real woman![5] She argues that being "responsible"

---

[3]Susan Austin, "The Aborting Community," *The Human Life Review*, Vol VIII, No. 4, Fall 1982, p. 55.

[4]Janet Smith, "Abortion as a Feminist Concern," *The Human Life Review*, Vol. IV, No. 3, Summer 1978, p. 71.

[5]Doris Anderson, "R.E.A.L. women don't want real responsibility," Toronto *Star*, March 2, 1985, L1. "The Real Truth about R.E.A.L. [Realistic, Equal, Active, (pro) Life] Women is that they are not women at all. They want

demands that a woman be open to the possibility of aborting her child. By rejecting the freedom to choose one option or the other, a woman rejects both true moral responsibility as well as her own womanhood. Women who are against abortion, therefore, are afraid of taking full responsibility for their pregnancy and hence are not real women at all, but dependent children (would that such thinkers accorded the status of "child" to the child in the womb). Some feminists are thus disexistentializing women in the same way they disexistentialize the unborn.

This subjective perspective is strongly reinforced by present-day consumerism which establishes the mind-set that a consumer should be free to choose or reject whatever products he finds available. The unborn child becomes just another product that is chosen or not chosen, according to the subjective disposition and current financial situation of the purchaser. Economists routinely advise couples not to have a child unless it is a "well thought-out investment." The decision to allow children to come into the world, like arranging weddings, vacations, and career changes, must be cleared through the household's Department of Planning.

The objective perspective, which tends to reduce the value of all life, is shaped largely through scientific-analytic thinking and the impact of technology. It represents a tendency toward the abstract, an attempt to reduce everything to its lowest common denominator. In this instance, we are exposed to the one-sidedness that results when the masculine is separated from the feminine. On the other hand, the subjective perspective is more associated with the elevation of a single factor—subjective preference—above all else. This, to a significant degree, reflects the one-sidedness associated with secular feminism, the manifestation of the feminine principle severed from the masculine. Speaking of two of the greatest and most balanced Christian thinkers in the history of the West, Martin Buber remarks that, "It is not irrelevant that beside Augustine stood a mother and beside Pascal a sister, who maintained the organic connection with the world as only a woman as the envoy of elemental life can."[6]

Both these perspectives—objective and subjective—are essentially and incontrovertibly *disorganic*. With respect to the abortion controversy, these disorganic perspectives provide an existential affirmation of the present disharmony between the sexes. Abortion is symptomatic of a problem between the sexes. Only in an organic perspective in which the masculine and feminine principles harmonize, is it possible

---

to be dependent. And dependents are not adults. Dependents are children."
 [6]Martin Buber, *Between Man and Man* (New York: Macmillan, 1965), p. 40.

to evaluate the nature and worth of unborn human life in a context of wholeness, realism, and truth.

The personalist thinkers (Martin Buber, Nikolai Berdyaev, Gabriel Marcel, Jacques Maritain, and others), have a strong and clear sense of the organic reality of human beings and human society. For Buber, the organic concept of "I-Thou" is a primary word. It is the individual that is the secondary phenomenon; or, as Buber expresses it: "There is not *I* taken in itself, but only the *I* of the primary word *I-Thou* and the *I* of the primary word *I-It*."[7]

According to personalist thinkers, *I-Thou* can only be spoken with the whole being. Hence, the organic structure of *I-Thou* represents human wholeness, whereas the *I* alone is fragmentary. Indeed, the singularized *I* is an aberration.

Modern personalists are by no means alone in their perception of the organic nature of the human person. Solomon understood well the special bond between mother and child. In dealing with the disputing women who claimed the babe to be theirs, he knew that the real mother, because of her organic relationship with her child, would prefer that it live in the custody of another than be divided in half in the interest of an abstract and arithmetic conception of fairness. According to the Talmud, "He who has saved a single life, it is as if he has saved the entire world."

The pagan Terence stated that he was human, and nothing human was alien to him. Kierkegaard maintained that "unum noris omnes" (if you know one, you know all). In his book *On Love*, Josef Pieper concludes that if a person truly loves one human being, he cannot hate anyone. Even in Camus' attitude of the rebel—"Je me revolte, donc nous sommes"—there is the simultaneous affirmation of the self and the other.

A wise maxim for successful family living advises that the best thing a father can do for his children is to love their mother. There is no need to ask "for whom the bell tolls," writes the poet John Donne, "it tolls for thee." And Pope John Paul II instructs us that "The ability to share in the humanness itself of every man is the very core of all participation and the condition of the personalistic value of all acting and existing together with others.' "[8]

All these notions are organic, emphasizing the fundamental inseparability of one human being and another. They are historical in that they represent the common wisdom of the cross-section of mankind, universal because they apply to all human beings, and realis-

---

[7]Martin Buber, *I-Thou* (New York: Scribner, 1958), p. 4.
[8]Karol Wojtyla, *The Acting Person* (Boston: Reidel, 1979), p. 295.

tic since they describe the fundamental structure of the human person. Moreover, these organic notions apply, naturally and properly, to a mother's relationship with her child. Indeed, conventional wisdom throughout history has consistently recognized the incontestable validity of the expression "with child" as a description of the pregnant woman.

The Luke narrative (1:41) speaks of the "babe," John the Baptist, leaping in his mother's womb at Mary's salutation. The Greek word for "babe" in this text is "*brephos*," the same Greek word used in Luke 2:12, 16 to describe Christ in the manger. According to a mythical saying of the Jews, "In the mother's body man knows the universe, in birth he forgets it." Doctors understand intuitively as well as scientifically that when they treat a pregnant woman, they are treating two patients. Books appear on newstands with titles such as *Caring for Your Unborn Baby*, and *The First Nine Months of Life*. When people are not acting as polemicists for abortion, they affirm the human and organic connection between the mother and her unborn child. It is the denial of this organic bond that is narrow, arbitrary, and doctrinaire. Joseph Sobran writes:

> Our civilization's real attitude toward abortion is revealed in its causal idioms, not in the artificial responses it is currently fashionable to make—the rigid euphemisms about 'terminating a pregnancy' and 'nonviable fetuses,' 'a woman's right to choose' and 'reproductive freedom.' These phrases are not the stuff of hymns and poems and myths. They are attempts to conceal disgust.[9]

The truth of any being is found in its wholeness, and its worth is revealed in the experience of that wholeness. In the case of the human person, his wholeness is organic, involving positive relationships of love and care with other persons. It is in this organic context that one directly apprehends the worth of another, an experience that naturally translates itself into a sense of joy. Where joy exists, the presence of inconvenience, hardship, and even personal risk seem unimportant. The example we offer here may seem somewhat unorthodox, since it is taken from the cinema. Nonetheless, it is one that represents such immediacy and symbolic richness that it never fails to communicate its essential message to the mind and heart of the viewer.

One of the most unforgettable scenes in the history of the cinema is Gene Kelly's performance of the title song in "Singin' in the Rain." Rain is usually regarded as an inconvenience. But not for Kelly, who exults in it. He is not only singing in the rain, but dancing and splashing

---

[9]Joseph Sobran, "An Open Letter to Governor Cuomo," *The Human Life Review*, Vol. XI, Nos. 1 & 2, Winter/Spring 1985, pp. 100-101.

ecstatically in it. A policeman wanders by and wonders whether he should lock up this apparent madman who is virtually bathing himself, body and soul, in the wet and chilly condensation. "What a glor-ious feel-ing, I'm hap-py again." The officer, after some hesitation, succumbs to his better judgment and continues on, though scratching his head. This kind of joy is *almost* illegal.

But what is its secret? Why is it that a scene in which a man sings in the rain and stomps and splashes through puddles is so memorable, perhaps the most memorable of all dances that have ever been immortalized in celluloid?

In the film, Gene Kelly has just become engaged to Debbie Reynolds. He now has an organic link to another person, his fiancée, and visions of marriage, children, family, are flooding him with irrepressible joy. His joy is too large for rain to dampen. In fact, it is so large that it transforms the rain and incorporates it into his joy. This is why the scene is so magical, because it choreographs in delightful detail the natural ease with which a loving person can conquer inconvenience. It is the kind of triumph over fate that is possible and meaningful only to organic man.

Today we frequently hear about how women need abortion, since an ill-timed pregnancy can be so inconvenient. The tragedy here is not the inconvenient pregnancy but the lack of an organic context in which the woman's love can overcome the attendant difficulties. It is not likely that the woman who loves and is loved by her husband, and loves her child is going to choose abortion. The organic woman chooses her family.

The disorganic woman, thrown back on her mere individuality, cannot "sing in the rain" or "sing in her pain." Without the support that an organic context of personal love and care can provide, mere individuality is not strong enough to withstand the burden of inconvenience. The right to be loved is more fundamental and human that the right to abort.

"Pro-choice" does a profound disservice to women, not only by reducing them from organic persons to disorganic individuals, but by conveying the message that their real need is not to broaden their life through love, but simply to secure the right to cut from themselves their own living link with love that beckons from within.

A second example comes from the lived experience of husband and wife. Malcolm Muggeridge recounts an episode that took place nearly fifty years ago involving "the person I most loved in this world, my wife Kitty."[10]

---

[10]Malcolm Muggeridge, "The Humane Holocaust," *Ronald Reagan,*

Kitty was desperately ill and her attending physician gave her only an outside chance of surviving. An emergency operation was necessary. But before the operation could take place, a blood transfusion was needed since Kitty's blood had been severely thinned as the result of a long spell of jaundice. At the very prospect that he could be the blood donor, "an incredible happiness amounting to ecstacy" surged up within her husband. His blood count was taken and found to be suitable. Husband and wife were then united through a simple glass tube with a pump in the middle, and the health-giving blood began to flow from one to the other. "Don't stint yourself, take all you want," Muggeridge shouted to the doctor, as he perceived the immediate and salutary effect his gift had in restoring life to her face. It was the turning point; from that moment Kitty began to recover.

Looking back on this incident, Muggeridge writes: "At no point in our long relationship has there been a more ecstatic moment than when I thus saw my life-blood pouring into hers to revivify it." To give life is what love is for; its denial is the antithesis of love.

The organic link between a mother and her child in the womb is established on a less dramatic plane. However, its meaning is not thereby diminished. It is natural enough to commence without even drawing attention to itself. It is sufficiently stable to endure, on the average, for a period of nine months. But even more significantly, it is prototypic, offering a symbol in substance of the organic "we" that describes the essence of personhood and at the same time announces both the origin and destiny of all human beings.

Whenever pre-natal human life is included within the web of an organic relationship, whenever it is affirmed in its fundamental worth as a member of the human family, there is no question of abortion, since abortion presupposes disunity, alienation, and private individuality. But these presuppositions—each disorganic in its core—signal an aberrated and fragmentary view of the human person, one within which a recognition of his real worth is not possible.

The real question today is not whether or not the human unborn has human worth and should be protected from arbitrary and premature death, but why is there abortion. And there is abortion primarily because people have abandoned the fundamental reality of their own organic structure, having forsaken their God-given roles as persons, family members, community members, caring citizens of society, and, as believing Christians, members of the Mystical Body of Christ.

Abortion and the Conscience of the Nation (Nashville: Nelson, 1984) pp. 92-3.

Abortion and the Family

The family is the fundamental unit of society. As such, it shapes or misshapes the pattern of social life. We all know this, though its common treatment as a textbook *cliché* has dulled the sharper edge of the truth that the family—and not the individual—is the basic unit, that plurality precedes singularity, that two, or three, or more, becomes before one. The primacy of the family in society is more mysterious than the simple arithmetic could ever suggest.

We begin to understand something of this paradox when we reflect on the fundamental human importance of love. Love binds us to one another and perfects us on the level of our humanness. Where there is no relationship and no love, humanness is lacking. This is why the solitary individual, looked upon as a closed entity in himself, is not properly humanized and therefore, of himself, not capable of assisting in the process of humanizing society.

The family is the fundamental unit of society because it is the most elementary source of human and humanizing energy whose natural ordination is the good of society. An intimate love begins between husband and wife and is continuous as it extends from parents to children, children to parents, all family members to each other, and the family as a whole to society. The family is the micro-community that makes the macro-community of society a possibility. The individual as such is not a social unit. In fact, the more individuated one is, the more he is cut off from society. The more one turns in on himself, the more he turns away from society. Individualism is ant-social in its essence.

The family as fundamental unit is the reality. But legislators and judges, knowingly or unknowingly, can and do ignore this reality. A great deal of judicial thinking in recent years has been grounded in the premise that the individual is the fundamental social unit. A prime example is a woman's newly-created 'right' to individual privacy in the matter of abortion. In giving a woman the nearly absolute right to abort her child, the courts have undermined the integrity of the family by separating the child from its mother, the father from his child, minor children from their parents, mother from the father, and siblings from each other.

Until quite recently, the Judaeo-Christian tradition still prevailed. A woman's duty to safeguard the life of her unborn child was considered paramount. Abortion was justified only when childbirth would be fatal to her. Yet, as social opinion took an increasingly sympathetic view of the woman in her individuality, it began to consider her freedom, her "liberation," even her career, as of more fundamental value. When the United States Supreme Court decreed virtual abortion on demand in 1973, it based its ruling on a "constitutional right" of the individual woman to her privacy. Thus, the life of an unborn child was no longer protected by law, either in the interest of his own life or the familial values his relationship with his mother implied. His life was redefined as one which intrudes upon his mother's right to remain an individual. Legal abortion for convenience, therefore, demotes the family to the status of being a private option that is of secondary importance to society, while establishing individuality as the fundamental social right.

Some would argue that in many cases abortion can be in the best interest of the family, e.g., when another child would be a severe economic or emotional burden to the parents. Yet the "right" on which the Court based its thinking does not depend on any "right" not to be severely burdened economically or emotionally by one's children, but the "right" to privacy, which gives the individual a more sacred and fundamental place in society than the family.

The full extent to which abortion menaces the family structure has become increasingly apparent as courts and legislatures follow out, step by step, all the implications of placing individuality before family. Once the mother was legally relieved of the duty to care for her unborn child, and was given the liberty to destroy him, the stage was set for the severing of every other family relationship. In order to secure the mother's legal right to separate her child from herself, it became necessary to separate the father from his unborn child, the mother from the father, a minor daughter seeking an abortion from her parents, and finally, children already born from their brother or sister in the womb.

If such law does not follow the order of nature, it does follow the order of logic. For if individuality precedes family, then every relationship within the family can be shattered by the insistence that individuality comes first. As the well-known legal scholar John T. Noonan, Jr., puts it, the childbearing woman has come to be regarded as "a solo entity unrelated to husband or boyfriend, father or mother, deciding for herself what to do with her child. She was conceived atomistically, cut off from family structure."[1] The rationale that justified abortion became the rationale that shattered the family into a collection of unrelated individuals—at least in the viewpoint of the law.

When the U. S. Supreme Court ruled that it was unconstitutional to prevent a woman from seeking an abortion, it left open the question of what constitutional right the father might have to prevent the abortion. In Missouri, a statute required the written consent of the spouse of a woman seeking an abortion during the first twelve weeks of pregnancy unless the abortion was necessary "in order to preserve the life of the mother."[2] Planned Parenthood of Missouri challenged the constitutionality of this statute and the case was eventually heard by the Supreme Court in 1976. John C. Danforth, then Attorney General of Missouri, rested his case on the state's long-standing interest in "marriage as an institution, the nature of which places limitations on the absolute individualism of its members." In support of the state's legitimate interest in "marriage as an institution," he cited a number of other "joint consent" requirements that were laws of Missouri and other states as well: joint consent to begin a family; joint consent to allow the adoption of a child born out of wedlock; joint consent for artificial insemination and as a condition of legitimacy for children so conceived; spousal consent for voluntary sterilization, and joint consent for disposing of an interest in real property. If joint consent is required by law in such instances in the interest of preserving the *bond* of marriage, Danforth argued, it should also be required, and in the same interest, for abortion.

The Court, however, ruled that the state cannot "delegate to a spouse a veto power which the state itself is absolutely and totally prohibited from exercising during the first trimester of pregnancy." It also argued that the state has "no constitutional authority to *give* the spouse unilaterally the ability to prohibit the wife from terminating her pregnancy when the State itself lacks that right"

Of particular importance here is the assumption on the part of the Court that the father is not so much the father of the child as he is a "delegate" of the state, which cannot delegate to the father a power that it does not itself have. That the Court construed the father primarily as a "delegate" meant, in effect, that he had already been legally divested of his natural and real claim to fatherhood. It is important to

---

[1] John Noonan, Jr., *A Private Choice* (New York: Free Press, 1979), p. 95.

[2] 428 U. S. 67-68 (1976).

note here that the Court not only ruled that the father could not veto his wife's abortion decision, but he had no right even to be *informed* of her decision, and thereby given the opportunity for consultation in a matter of great importance to him and his marriage.

The Court's ruling, therefore, refused to recognize that the father has any legitimate interest of his own in the life of his unborn child. A woman's "right" to abort outweighed a father's preference that his child live, even though, in a given case, it may very well be that a father's interest in having a child—perhaps his only child—is unmatched by any other interest in his life.

In dissent, Justice Byron White stated: "It is truly surprising that the majority finds in the United States Constitution, as it must in order to justify the result it reaches, a rule that the State must assign a greater value to a mother's decision to cut off a potential human life by abortion than to a father's decision to let it mature into a live child."[3]

Thus, in the eyes of the Court, the father has less right to protect his own unborn child from premature death than abortion referral agents have to arrange the abortion, or the aborting medical staff to abort the child, or the State to declare unconstitutional the father's involvement in that child's welfare. Moreover, the father's relationship to the life of his unborn child was deemed to be much less important than his relationship with, say, a half-acre of real estate, or the family picnic table, which he co-owned with his wife. If fatherhood was left to have any meaning whatsoever here, the Court did not specify what that meaning might be.

The Court's decision favoring *Planned Parenthood* depended on a conception of marriage in which husband and wife are regarded not as forming a *union* with each other (much less the biblical "two in one flesh") but as retaining absolutely independent identities. The Court viewed the case not in terms of upholding sound interest in respecting the marriage bond, but as a conflict of "rights" between two individuals wherein the woman has a right which her husband cannot veto.

The Court's insistence on viewing people primarily, even exclusively, as individuals has been noted by political scientist Francis Canavan, S. J., who writes:

> Justice Blackmun and the majority erred because they asked the wrong question and thereby ignored the family as a natural community and the basic unit of society. And this they did not because the constitution made them do it, but because their minds are still dominated by the

---

[3]428 U. S. 93 (1976).

suppositions of an outmoded political theory.[4]

Professor Canavan, here, is referring to such philosophers as Rousseau, Hobbes, and Locke, who argued that the individual *is* the "natural" unit of society.

In Canada the situation is much the same. Given the laws relating to abortion and the way a number of court cases on the subject have been resolved, it is clear that therapeutic abortion committees at Canadian hospitals are not accountable to husbands of women seeking abortions. In fact, husbands who seek to save the life of their own child are regarded as "third parties" who are exerting "pressure" and "interfering" with the hospital's prerogative to allow and carry out the abortion.

Dr. Bernard M. Dickens, writing in the *Canadian Medical Association Journal*, goes so far as to say that a man seeking to prevent a medically-indicated abortion for his wife could place himself at odds with the Criminal Code of Canada by refusing to provide "necessities of life" to his spouse—a term that might include medical treatment, and thus the "treatment" of abortion. It is important to note here that therapeudic abortion committees often regard pregnancy itself as a condition that threatens a woman's health. When the Canadian Press wire service carried a summary of Dr. Dickens' article, it introduced it with these words in large, boldfaced type:

> "Hubbie's view in abortion irrelevant." The term "hubbie," needless to say, apart from being frivolous, does not in any way imply or suggest the notion of father. If the father of the child who is about to be aborted is not a "delegate" or an "interfering third party," he is merely a "hubbie."

One case in particular, decided by the Ontario Supreme Court, well illustrates the legal irrelevance of the father's concern for the welfare of his unborn child. In March of 1984, Alex Medhurst made an unsuccessful legal attempt to prevent his wife from aborting their child. Ontario Supreme Court Judge Robert Reid stated that this was "the first occasion when the issue presented here [the abortion] has been disputed between man and wife . . ." Mr. Medhurst had agreed to assume all financial, moral, and educational responsibilities for the child in the event his wife continued to reject him after the child's birth. The Canadian Abortion Rights League (CARAL) paid all of the legal fees incurred by Mrs. Medhurst, who finally obtained her abortion. The de-

---

[4]Francis Canavan, S. J., "The Danforth Case," *The Human Life Review*, Fall 1976, p. 14.

cision reached by the Court was that the father of an unborn child has no legal status to prevent it from being aborted.[5]

In the above-mentioned *Planned Parenthood of Missouri v. Danforth* case, the plaintiffs also opposed a Missouri statute which required an unmarried woman under the age of 18 (and within the first twelve weeks of pregnancy) to obtain the written consent of a parent or person in *loco parentis* before obtaining an abortion, unless her life was in danger. The State, in defending its statue, argued that girls as young as ten and eleven had sought abortions, and that permitting such children to obtain an abortion without the consent of a parent or guardian "who has responsibility for the child would constitute an irresponsible abdication of the State's duty to protect the welfare of minors."[6]

The Court, nonetheless, ruled in favor of Planned Parenthood, arguing that, "the State does not have the Constitutional authority to give a third party an absolute, and possibly arbitrary, veto power over the decision of the physician and his patient to terminate the patient's pregnancy, regardless of the reason for withholding consent."[7]

In another case in 1979, *Bellotti v. Baird*, the Court found unconstitutional a Massachusetts statute which required an unmarried pregnant woman under 18 to obtain the consent of her parents before obtaining an abortion. The Court held that: "Under State regulation such as that undertaken by Massachusetts, every minor must have the opportunity—if she so desires—to go directly to a court without first consulting or notifying her parents. If she satisfies the court that she is mature and well-informed enough to make intelligently the abortion decision on her own, the Court must authorize her to act without parental consultation or consent."[8]

The Court expressed its concern that the minor seeking an abortion receive help, but from a judge or bureaucrat rather than from either of her parents. Professor Noonan has argued that such a decision which separates the minor from her parents is not only an "invasion of parents' rights" but also "an invasion of what most people have considered an absolutely essential element of due process of law" since the parent will not be notified of a judicial proceeding in which he or she has a legitimate interest.[9]

---

[5]Kitchener-Waterloo *Record*, "Court rules father of fetus doesn't have say in abortion." March 23, 1984. See also *The Interim*, April 1984, p. 1.

[6]428 U. S. 72-73 (1976).

[7]428 U. S. 74.

[8]*Bellotti v. Baird*, 428 U. S. 24 (1979).

[9]John Noonan, Jr. "Is The Family Constitutional?" (Washington, D. C.: American Family Institute, 1979).

Expressing its distrust of parents, the Court stated: "We may suspect, in addition, that there are parents who would obstruct, and perhaps altogether prevent, the minor's right to go to court. This would seem but a normal reaction of persons who hold strong anti-abortion convictions."[10]

Such thinking by the Court creates a liberty for abortion which is greater than any liberty located within the family. Nonetheless, the logic holds: if the liberty of the individual is more basic to society than the unity of a good family, then minors would be free to obtain abortions without parents having even the right to consultation or notification.

In another case, *Women's Community Health Center v. Cohen* (1979), a federal district judge found a Maine statute requiring parental notification unconstitutional. He based his decision, in part, on affidavits submitted to him by various doctors who testified that parental notification would "in some instances . . . be harmful to both the minor and the family relationship;" that "in some cases parents will pressure the minor, causing great emotional stress and otherwise disrupting the family relationship"; and finally, that "notifying some parents of a child's pregnancy can create physical and psychological risks to the child."

The State replied that laws regarding child abuse and neglect were sufficient to protect the child against enraged parents. To this, the federal judge replied that such laws fail to protect children from parents who coerce a child's abortion decision in ways that are neither abusive nor neglectful![11]

The practical outcome of "liberating" the minor to have an abortion by separating her from her parents and the support, counsel, or alternatives they could provide, is revealed in a most dramatic way by the testimony of two parents, Thomas and Catherine Yassu.[12]

The Yassus' presented their testimony to a Senate committee of the Oregon state legislature on May 8, 1979, in support of a bill to require that parents be informed before a minor daughter obtains an abortion (the bill was subsequently defeated). The Yassus told of how they tried to see their 15-year-old daughter before an abortion was performed on her at the Lovejoy Specialty Clinic: they arrived at the clinic in time to speak with their daughter before the abortion, but were "lied to" and intimidated by staff members; the administrative director gave

[10]*Bellotti v. Baird*, 450 F. Supp. 997, 1001.

[11]See Senator Jake Garn and Lincoln Oliphant, "Abortion and the American Family," *The Human Life Review*, Spring 1980, pp. 33-4.

[12]Thomas and Catherine Yassu, "A Family Betrayed," *International Review of Natural Family Planning*, Spring 1980, pp. 35-39.

them her reasons why parents should not be informed or allowed to interfere in the decisions of their children—not the least of which was their "over-emotionalism."

The Yassus stated: "It is our firm conviction that we were deliberately lied to, prevented from seeing or talking to our daughter. . . . The only possible motive they could have had for preventing us from seeing our daughter was the distinct possibility that she would not have had the abortion and that therefore they would have suffered the loss of $158." Their daughter informed them later that had she known her parents would have been willing to take care of her and her baby, she definitely would not have undergone the abortion.

In Canada at the present time, parental consent is required before a minor can be aborted. However, there have been attempts to change this, including one in 1980 by the Ontario Medical Association. It is impossible to foretell how the Supreme Court of Canada might rule on a lawsuit claiming that under the new Constitution a minor has the "right" to abort without parental consent or notification.

Ellen Picard, however, a University of Alberta law professor, maintains that children under the age of 16 cannot be denied abortions even if their parents disapprove. She interprets the Criminal Code statement that parents are responsible for providing children "the necessities of life" as including abortion. She argues that once a child has consented, parents who interfere could be accused of "failing to provide necessary medical treatment," and might even run the risk of being charged with child neglect and face the possibility of losing custody of their child to provincial child care authorities.[13]

Contemporary abortion has its genesis in the notion of the unwanted child. But this notion subsumes a more fundamental one, namely that a mother and her child may be separated from each other for reasons of convenience. If a mother can separate her unborn child from herself, a minor daughter can initiate a similar separation in reverse. The unwanted child inevitably produces its own shadow in the form of the unwanted parents. But this latter form of unwanting is particularly devastating since it proceeds from two directions at once. Not only does the child "unwant" her parents, but society stands most eager to replace them with any judicial, bureaucratic, medical, or mere mercenary stranger who happens to be available and/or willing. And what can we expect of these parental replacements? Will they be motivated by parental love, or by financial interests? Will their judgments be based on a life-long knowledge of the child, or on a brief and superficial interview? Will their interest in the child be part of a long-term per-

---

[13]Pro-Life News, "Twisted Logic," Vol. 8, No. 6, January 1984, p. 5.

sonal commitment, or simply a small part of one day's work?

Whenever the father is legally powerless to prevent the abortion of his child and lacks even consultation in the matter, his relationship with the pregnant mother is obviously weakened. A marriage bond cannot mean very much when parents have so unequal a relationship with their unborn offspring that one party's decision is sovereign while the other's is simply irrelevant.

Author Suzanne Gordon reflects this weakened spousal relationship when she describes her own abortion:

> I didn't even call my husband to tell him I was pregnant, nor did I ask his consent before making an appointment with the local abortionist. There was no question in my mind as to what we would do. We could not have a baby. I am a very liberated woman. My decision to have the abortion was made without the slightest trace of emotional conflict. I had no qualms that what I was about to do would make me feel any less a woman. Besides, I have a career. My husband has a career. We have our life-style, our spontaneity, our dog to protect.[14]

In the unbalanced relationship between the pregnant woman and her child's father, it seems grossly unfair that the woman need not be burdened by an unwanted child, but the father—at least financially—should. If the parents of an unborn child are to retain their separate individualities, the woman should owe no favors to the man concerning his child and, logic would dictate, the man should owe nothing to the woman either.

The family can remain strong and whole only when relationships within the family are strong. And, being organic, the family must be whole in order to do for its members, and for society, what it is meant to do.

Abortion fractures the family. It sets in motion a tendency whose logical end is the collapse of the family into a collection of alienated individuals. Author Eda LeShan tells of a four-year-old boy whose mother suffered a miscarriage. The mother did not explain the unfortunate occurrence to her child and thus allowed, though unintentionally, the abortion to have its impact on him. The boy became increasingly disturbed. He cried every morning and did not want to go to nursery school. He became fearful and could not sleep. He would not dress or feed himself and clung to his mother all day. In his own fearful way, he had decided that his mother had gotten rid of the baby because she was afraid the baby might be as bad as he sometimes felt he was. Fortu-

---

[14]Suzanne Gordon, "A Not-So-Simple Operation," *The Human Life Review*, Winter 1976, pp. 11-12.

nately, when the mother understood the situation, she could reassure her son that she did want her baby and had, in fact, grieved over losing it.[15]

But what does a mother who chooses abortion tell her other children?

Several years ago a group of doctors reported in the *Journal of Psychosomatic Medicine* [16] the reactions of 87 children whose mothers had abortions. These reactions were identified as of an immediate type, characterized by anxiety attacks, nightmares, stuttering, running away, death phobias, increased separation anxiety, sudden outbursts of fear or hatred against the mother, and even suicide attempts, and a late type including a range of effects from isolated fantasies to crucial disabling illnesses.

Thus the "right" of abortion has become a primary cause of the decline of family values. The institutionalizing of such individualism is clearly antagonistic to the family. And yet, paradoxically, people who defend the isolated individual's right to remain an individual, form a kind of family of their own. For example, the abortion clinic that fought the Massachusetts statute requiring parental notification of a minor seeking an abortion, calls itself *Parents [sic] Aid*. Another arbortorium called *Parents Aid* operates in Missouri. In Chicago there is one abortion clinic that identifies itself as *Family Guidance* and another that calls itself *Pre-Birth*. In addition, there is *Family Foundation*, the *Orlando Birthing Center*, and the *Center for Human Reproduction*, all of which are dedicated to preventing a child from being born into a real family. In the end, our choice is between a real family, with its love, intimacy, acceptance, and lifelong commitments to each member, and the socialized, pseudo-family made up of judges, bureaucrats, and other (often self-interested) professionals.

So long as permissive abortion continues, its ill effects will continue to tear at the family and society, making it increasingly clear that there can be no adequate substitute for a good family. It should already be abundantly clear that the family is the only department of health, education, and welfare that really works. A realistic society, then, would make every effort to solidify the family, to strengthen spousal and parental love, and create an atmosphere that will produce loving children. The family itself will survive, because it has reality on its side. But at the present moment, that reality demands the support of society, for

---

[15]Eda LaShan, "What Every Child Should Know about Grownups," *Woman's Day*, Feb. 12, 1980, p. 28.

[16]Cain et al. "Children's Disturbed Reactions to Their Mother's Miscarriages," *Psychosomatic Medicine*, 26:58-66, 1964.

we have reason to fear that our present society itself, at least as we know it, may *not* survive today's anti-social assault on its fundamental unit.

Given the organic structure of the family as well as its indispensable significance to the health of society, it is particularly distressing that an organization that calls itself Catholics for a Free Choice could appear on the social scene as a promoter of abortion. For Catholics should know, perhaps better than any other group of people, the dangers inherent in separating the human person from his organic relationship with a community and abandoning him, naked and vulnerable, to his mere individuality. According to a fundamental doctrine of the Church, The Mystical Body, each member of the Church is united to the body of Jesus Christ. In a real way, the Church is Christ, being one with Him as His Mystical Body.[17] Moreover, as St. Paul states, "Christ is the head of the body of the Church" and "we are members of his body" (Eph. 5:30). As Christians, people are not isolated or alienated from one another, but organically linked to each other, through Christ, as parts of a body are united in one living organism.

In his encyclical on *The Mystical Body of Christ*, Pope Pius XII writes:

> But a body calls also for a multiplicity of members, which are linked together in such a way as to help one another. And as in our mortal composite being when one member suffers, all other members share its pain, and the healthy members come to the assistance of those ailing; so in the Church the individual members do not live for themselves alone, but also help their fellows, and all work in mutual collaboration for their common comfort and for the more perfect building up of the whole Body.[18]

By sharing life, in its sorrows as well as in its glories, people live no longer as mere individuals, but as *persons*, retaining their individualities, but also uniting them with others in a community of persons. The family is an organic community of persons, each deeply concerned with the welfare of each member. The Catholic family should be more consciously and emphatically this kind of community because of its intimate involvement with the Mystical Body of Christ.

For Christians, there are no pure individuals, only caring persons. The distinguished Catholic theologian Reginald Garrigou-Lagrange calls attention to the crucial distinction between *individual* and *person*,

---

[17] Ronald Lawler *et al.*, *The Teaching of Christ*, 7th printing (Huntington, Indiana: Our Sunday Visitor, 1980), p. 195.

[18] *Mystici Corporis*, sec. 19.

and how the former leaves man undeveloped and unprotected, the inevitable victim of a thousand passing temptations:

> Man will be fully a person, a *per se subsistens* and a *per se operans*, only in so far as the life of reason and liberty dominates that of the senses and passions in him; otherwise he will remain like the animal, a simple *individual*, the slave of events and circumstances, always led by something else, incapable of guiding himself; he will be only a part, without being able to aspire to be a whole...
>
> To develop one's *individuality* is to live the egoistical life of the passions, to make oneself the centre of everything, and end finally by being the slave of a thousand passing goods which bring us a wretched momentary joy.
>
> *Personality*, on the contrary, increases as the soul rises above the sensible world and by intelligence and will binds itself more closely to what makes the life of the spirit.[19]

Abortion is demonstrably a grave evil—apart from any consideration of the nature of the fetus—because it shatters the organic unity of the family, itself a great good. It is a grave evil to the individuals directly involved, to the integrity of the family, to the larger community, and to society as a whole. Abortion is also a grave evil because it is antagonistic to the affirmation and development of genuine personhood. In addition, it strikes at the heart of Christianity because it places isolated individualism above Christian community, particularly that form of organic community described as the Mystical Body. Abortion is opposed to personhood, family, community, and society. But most of all, it is opposed to that essential factor which binds all communities together—love. Abortion is not a blessing because it keeps unwanted children out of the world; it is a calamity because it prevents needed love from coming into the world.

---

[19]R. Garrigou-Lagrange: *Le sens commun*, 2nd ed. (Nouvelle Librairie Nationale), pp. 332-333.

Abortion and Contraception

There is much talk today of making contraceptives more readily available, especially to teenagers, than they are already. The principal purpose of this greater availability, so it is claimed, is to reduce the incidence of abortion. Virtually everyone, even those who approve abortion for one reason or another, recognize it as a highly undesirable eventuality, and one that brings with it a train of equally undesirable consequences. In the hope of avoiding abortion, or at least sharply reducing the number of abortions performed, many people strongly advise the use of contraceptives. In Canada, for example, the religion editor for the Toronto *Star* fully supports the 1982 Synod decision of the Anglican Church of Canada to develop and encourage more contraception education for teenagers in schools. In his June 12, 1982 column, Tom Harpur states:

> Surely to oppose abortion on the one hand while on the other fiercely opposing sex education and the very contraceptives which could prevent unwanted pregnancies, as many religious groups of varying persuasion do, seems an illogical—and often tragic—mistake.

In the United States, Marjory Mecklenburg, the Deputy Assistant Secretary of Health and Human Services for Population Affairs, says that the Reagan Administration hopes that teenagers will avoid sex, but adds that "if teenagers are sexually active, we want them contracepted safely and effectively."[1] She ardently believes, as does Planned Parenthood, that contraception is the simple and sensible way to prevent unwanted teenage pregnancies and therefore eliminate the need for teenage abortions.

Dr. Carol Cowell, chief of pediatrics and adolescent gynecology at

---

[1] The *Review of the News*, March 24, 1982, p. 19.

the Hospital for Sick Children in Toronto, wants contraception advertising in places frequented by teenagers, such as fast food chains, jean stores, and record shops. American author Eda LeShan says: "Birth control information and *resources* should be easily available whenever a teenager wants them—not from his parents but through the school health service or the family doctor." And Ellen Peck, author of the best seller, *The Baby Trap*, believes contraception should be regarded as natural, not artificial "and just casually part of a girl's tote-bag equipment or make-up paraphernalia." (p. 150) Currently, Planned Parenthood in the United States is vowing to sue the government, takes its case to Congress, and even give up federal funding (which includes about $30 million annually from the Department of Health and Human Services) in its fight against a proposed governmental regulation to inform parents when teenagers receive contraceptive prescriptions.[2]

Similar views are expressed throughout North America, while many people blithely accept them without giving the matter further thought. The plausible hypothesis that contraception will prevent unwanted pregnancies remains largely unchallenged. Yet the fact that competent thinkers *do* find reasons to oppose the promotion of greater contraceptive availability, particularly for teenagers, is itself an indication that this matter warrants closer inspection. Consider, for example, the statement by the researcher Kingsley Davis, in his report to the United States Commission on Population Growth and the American Future when, on the subject of illegitimacy, he stated the following:

> The current belief that illegitimacy will be reduced if teenage girls are given an effective contraceptive is an extension of the same reasoning that created the problem in the first place. It reflects an unwillingness to face problems of social control and social discipline, while trusting some technological device to extricate society from its difficulties. The irony is the illegitimacy rise occurred precisely while contraception was becoming more, rather than less, widespread and respectable.[3]

In short, more contraception leads to more illegitimacy.

What is true for illegitimacy is just as true, though the figures may

---

[2]Washington *Post* story carried in the Kitchener-Waterloo *Record*, April 19, 1982, p. 35.

[3]Kingsley, Davis, "The American Family in Relation to Demographic Change," Research Reports, U. S. Commission on Population Growth and the American Future, Vol. I, *Demographic and Social Aspects of Population Growth*, edited by R. Parke, Jr. and C. Westhoff (Washington, D. C.: U. S. Government Printing Office), p. 253.

be more startling, for venereal disease. For some years now physicians and researchers have spoken openly of a veritable explosion of venereal disease, a rampant and still uncontrollable blight that has affected untold millions of people in North America alone. The extensively researched cover story of the August 2, 1982 edition of *Time* magazine informs us that current researchers estimate that 20 million Americans now have infectious, incurable, herpes, with half a million new cases in 1982. Some critics believe that this tragic consequence of the contraceptive mentality may shock many into a new respect for traditional sexual morality. Says *Time*:

> . . . in the age of the Pill, Penthouse Pets, and porn-movie cassettes, the revolution looked so sturdily permanent that sex seemed to subside into a simple consumer item.

Ironically, eight years ago, Alex Comfort—author of *The Joy of Sex* and *More Joy*—had said of sexual permissiveness: "There is nothing to be afraid of, and never was." Now even magazines which champion permissiveness such as *Rolling Stone* have gotten the message. In its March 4, 1982 issue, it fully acknowledges the failure of contraception, the epidemic of venereal disease and other sexual miseries, while speculating that "some wrathful deity is exacting revenge for our decade-long orgy."

If the widespread use of contraceptives has brought more illegitimacy rather than less, and if it has given society a veritable plague of venereal disease with all its unhappy consequences, we do well to examine the constantly repeated but as yet unsubstantiated claim that a greater use of contraception will reduce the incidence of abortion.

Contraception is the prevention, by mechanical or chemical means, of the possible natural and procreative consequences of sexual intercourse, namely, conception. The purpose of contraception is to separate intercourse from procreation so that the contracepting partners can enjoy the pleasures of sex without the discomforting fear that their sexual activity could lead to the procreation of another human being. The "contraceptive mentality" results when this separation of intercourse from procreation is taken for granted and the contracepting partners feel that in employing contraception, they have severed themselves from all responsibility for a conception that might take place as a result of contraceptive failure. Somewhat ironically, this practice of using contraception to relinquish responsibility for one's own offspring is, in the minds of many, consistent with "being responsible" and even with "responsible parenting."[4] At any rate, the "contraceptive mentality"

---

[4] See K. D. Whitehead, "The Responsibility 'Connection': Divorce, Con-

implies that a couple has not only the means to separate intercourse from procreation, but the right or *responsibility* as well.

The first person to draw attention to the "contraceptive mentality" and offer statistical evidence to support its widespread existence was the Jesuit sociologist Stanislas de Lestapis. In his book, *La limitation des naissances*, published in 1960, de Lestapis provided sociological data that indicated the presence of what he termed a "contraceptive state of mind."[5] As early as the 1930s, the historian Christopher Dawson expressed the fear that widespread contraception would be a threat to marriage. He pointed to the need to re-spiritualize sexuality in order to preserve its true meaning.[6] However, Dawson was regarded as an alarmist for expressing such views. Also in the 1930s, Dr. Paul Popenoe complained in his book, *Modern Marriage*, of real difficulties in marriage that were "intensified by an emotional propaganda, much of which was associated with the earlier years of the birth-control movement." He went on to say that:

> For well over a quarter century, America was assailed with propaganda painting the evils of large families, the dangers of child-bearing, the misfortunes of the "unwanted child" (without taking much trouble to inquire why he was unwanted). . . . From a good deal of modern discussion one would think that children were a misfortune; that the smallest number was a desirable number; that each additional child was for the mother a step toward the grave, for father a step toward bankruptcy, and for both a step toward misery.

As time went on, a variety of thinkers sensed the gradual unfolding of the "contraceptive mentality" and voiced their criticisms. Among these thinkers were such diverse personalities as the humanist philosopher-sociologist Max Horkheimer, founder of the Frankfurt School in Germany,[7] and the Catholic Cardinal Suenens of Belgium who in the 1950s declared that "the instability of family life and the disturbing increase of divorce can, of course, be traced back to the corrosive and shattering

---

traception, Abortion, Euthanasia," *International Review of Natural Family Planning*, vol. IV, no. 1 (Spring 1980), pp. 62-66.

[5] Stanislas de Lestapis, S. J., *La limitation des naissances*, 2nd ed. (Paris, 1960), pp. 63-65.

[6] Christopher Dawson, *Enquiries into Religion and Culture* (1933). See *The Dawson Newsletter*, vol. 1, no. 2 (Fall 1981).

[7] Horkheimer believed that the Pill transforms Romeo and Juliet into a museum piece, and the price of the Pill consists in the acceleration of the loss of longing and finally the death of love. See Rudolf J. Siebert, "The Future of Marriage and Family," ed. Andrew Greeley (New York: Seabury Press, 1979), p. 45.

effect of contraception."[8]

There can be no doubt that contraception has become a dominant feature of sexual behaviour in the Western world. In the United States, in 1975, ten million women were using the Pill (64 million annual prescriptions); in 1974 two million were using the now outlawed Dalkon shield; while sales from condoms reached $150 million a year.[9] But the contraceptive culture is by no means restricted to the United States. By the mid-seventies, 40 million women throughout the world were using the oral contraceptive, to name but one form of contraception. In England, for example, a 1972 Report of the Royal College of Obstetricians and Gynaecologists stated that "over 90% of married couples are believed to have practiced contraception in some form at some time in their married lives."[10] Germaine Greer, the noted feminist, observed that, in Australia, mothers now put birth control pills in the morning tea of daughters aged as young as 12 or 13 years. In India contraceptive advice and information is delivered with cans of milk. In Canada, 24% of all women aged 18 to 44 years were on the Pill by 1976. Clearly, the "contraceptive mentality" has achieved a nearly global acceptance and the push continues to make that acceptance even broader especially among the young.

In his study of the history of the birth control movement in the American society, author James Reed maintains that the major obstacle to wider acceptance of contraception was less technological than psychological. Similarly, he argues that the development of the Pill and other contraceptive devices owed more to changes in social values than to technological opportunity. This psychological barrier was overcome primarily by the effect of intense and relentless propaganda. But the leading propagandists carefully avoided or suppressed the fact that contraception contains an implication of abortion. This they revealed only at such time when the public was ready to accept abortion on its own.

In the United States two very powerful organizations, the American Civil Liberties Union (ACLU) and the Planned Parenthood Federation (PPF) worked together hand in glove to establish the right to contraception which became law in 1955.[11] Thus they helped establish the contraceptive mentality as an important feature of the American way of life. Significantly, both groups ostensibly viewed abortion as an undesir-

---

[8]Leon Cardinal Suenens, *Love and Control* (Westminster, Maryland: The Newman Press, 1960), p. 16.

[9]"Birth Control: New Look at the Old," *Time*, January 10, 1977.

[10]*Unplanned Pregnancy: Report of the Working Party of the Royal College of Obstetrics and Gynaecologists*, London, February 1972, p. 51.

[11]The United States Supreme Court Decision, *Griswold v. Connecticut*.

able objective. They saw an increase in contraceptive practice resulting in a decrease of abortions. But their public campaigns to promote contraception were kept free of any endorsement of abortion, not because their leaders opposed abortion but because the public was not ready for pro-abortion propaganda.

Margaret Sanger, the foundress of Planned Parenthood in the United States, had condoned abortion in her 1916 edition of *Family Limitation*, stating the "No one can doubt that abortion is justifiable."[12] But her colleague, Havelock Ellis, helped persuade her to change her public stance on the matter, shrewdly advising her that the "right to create or not create new life" had better propaganda value than the "right to destroy." As a result, Margaret Sanger began using abortion as a lever to make contraception more acceptable, arguing that contraception would put an end to abortion. Abortions are "barbaric," she then exclaimed, and classified it with infanticide as "the killing of babies."[13]

As late as 1961, Alan Guttmacher, president of Planned Parenthood in the United States, wrote concerning the origin of human life: "Fertilization, then, has taken place; a baby has been conceived."[14] This remark was consistent with an observation he had made in an earlier work, *Having a Baby* (1947), where he referred to the being who was produced by fertilization as "the new baby which is created at this exact moment." But in 1968, when he was international president, the time was ripe for endorsing abortion; consequently, he changed his tactics and declared that "My feeling is that the fetus, particularly during its intrauterine life, is merely a group of specialized cells that do not differ materially from other cells."[15]

One may note that a similar evolution is associated with Dr. John Rock whose book, *The Time Has Come: A Catholic Doctor's Proposals to End the Battle Over Birth Control* (1963), made him, almost overnight, a national celebrity. Although the New York *Times* quoted him in 1966 as saying he would never prescribe or recommend abortifacients, by 1973 he was ridiculing Catholic teaching on abortion and predicting it would eventually be changed. Given the extent of malnutrition in the

---

[12]Elasah Drogin, T.O.P., *Margaret Sanger: Father of Modern Society* (Coarsegold, California: CUL Publications, 1979), p. 69.

[13]Margaret Sanger, *My Fight for Birth Control* (New York: Farrar & Rinehart, 1931), p. 133.

[14]Alan F. Guttmacher, *Birth Control and Love: The Complete Guide to Contraception and Fertility* (New York: Macmillan, 1961), p. 12.

[15]Alan F. Guttmacher, "Symposium: Law, Morality, and Abortion," *Rutgers Law Review* 22 (1960) : 415, 416.

world, he called efforts to prevent abortion a blasphemy.[16]

The contraceptive mentality contained the seeds of the abortion mentality. But certain morally revolutionary events were needed in order to prepare the ground for public acceptance of abortion. These events were mainly four. The first was connected with the moral and ideological turmoil of the 1960s which led to a rethinking (some would say a "doing away with thinking") of traditional views of sexual morality. The other three were more specific: the rise of feminism, the recognition of the hazards of the Pill, and the appearance of anxious world population watchers to check the "population explosion."

The feminist movement which put forward a view of women's liberation that included the right to abortion had a decisive impact on the ACLU (American Civil Liberties Union). As a result of feminist influence the ACLU adopted a pro-abortion stance and dispatched its best constitutional lawyer, Norman Dorsen, to the appeal of *Roe v. Wade* in the United States Supreme Court which was to legalize abortion on demand for the first trimester.[17] The well publicized news of the dangers of the oral contraceptive led many to abandon the "ideal contraceptive" and either resort to lesser effective contraceptive measures or assume the risk of an unwanted pregnancy. The so-called "population explosion" gave rise to a panic rhetoric that was largely accepted without question by the media. Historian James Hitchcock remarks that, "The control of population was, in countless articles and radio and television broadcasts, presented as an imperative which could neither be denied nor compromised. It soon became one of the new moral absolutes, spawning its own far-flung orthodoxies."[18]

All four events are intricately interwoven. The rejection of traditional values was largely a preference to separate sex from marriage, children, and religious dogma, that is, to make sex more "personal" or, in the language of the courts, "private." This preference was congenial to feminists who were demanding a liberation that was to proceed independently of any traditional expectations or values, one that was purely on the individual woman's own terms. The need for an effective and safe contraceptive was a crucial and obvious step along this road to personal and sexual liberation. It may be observed that the United States Supreme Court decision, *Griswold v. Connecticut*, established the

---

[16]Reprinted from the *Boston Sunday Globe Magazine* in the St. Louis *Post Dispatch*, August 20, 1973, p. 28.

[17]See John Noonan, Jr., *A Private Choice* (New York: Macmillan, 1979) p. 36.

[18]James Hitchcock, 'The American Press and Birth Control: Preparing the Ground for Dissent," *Homiletic and Pastoral Review*, July 1980, p. 11.

right to contraception on the basis of the right to privacy. Thus it offered the philosophical basis used in *Roe v. Wade* in 1973 to legitimize abortion on demand in the first trimester. Writing for the Court in 1973 Justice Douglas wrote: "We deal with a right of privacy older than the Bill of Rights—older than our political parties, older than our school system."

The Pill was also viewed as a way of solving the "population crisis" and this fact shaped the minds of people who were influential in approving the Pill for widespread distribution. Louis Hellman, chairman of the Food and Drug Administration's Advisory Committee on Obstetrics and Gynecology interpreted the law to permit the Pill's distribution—despite warning from the scientific community that it was not safe for some women—by balancing the *social* against the risk to the *individual*. Hellman testified before a Congressional Hearing on "Oral Contraceptives" (Jan. 22, 1970) that he had chosen the Administration because "the threat of population growth" was "real to each and every individual of this country." Nevertheless, the Pill which produced diseased conditions in millions of women proved not to be the ally it was presumed to be in the feminists' quest for sexual liberation.

The promoters of the contraceptive mentality were not about to back down when signs of contraceptive failure appeared everywhere. Failure seemed to arouse in them only a greater commitment to the very principles that brought about such disappointing consequences. A survey done between 1965 and 1970 by Princeton sociologists Ryder and Westhoff revealed a contraceptive failure rate of approximately 34%. Four to five percent of Pill or IUD users failed to prevent an unwanted pregnancy. But 10% of condom users, 17% of diaphragm users and 40% of douche users also had the same failures. In response to this study, Planned Parenthood vice-president Frederick Jaffe declared: "To cope with this epidemic we need new conception control methods more effective and acceptable than the Pill and higher program priority and greater financial resources for biomedical research."[19] The new forms of conception control, however, would inevitably mean abortion on greater scale than ever before.

As word circulated, announcing the serious and high risks of the Pill, medical and scientific journals were producing a small tidal wave of studies explaining the diverse factors, conscious and unconscious, that accounted for the rejection and misuse of contraception. Kristin Luker's book, *Taking Chances: Abortion and the Decision Not to Con-*

---

[19]Washington *Post* story appearing in the Kitchener-Waterloo *Record*, October 1, 1973. The Ryder-Westhoff survey was done among 6752 married women.

tracept (1975), presented the clearest picture and supplied the most compelling documentation that had been provided up to that time as to why women routinely chose not to contracept. Sociologist Luker discovered that, given all the personal, emotional, medical, and psychological "costs" of contraception, it was quite rational for a woman to shun contraception and risk an unwanted pregnancy. Luker concluded that the failure of contraception necessitates the full acceptance of abortion:

> We would argue that since abortion has become a primary method of fertility control, it should be offered and subsidized in exactly the same way that other contraceptive services are. (p. 144)

Luker's point is now routinely confirmed by government fiat. The United States government requires each Pill package to come with a detailed two-page insert that spells out the dangers of the Pill in easy-to-understand language. Significantly, it includes a chart claiming that the barrier methods—backed up by abortion in the event of failure—pose the fewest risks for all age groups.[20]

In Canada, the government sponsored Badgley Report (1977) showed that 84.8% of women who had abortions had contraceptive experience. Another government sponsored publication a sex education pamphlet entitled *Birth Control and Abortion* (1976), presented abortion as an inevitable adjunct to failed contraception:

> As long as contraception methods are not 100% effective and safe, and as long as women wish to control their fertility, requests for abortion can be expected to continue. . . . Today abortion is the most widely used birth-control method in the world.[21]

At the 1982 annual meeting of the National Abortion Foundation, Philip Lee, M.D., forecast that in coming years, 50 to 60% of all abortions will be performed on repeat customers. In addition, he stated that even "consistent use of contraceptive methods considered most reliable produces not insignificant failure rates."[22] Biostatistician Christopher Tietze calculates that between 2-5% of women using the Pill with a reasonable degree of motivation are likely to have a repeat abortion within a year of the first abortion, and, within ten years of the first abortion,

---

[20]*Maclean's* "Living Without the Pill," March 15, 1982, p. 45.

[21]Robertson et al., *Sex Education: a teacher's guide*, published by the authority of The Minister of National Health and Welfare, vol. 4, pp. 24-5.

[22]Andrew Scholberg, "Abortionists Meet: 1982," *Life and Family News*, June-July, 1982, p. 1.

between 20-50% of Pill users may be expected to experience at least one other unplanned pregnancy.[23]

Professors John Kantner and Melvin Zelnik of John Hopkins University have done three separate national (U.S.) surveys of teenage sexual activity, contraceptive use, and pregnancy. These surveys, all similar, were conducted in 1971, 1976, and again in 1979. The results are most interesting and serve to confirm the finding that contraception is linked with abortion.

Kantner and Zelnik report that in 1970 there were 190,000 out-of-wedlock births to teenage mothers. By 1978 this figure rose to 240,000. Also in 1970 there were 90,000 abortions performed on teenage women. But by 1978 this figure mushroomed to about 500,000.

The researchers noted a steady rise in the number of teenagers having at least one premarital pregnancy from 8.5% in 1970 to 13% in 1976 to 16.2% in 1979. At the same time, they noted that the percentage of teenagers engaging in sexual intercourse also increased: from 21.8% in 1970 to 30% in 1976 to 32.5% in 1979.

Along with an increase in unwanted pregnancies, abortions, and premarital intercourse, however, was a decline (between 1976 and 1979) in teenagers never using contraception by about one-fourth, and an increase in the number who always used contraception by about one-fifth. More startling, perhaps, is the fact that almost one-third (31.5% of the unintended pregnancies in 1979 occurred while a contraceptive method was in use—a proportion almost four times as high as the 1971 figure of 8.6%. And nearly half the unintended premarital pregnancies (49.7%) occurred among young women who had used a contraceptive at some time. Moreover, Kantner and Zelnik discovered that young women who became pregnant while using contraception were twice as likely to seek an abortion as those who became pregnant in the absence of contraception.

Unintended pregnancies and abortions increased significantly among teenagers despite their using more effective forms of contraception and employing them more frequently and more regularly. Part of the explanation of this paradox lies in the fact that the incidence of teenage intercourse rose to a level that offset whatever advantage contraception may have represented. Indeed, the increase in premarital sex was so great that it surpassed the limits of effectiveness of the birth control and abortion clinics in holding down out-of-wedlock births.

But another part of the explanation has to do with a contraception-abortion mentality that was fostered by federally subsidized birth

---

[23]Paul Marx, "Theological Tomfoolery and Contraception," *Restoration*, February 1979.

control clinics. Since there is a moral and cultural link between contraception and abortion, it is not surprising that evidence for this link would appear on a statistical level.

Michael Schwartz and James Ford, M.D., who studied the Kantner-Zelnik surveys in detail concluded that "it is clear that the family planning programs have contributed directly to an increase in the rate of abortion among teenagers." In providing teenagers with a program of contraception and tacitly encouraging them to engage in sexual intercourse, family programs in the United States not only failed to realize their objectives, but brought on more of the disease.[24]

What should be noted in all the above is that as long as the contraceptive mentality continues, more and more teenagers will follow the cues provided by a contraceptive culture and participate in premarital sexual adventures. In other words, a pervasive and unchecked contraceptive mentality creates a wider clientele that is susceptible to sexual experimentation and all the ills such activity produces: unwanted pregnancies, illegitimacy, abortions, venereal disease, promiscuity, cervical cancer, reproduction problems, sterilization, sexual exploitation, and so on. In a word, the more troops you send into battle, the more casualties you will incur. Thus the widespread use of contraceptives leads to more and not less abortion. Using the contraceptive mentality to fight the abortion mentality confuses cause and effect. It is like trying to put out a fire with matches. *The contraceptive mentality is not the cure but the cause of the abortion mentality.*

All of the above has been amply demonstrated through innumerable research studies. In England, for example, the Royal Commission on Population noted that in 1949 the number of procured abortions was 8.7 times higher among couples who habitually practiced contraception than among those who did not. In Sweden, after contraception had been fully sanctioned by law, legal abortions increased from 703 in 1943 to 6,328 in 1951. In Switzerland, where contraception was almost unrestricted, abortions were alleged to equal or outnumber live births by 1955, and so on.[25] Such figures offer compelling evidence for the claim that de Lestapis was advancing in 1960, namely, that increased contraception does not reduce the incidence of abortion. In fact, contraception tends to establish a "contraceptive state of mind" which leads to absolving responsibility for children conceived, which, in

---

[24]Ford and Schwartz, "Birth Control for Teenagers: Diagram for Disaster," *Linacre Quarterly*, February 1979.

[25]John Noonan, Jr. *Contraception: A history of its treatment by the Catholic theologians and canonists* (New York: New American Library, 1965), p. 614.

turn, leads to *more* abortion. Consequently, Joseph Boyle could write in his article "Contraception and Natural Family Planning":

> ... the approval of contraception leads—though not in such a direct and logical way—to acceptance of abortion. Contraception is an attempt to prevent the handing on of life, and one who turns against life as it is passed on is likely to remain against it if the unwanted new life begins. The resolve to prevent a child from coming to be is often sufficiently strong that one will eliminate the child whose conception was not prevented. This anti-life attitude is often regarded as a "responsible" stance; it often includes the denial that human life is a basic good and the determination that one can do whatever is necessary to execute one's resolve to prevent a person from coming to be.[26]

Dr. Wanda Poltawska, a psychiatrist and director of Marriage and Family Institute in Krakow, Poland, writes:

> Paradoxically, however, as contraception was given the "green light" the number of abortions also increased. It seemed obvious that wherever the contraceptive mentality prevailed, abortion would be the logical outcome of contraceptive failure. Therefore, in countries that admitted contraception for general use, the increasing number of abortions compelled authorities to make them legal. This second green light escalated the worldwide number of abortions to millions and millions each year.[27]

Former Supreme Court Justice Tom Clark put the matter rather tersely in an article he wrote for the *Loyola University of Los Angeles Law Review* (2, no. 1, 1969): "If an individual may prevent conception, why can he [*sic*] not nullify that conception when prevention has failed?" In view of the figures de Lestapis noted, and those culled from several other sources, John T. Noonan, in his widely acclaimed book on the history of contraception, remarked that "it was dangerous to create the idea that offspring were to be avoided."[28] It is indeed true, as Australian physician R. S. J. simpson has pointed out, that "the acceptance of contraception carries with it the virtual certainty that soon you will have to face up to a wide range of individual, family and community evils which are the inevitable consequence of the contraceptive mentality."[29]

---

[26]*International Review of Natural Family Planning*, vol. IV, no. 4 (Winter 1980), pp. 311-312.

[27]Wanda Poltawska, "The Effect of a Contraceptive Attitude," IRNFP, vol. IV, no. 3 (Fall 1980), p. 188.

[28]Noonan, *Contraception*, p. 616.

[29]R. S. J. Simpson, *Contraception: The Camel's Nose*," IRNFP, vol. I, no.

It is important to remember that at the very core of the "contraceptive mentality" is a fear of something which is perfectly natural—babies. The present "contraceptive mentality" make this point difficult to remember since the popular cry to permit teenagers to use contraceptives when they fornicate is based on an understandable desire to reduce the incidence of teenage abortion. Yet the historical root problem which has led to the present teenage crisis is the fear on the part of married couples that their acts of intercourse would be fruitful.

The anti-baby root of the "contraceptive mentality" was brought home in a surprising way a few years ago when G. D. Searle and Company was trying to market its anovulent contraceptive in Turkey. The chief obstacle it ran into was that there was no word for contraception in the Turkish language. So the Pill was marketed to the Turkish people under the equivalent of the "have no baby" pill. A more startling and direct illustration of the anti-baby essence of the "contraceptive mentality" is offered by Montreal's Dr. Lise Fortier at the 1980 meeting of the National Abortion Federation. At her banquet address, Dr. Fortier stated that "each and every pregnancy threatens a woman's life" and that from a strict medical viewpoint "every pregnancy should be aborted."[30]

The "contraceptive mentality," which begins in the dissociation of intercourse from conception, logically and inevitably results in the dissociation of conception from life. As Malcolm Potts, the former medical director of the International Planned Parenthood Federation, accurately predicted in 1973: "As people turn to contraception, there will be a rise not a fall, in the abortion rate."[31] It was an easy prediction to make in the light of what had transpired in other countries. To cite but one more example, Japanese research had shown that women who use contraception have six times as many abortions as other women.[32]

There is virtual universal agreement that abortion is highly undesirable. But repeatedly, as shown above, opponents of abortions who are themselves victims of the contraceptive mentality defend the indefensible thesis that contraception will reduce abortion.

There is only one way to reduce abortion and that is to reduce its cause which is in the contraceptive mentality. And the contraceptive mentality can be reduced only by recognizing that procreation is good and by repudiating the attitude that endorses the violent negation of

---

3 (Fall 1977), p. 236.

[30]Andrew Scholberg, "The Abortionists and Planned Parenthood: Familiar Bedfellows," IRNFP, vol. IV, no. 4 (Winter 1980), p. 308.

[31]Scholberg, p. 298.

[32]Poltawska, p. 188.

that good. It is surely illogical and unrealistic to try to establish a truly humane civilization where every human being has a right to live by beginning with the idea of reducing abortion and remaining unconvinced that the natural and procreative consequence of sexual intercourse is a real good. We cannot restore civilization merely by eliminating something that is bad; we can restore it only by loving and embracing what is fundamentally good. We begin to build a humane civilization not backwards from the charred remains of a burned-out civilization, but forwards from the realization that new life is a great good. The Russian existentialist philosopher Nicolas Berdyaev is right when he says, "If there were no childbearing, sexual union would degenerate into debauchery."[33] It is precisely the possibility of invoking new life that raises sexual intercourse to a supra-personal, transcendent level and gives to the married couple a focus for their commitment that is truly theirs and not something that belongs exclusively to one or the other.

Let us express it another way. It is far more logical and realistic to revolutionize society by teaching men to be virtuous, since virtue is a perfection of something natural, than it is to effect the same revolution by being indifferent to virtue and trying to suppress the evil consequences of man's vices through technological interventions. This is not to say that virtue or civilized society comes easily; in fact, their achievement demands the development and pooling of every gift men have. But it is to say that it is the only way that is logical and realistic. It was the essential insight of Huxley, Orwell, and others that the amoral technological approach produces a dehumanized social nightmare.

In reading the Westhoffs' book, *From Now to Zero* (1968), in which they write lyrically about the "Perfect Contraceptive Society"[34] where contraception is "completely effective" and "completely acceptable," the sensible reader is not impressed with the authors' realism, but on the contrary is puzzled at their apparent total unfamiliarity with real life and the nature of the human condition. Indeed, much modern sociology in this respect is indistinguishable from science fiction (*bad* science fiction, that is).

The true realist looks at man and discovers that sexual pleasure separated from procreation does not succeed in bringing about the happiness it promises because it fails to correspond to the inner rules of sexuality. These rules demand wholeness, integrity, surrender and fruitfulness. No matter how gratifying a reciprocal sexual relationship may be, if the drama and mystery of procreation is not celebrated, at least

---

[33]Nicolas Berdyaev, *The Destiny of Man* (New York: Harper & Row, 1960), p. 242.

[34]Westhoff, pp. 323-335.

symbolically, the partners will disappoint each other and will inevitably turn their attentions to others in the secret hope that next time they will find a relationship that will provide the deeper fulfillment they seek.

The realist is concerned about the difficulties of teaching or living by principles towards which the most influential powers of society are hostile. Although in principle these powers do not prevent us from distinguishing between the real nature of our sexual responsibilities, on the one hand, and the fraudulence of the current contraceptive mentality on the other, they do make things more difficult. Yet a clear distinction between reality and deception would be sufficient to inaugurate a moral revolution.

The story is told of a team of fishermen that was concerned about its dwindling clam harvest. When the fishermen realized that their crop was being ravaged by starfish, they applied a plausible solution to the problem by hauling the predators onto their boats, chopping them in half, and tossing the severed remains back into the sea. Yet they were astonished to discover that the more starfish they bisected, the more clams they lost. Their critical error was failure to understand the real nature of their enemy. Since starfish have the capacity to regenerate, the fishermen were actually increasing their problems all the while they believed they were reducing them. In effect, they had become their own enemies.

The story is a parable for fighting abortion. Since abortion thrives on the contraceptive mentality, we fight abortion realistically not by doubling our efforts to intensify the contraceptive mentality, but by working to eliminate it.

> We would rather be ruined than change,
> We would rather die in our dread
> Than climb the Cross of the moment
> And see our illusions die
>
> *W. H. Auden*

The first step is the realistic assessment of the enemy.

Abortion and Bio-engineering

In May of 1983, a court case in defense of the unborn from abortion opened in Regina, Saskatchewan. This case is the first of a series of cases scheduled to culminate in the Supreme Court of Canada, a combined effort many Canadians refer to as "The Trial of the Century." The purpose of the Regina case was to show that the unborn who develop within human females are themselves human and therefore protectable under the Canadian Charter of Rights which holds that every individual has the right to equal protection and equal benefit of the law without descrimination. To this end, Morris Shumiatcher, a distinguished civil rights lawyer, who spoke of charting "the voyage of the unborn to prove they are human beings.,"[1] called upon nine expert witnesses to prove that the unborn of human beings are themselves human beings.

Among the witnesses for the unborn was the late Sir William Liley of New Zealand, known throughout the medical world as the "father of fetology" and knighted for his pioneering work in amniocentesis. Dr. Liley stated that the unborn is not a part of the mother's body but a separate person who dictates his own growth and determines when he is to be born. He pointed out that the foetus produces its own blood at 17 to 20 days after conception, develops a heart beat at 24 or 25 days, and exhibits recordable brain wave activity by 35 days.

In addition, Dr. Liley made a comment that cut to the very essence of the abortion controversy. He objected to the popular phrase "unwanted children"—which for many is sufficient justification for abortion—because it attaches a stigma to the unborn, whereas the stigma belongs more appropriately to the "unwanting parents." "After all," he said, "we do not blame stolen goods for being stolen."[2] Liley's remark complemented one which attorney Shumiatcher had made ear-

---

[1]Alphonse de Valk, *Joseph Borowski and the Trial of the Century*, Life Ethics Centre, St. Joseph's University College, Canadian Pamphlet No. 10, October 1983, p. 4.
[2]*Ibid.*, p. 5.

lier when he contended that Canada's present abortion law creates "a punishment without a crime and a death sentence without a trial."[3]

The reason we do not blame stolen goods for being stolen is that blame always follows upon culpability. If there is no culpability there can be no blameworthiness. There is nothing that goods can *do* to cause their being stolen, the blame falls solely on the burglar who chooses to steal them. Justice grounded in common sense demands that the burglar be punished for his theft, not the jewels for their being stolen. Similarly there is nothing the unborn can *do* in order to warrant their being "unwanted"; it is the parents who do the unwanting. Nonetheless, it is the unborn who is punished, while the parents are not enjoined to change their act of unwanting their own offspring. It is the innocent who are punished by abortion, while the culpable go unchastized, a practice that makes justice the prerogative of the powerful.

Socrates, the Father of Moral Philosophy, made the same point more than 2,000 years ago. The "gadfly" of Athens explained that when we speak of something in the passive voice we do not reveal anything about its own nature, but simply describe how something else acts on it. Something "is carried" or "is led" or "is seen" because something else carries it or leads it or sees it. "Whenever an effect occurs, or something is effected" he said, "it is not the thing effected that gives rise to the effect; no, there is a cause, and then comes this effect."[4] The principle that Socrates is explaining is that we know something only when we discover what it is in terms of its own inherent principle of activity, and not how it is treated or how other people might happen to evaluate it arbitrarily. It is the nature of the thing that tells us what it is, and not how it is acted upon. To answer the question "what is the unborn" with the answer that it is "unwanted" is to avoid spotlighting what the question directs us to think about. And we must know what a thing is in its own right if we are to render it justice. There is no justice if there is no truth.

Socrates was an enemy of the *status quo* and the various myths and superstitions that blind people and prevent them from seeing what things are in their truth. And he was a relentless opponent of all those who viewed reality as merely a reflection of their own judicial, political, or religious power.

In the Regina trial, Shumiatcher and his expert witnesses for the unborn were following the realism of Socrates, unconventional as it may still be in 20th century North America. They were placing the focus in the proper place, on the nature of the unborn, and not on whatever arbitrary attitudes certain individuals may have towards the unborn or

---

[3]*Ibid.*, p. 3.
[4]Plato, *Euthyphro* 10c.

what dubious opinion polls might have reported on the matter. They insisted on speaking of the unborn in the active, not passive voice. Like Socrates, they were more concerned about truth than power; and their reasoned and scientific conclusion was that the unborn is first and foremost a human being. Nonetheless, Justice Matheson concluded that the unborn are not persons, and their lives should not be counted among those individuals whom the Charter of Rights protects.

The controversy, of course is not about the human nature of the unborn or when human life begins, but whether the unborn should be protected in an upwardly mobile, presumably "liberal" and "enlightened" society that feels they should not. The real controversy has to do with whether contemporary society will render justice to its own unborn or exert power over them.

The *Roe v. Wade* ruling in the United States in 1973 consciously avoided the issue involving the nature of the unborn: "We need not resolve the difficult question of when life begins." The ruling had nothing to do with the nature of the unborn, but with the pregnant woman's right to privacy, that is, how she felt about the child she carried. It was as one dissenting judge described it, an exercise in "raw judicial power."

Recent judicial decisions regarding the human unborn in North America have established a most dangerous precedent in which the value of some humans is derived exclusively from how certain other humans view them and not in terms of what they are in their own right. Society is no longer uncompromisingly committed to the principle that all human life must be respected because it is good, but is beginning to adopt the reverse notion that human life is good only because it may happen to be respected. This reversal is most dangerous because it ignores the good inherent in all human beings, a negative violation of justice, and permits some humans to exercise power over the very lives of others, a positive violation of justice. Moreover, by making "being respected" or "being wanted" a primary condition for continued life, society begins to view human life in a passive way, as something tenuous that can be manipulated, rather than in a positive way, as something of value that commands protection. How far this precedent will advance and how many victims it will ultimately claim is open to speculation; theoretically, it could claim everyone, though its advance is incremental and for most people, imperceptible. But the sphere of victims has already enlarged to include infants, the elderly, the terminally ill, and those who are severely handicapped. As society consents to withdrawing life protection from some humans, it begins to see human beings in a new light as subjects to be manipulated. "There are important voices in our society," writes one social critic, "including the U. S. Supreme

Court, which are consciously or unconsciously dedicated to norms of life, dignity, and freedom external to the human being."[5] We are beginning to view members of our own species not as having their own inherent dignity and value, but as objects that must measure up to certain external and arbitrary standards before value is conferred upon them. The original impetus for this new view is provided by the abortion mentality which is now having a decisive influence in other areas of society, particularly, in the area of bio-engineering.

The moral issue at the heart of bio-engineering centers precisely on how human beings are conceptualized. If we view human life as a primary good, although in individual cases defective and in need of therapeutic intervention, we understand the role of bio-engineering as helping man to attain the fullness of that good to which he is naturally inclined. On the other hand, if we regard certain images of human life which exist in the minds of social engineers as a primary good, then bio-engineering embarks on a dangerous course because it aims at subordinating and sacrificing real human lives for a life that is bio-engineered.

In vitro fertilization is an immensely controversial instance of bio-engineering because the many human lives that are sacrificed are obscured by the few that are born. Shortly after Louise Brown, the world's first "test tube" baby, was born in 1978, national opinion polls and popular magazines announced that the general public was most accepting of this event. What the public saw was an apparently healthy and normal baby that brought great joy to parents who were otherwise unable to have children. It was unlikely that the public would react against such positive, life-connoting images. What was not well known to the public, and certainly not depicted, were less savory realities that preceded the birth of Louise Brown.

It has been estimated that doctors Edwards and Steptoe, who engineered the first "test tube" baby, discarded 99.5% of all fertilized ova produced in their laboratory over a period of 12 years because of various problems including obvious abnormality and development beyond the optimum stage for implantation.[6] In 1975, Edwards and Steptoe published a report on their early *in vitro* fertilization research, admitting that they had failed in at least 200 attempts at transferring the embryo to the uterus. Steptoe's research had been financed by his lucrative abortion practice,[7] and the British Medical Research Council cut off

---

[5]Robert Brungs, S. J. "Life and Personhood," *The Human Life Review*, Summer 1982, pp. 76-7.

[6]Eugene Diamond, "A Call for a Moratorium on *In Vitro* Fertilization," *Linacre*, November 1979.

[7]*Time*, July 31, 1978.

Edwards' grants when it discovered that Steptoe and Edwards proposed to bypass what was considered to be the next necessary step in *in vitro* fertilization research—experiments with non-human primates such as monkeys—and proceed directly to experimenting with human beings. Dr. Steptoe required the parents of Louise Brown to agree to abort their child if there was even a suspicion that it was deformed; and he and his partner, Edwards, kept a close eye on Louise throughout her mother's pregnancy.

In a society that receives most of its information, and forms most of its moral convictions through media images, there is a pervasive tendency for people to believe that all that counts is the "bottom line"—the apparently happy ending. The birth of a child who was conceived *in vitro* often obscures all else as if morality did not include anything that could not be captured in a single photograph. Morality is largely about means, and it cannot be assumed that the end justifies the means. The camera is often oblivious to the moral dimension (though not to the aesthetic dimension). There may be nothing wrong with desiring wealth, but how we obtain it is the very substance of the moral question. The lady in the mink coat, or the gentleman in the pink cadillac may disport enviable images of success, but the invisible moral dimension raises deeper questions such as: are they entitled to their possessions, and did they exploit anyone in the process of acquiring them?

Ethicist Paul Ramsey of Princeton University, fully aware that morality is far broader than any single image that certain people might endorse, submitted an impressive protest against *in vitro* fertilization to the Ethics Advisory Board of the U. S. Department of Health, Education and Welfare. He said:

> *In vitro* fertilization and embryo transfer should not be allowed by medical policy or public policy in the United States—not now, not ever.
>
> I offer four reasons in support of this verdict:
>
> 1) The need to avoid bringing further trauma upon this nation that is already deeply divided on the matter of the morality of abortion, and about when the killing of a human being (at tax expense) can occur;
>
> 2) The irremovable possibility that this manner of human genesis may produce a damaged human being;
>
> 3) The immediate and not unintended assault this procedure brings against marriage and the family, the immediate possibility of the exploitation of women as surrogate mothers with wombs-for-hire, and the immediate and not unintended prospect of beginning right now to 'design' our descendants; and
>
> 4) The remote—but still very near—prospect of substituting laboratory generation from first to last for human procreation. We ought

not to choose—step by step—a world in which extracorporeal gestation is a possibility.[8]

Apart from the moral dimension, the technique of *in vitro* fertilization poses a number of other serious problems. There is a high rate of prematurity associated with IVF; the mother-to-be must undergo laparoscopic surgery so that doctors can obtain ripe eggs, and she is often superovulated so that multiple births are commonplace; and the financial costs remain high while the success rate is very low. Given these and other drawbacks, some scientists are championing a technique designed to supersede IVF, called Embryo Transfer. In this technique, a woman is fertilized through artificial insemination and surrenders her newly formed embryo which is then implanted in the woman who will gestate and bear the child. Yet even Embryo Transfer is fraught with formidable problems. The attempt to recover embryos from the woman who conceived them often fails and is sometimes followed by induced abortion. Spontaneous abortions sometimes take place, and there are occasions when the woman who surrenders her embryo experiences a profound sense of loss. In addition, some embryos die in the attempt to implant them in the uterus of the gestational mother.

We ask the question: "What are the rights of embryos that are manipulated in an unnatural environment without their consent and exposed to unknown but real hazards in the process?" Given the impetus provided by the abortion mentality, society is inclined to believe that these embryos have no rights unto themselves, that their sole reason for being is to satisfy someone else's expectations. *In vitro* fertilization and embryo transfer are just two of many bio-engineering techniques that derive their philosophical justification from the unbalanced principle that some human brings have value only insofar as they fulfill certain functions. The abortion mentality has ushered in and proselytized the notion of the human being as a purely functional entity. This is the lethal connection between abortion and bio-engineering.

In vitro fertilization and embryo transfer have not improved the human condition as much as they have widened the sphere of human victims sacrificed on the altar of functionalism. In examining the available literature on the subject of prospective modifications of man through bio-engineering, it is chillingly evident that if certain scientists have their way, functional man will replace autonomous man. Some scientists have called for certain regressive mutations to enable man to

---

[8]Paul Ramsey, "On *In Vitro* Fertilization," Reprinted in *The Human Life Review*, Winter 1979, pp. 17-30.

survive in space, including legless astronauts who would take up less room in a space capsule and require less food and oxygen. Others anticipate a man with a larger head to accommodate an increased number of brain cells, or a man with an extra thumb or an extra set of hands, one with protruding eyes for improved peripheral vision, or one with a two-compartment stomach to digest cellulose. Still others envision a creature who is a hybrid of human and plant whose only need for food would be water and sunlight, or a race of humans only four inches tall who would cause less pollution and conserve more natural resources. Finally, there are scientists who would like to make it possible for women to lay eggs that could be hatched or eaten, and to see humans equipped with gills to facilitate underwater travel.

The abortion mentality that commences with "raw judicial power" and extends to "raw parental power" can easily lead to a bio-engineering mentality that thrives on "raw biological power." The great tragedy of our time is to applaud in the name of progress the advance of this mentality which victimizes more and more of us, while remaining blind to the essence of the problem which lies in the approval given to withdrawing the right to life from some humans in order to serve the interests and satisfactions of other humans.

The price of not becoming a casualty to the enlarging circle of "functional" man, is to recognize and respect the inherent dignity and equality of all human beings. In a way that perhaps transcends easy comprehension, we are all inter-related in a most inescapable and profound way. How we treat others inevitably determines how we ourselves will be treated. Our love for others will safeguard our love for ourselves.

The abortion issue cannot be contained. It will not remain merely an abortion issue, for its underlying principle, which sets humans against humans, threatens the security of all human beings. We witness in the area of bio-engineering the reincarnation of this same principle and realize that in opposing abortion we are involved in the formidable task of fighting to preserve humanity. Functional man is enslaved by things; he worships something lower than himself. Free man, the man of inherent dignity and value, must remain open to the transcendent if he is to preserve his essential nature. Thus, free must not tolerate the subjugation of any human to any other human. He must not tolerate this because it is unjust; but even more importantly, he must not tolerate it because he has a sacred responsibility not to allow the degradation of his own species.

Abortion and Compassion

"I am well aware that every human being is more or less one-sided," write Kierkegaard, "and I do not regard it as a fault. But it is a fault when a fashion selects a certain form of one-sidedness and magnifies it into a total norm." This observation of Kierkegaard, one of the most insightful thinkers of the modern age, provides us with an important key to understanding a fundamental moral dilemma that plagues our own time.

Philosophers write more books on alienation than on any other subject. The explanation for this lies in the fact that alienation is a clear and pervasive feature of our present age, and philosophers, almost *en masse*, are trying to shed light on this crucial problem. We need not discuss the sundry factors that have contributed to the current situation: the advance of technology, the rise of bureaucracies, increased mobility, the separation of workplace from home, and so on. We are primarily concerned here with the fact of alienation and how its existence and the proposed solutions for its eradication have brought about a critical one-sidedness.

Expressions that denote alienation, such as "out of touch," "not caring," "estranged," "lonely," "confused," "isolated," "cut off," "misunderstood," "victim of prejudice," "discrimination," and so on, are stock-in-trade descriptions that faithfully reflect this painful existential situation. Alienation poses so fundamental a malady in our contemporary world that moral leaders have been constantly prescribing a most fundamental remedy for its alleviation. This remedy is *compassion*. We may not understand what is happening to us; we may have lost our relationship with the moral law, with truth, and even with God; but we can at least be compassionate towards one another. As soon as people are compassionately disposed to each other, their very compassion frees them from the imprisonment of alienation.

Compassion in itself is unassailable. A "compassionate society" represents a higher mode of humanhood than a "competitive society." Certainly compassion is to be preferred to alienation. At the same time, however, compassion is but one virtue among many. It lacks the breadth to provide what is needed for the complexity of relationships that people have with one another. Justice, courage, prudence, and temperance—the time-honored *cardinal virtues*—are necessary for both the normal functioning of the person as well as of society. The inadequacy of compassion is soon realized when people try to make it do more than it can do, while suppressing the virtues that should complement it. In this way, a virtue, by being separated from other virtues actually becomes a vice. There is nothing intrinsically wrong with compassion, nor is there anything inherently wrong with sausages or shoes. But a person who lives by compassion alone is not prepared to meet the moral demands that life imposes. By the same token, a person who diets exclusively on sausages is not healthy, nor is a person who wears only shoes fully dressed.

G. K. Chesterton explains how one virtue (whether it be compassion or even charity), when severed from the rest of the virtues can become a vice and actually do more damage than ordinary vices do:

> The modern world is not evil; in some ways the modern world is far too good. It is full of wild and wasted virtues. When a religious scheme is shattered (as Christianity was shattered at the Reformation), it is not merely the vices that are let loose. The vices are, indeed, let loose, and they wander and do damage. But the virtues are let loose also; and the virtues wander more wildly, and the virtues do more terrible damage. The modern world is full of the old Christian virtues gone mad. Thus some scientists care for truth; and their truth is pitiless. Thus some humanitarians only care for pity; and their pity (I am sorry to say) is often untruthful. For example, Mr. Blatchford attacks Christianity because he is mad on one Christian virtue: the merely mystical and almost irrational virtue of charity. He has a strange idea that he will make it easier to forgive sins by saying there are no sins to forgive. Mr. Blatchford is not only an early Christian, he is the only early Christian who ought really to have been eaten by the lions. For in his case the pagan accusation is really true: his mercy would mean mere anarchy. He really is the enemy of the human race because he is so human.

Jacques Maritain saw at the very source of the modern disorder a *naturalization* of Christianity.[1] By tearing one Christian virtue away from its supernatural order and transposing it into the sphere of simple

---

[1]Jacques Maritain, *The Three Reformers* (New York: Crowell, 1970), p. 142.

nature, Christianity is corrupted in the process. Virtues which once kissed, as Maritain points out, will now forever hate each other. Thus, Martin Luther sought to exterminate reason in order to save faith. Likewise, Immanuel Kant was to say: "I had to suppress knowledge to make room for belief."[2]

The current obsession with compassion well exemplifies the one-sidedness of today's society. Magnifying an exclusive preoccupation with compassion into a social norm (*sans* understanding, *sans* reason, *sans* temperance, *sans* justice, *sans* everything else) not only enshrines one-sidedness but creates an atmosphere which is severely hostile to any balanced and integrated view of things. Blatchford was myopic and mono-dimensional, and therefore intolerant of Christianity, which is far-sighted and multi-dimensional. But today the legion of Blatchfords are alive and well and operating seemingly everywhere, including within the structure of Christianity.

Because of the widespread acceptance of compassion alone as a substitute for moral discourse, it is rare that ethical issues receive intelligent debate. Such is the case with the abortion issue. The "compassion" position views all philosophy, reason, theology, science, logic, and so on, as irrelevant and even inhuman. Compassion alone, so they contend, is all that is needed to resolve each individual abortion case. We should treat each woman who has a problem pregnancy with compassion; that is all we can be asked to do. Anything more would constitute an attempt to impose one's private morals, an act which is plainly incompatible with compassion.

Compassion reveals its inadequacy as an approach to the abortion question in several ways. We mention three of these limitations in particular, namely, that it is *partisan*, *unilluminating*, and *ideological*.

The fact that it is partisan (or selective) is demonstrably clear from the rhetoric of compassion that invariably supports a woman's decision to abort. It is commonplace, even in Christian circles, to perceive the debate as one pitting forces that are "pro-woman" against those that are "pro-fetus."[3] Since it is the woman who undergoes the "agonizing" struggle in reaching her decision (and not the fetus), it is she who is the natural object of compassion. And if one decides the abortion issue on the basis of compassion, one must necessarily be "pro-woman." To be "pro-fetus" is therefore seen to be both "anti-woman" and "anti-compassion." The father of the child, who is somewhat distanced from his offspring and is spared the experience of

[2] *Ibid.*, p. 143.
[3] Joy Bussert, "Can Abortion Be Life-giving?" *The Lutheran*, March 7, 1984, pp. 10-13.

aborting or carrying the pregnancy to term, is not in a very favorable position to receive much compassionate support. Compassion can be decisive only when it pre-selects one character in the conflict and excludes all the rest. To see the abortion reality in all its elements, including the interests of the fetus, the father, other members of the family, and society, requires a vision that mere compassion cannot provide. Nor does compassion contain within itself the justice that is required in order to resolve the issue fairly. Thus, compassion reduces a problem that involves many to one that involves just the woman. In this regard, compassion sees less than it should and is arbitrarily without compassion for all those parties other than its pre-selected favorite. In other words, it is discriminatory.

Compassion is also unilluminating. One may have all the compassion any human being could possibly have for the distressed woman in a particular situation. Nonetheless, this compassion does not provide any hint about what course of action should be taken. If the woman is confused and her compassionate supporter has perfect compassion and nothing more, he would be equally confused. In the practical realm of helping her to make the right choice, he would be entirely useless. Compassion may help alleviate a woman's sense of alienation, but it does not help in the line of intelligent decision making. It offers no direction and is stalemated at the level of feeling. Here we find Rousseau reactivated, a stance that exalts feeling and condemns thought. Confusion about what is right and what is wrong is at the heart of her dilemma. What she is struggling to achieve is enough moral clarity to provide a basis for her ultimate decision. The reason for her struggle is not that she is lacking compassionate support but that she is lacking illuminating light. Mere compassion cannot possibly furnish her with the illumination she is straining to acquire.

Finally, the rhetoric of compassion is set in an ideological context. There is no reason to suppose that "pro-woman" or "pro-choice" forces have a monopoly on compassion. The thousands of compassionate and practical support groups that help a woman to carry her pregnancy to term provide ample testimony to the fact that pro-life people are not without compassion. Yet the rhetoric of compassion propagandizes the notion that pro-abortionists are somehow morally superior to anti-abortionists because they have compassion whereas their opponents see things in terms of abstractions. The pro-abortionists hijack the term "compassion" and claim that it belongs to them by nature. Such an arbitrary appropriation is neither realistic nor fair. It is purely ideological, intended primarily as a strategy aimed at securing their position. The honest admission that there is a great deal of compassion on both sides would take away any leverage the compassion argument could have as a defense of abortion. If both sides are compassionate, the compassionate argument draws a blank. Thus the need for the ideological fiction that pro-abortionists alone are motivated by compassion.

The compassion argument is biased toward the pregnant woman, though it offers her no moral or intellectual illumination and places everyone to whom she is related in a fictitious ideological perspective. What this amounts to is nothing more than encouraging the woman to do what she wants. The compassion argument, therefore, is merely a thinly disguised version of the pro-choice argument. One grants the woman her choice because it would be contrary to compassion to oppose it and thereby add yet another burden to an already over-burdened situation.

Compassion, then, is not merely compassion; it is also permission—and even encouragement—for the woman to do whatever she wants to do. Since compassion lacks illumination it cannot advise a woman against one course of action or another. Consequently, the rhetoric of compassion frees a woman to do as she pleases.

We find a typical example of how the compassion approach works recorded in *The United Church Observer*, a magazine of the United Church of Canada. A 34-year-old married woman becomes pregnant despite having been sterilized the previous year. She goes to an Anglican priest for counseling. The priest, a woman, explains to her that she would have God's blessing "simply by going through this struggle of choosing." It was not important *what* she decided, only *that* she decided. In the end, the woman chose to abort. Because the woman is Christian and deeply religious, she needs to be at peace with God. God does not, in her view, "specifically will the life events or death of any one being," although He did "set in motion the physical laws of the universe eons ago" causing some babies to be born retarded and preventing some women from delivering babies successfully. By separating God's will from His creative act, she is able to abort the life He creates without being in conflict with His Will. She is free to do as she pleases and remain at peace with God because God does not will the life He creates. Christian counseling, therefore, consists in offering compassionate support while allowing the woman her freedom of choice. God's creative act and His Will are not necessarily in harmony with each other.

We find a theological argument for this separation in God of His creative Power from His Will in an article written by J. Philip Wogaman, a distinguished Protestant theologian. Dr. Wogaman's argument appears in a pamphlet he wrote in defense of *Roe v. Wade*, which he called "a landmark of humane spirit and practical wisdom." In the pamphlet, Wogaman asserts that many actual conceptions of human beings "are a frustration of God's will."[4] "Concerning such conceptions," he adds, "it is necessary to say that God probably never intended for them to occur at all, even though it is still God's creative general empowerment that made them possible."

God's creative empowerment brings the universe and all creation into being. Yet, according to Wogaman, God's Will may be at variance with His Power with regard to specific actual conceptions. There is no unity, as the Catholic Church teaches, between God's Power and His Will. His creative act may bring into life new human beings He really does not want. This notion of a divided, possibly even schizophrenic God, has important implications for the pro-choice position. If God does not want certain new human beings, abortion may actually be in harmony with God's Will. Therefore, Wogaman can declare that "abortion may be faithful obedience to the God of life and love."[5] At the same time, one who supports a particular new life may be contravening God's Will.

According to traditional Christianity, God's purpose is made plain through His creation. In other words, creation is God's mouthpiece through which His Will is expressed. There can be no contradiction between His Power and His Will, although the two are distinguishable in that Power executes while Will commands. Accordingly, Thomas Aquinas writes:

> In God, power and essence, will and intellect, wisdom and justice are one and the same. Whence, there can be nothing in the divine power which cannot also be in His just will or in His wise intellect.[6]

When God creates new life through His Power, He is expressing His Will that that particular being exist. God's Will remains faithful to His plan of creation. If there is discordance between God's Will and His creation it is not in Him, but in us. The person whose sexual actions invoke new life (and therefore invite the execution of God's Power), but whose will opposes it, is setting his own will against God's Power.

By separating God's Will from His Power, the order of creation provides us with no clue as to what His Will might be. If God creates

---

[4]J. Philip Wogaman, "Shall We Return to Absolutism?" reprinted in *The Human Life Review*, Vol. I, No. 2, Spring 1975, p. 33.
[5]*Ibid.*, p. 34.
[6]*Summa Theologica* I, 25, 5 ad 1.

life, He may not will it. However, well we scrutinize nature, we remain in the dark. Moreover, our darkness allows us the freedom to exercise our own will. If we cannot begin to discern God's Will through the medium of nature by interpreting the new life He brings into existence as being a manifestation of His Will, we are free to interpret His Will any way we please. As a consequence of such a position, it is logically possible that by performing abortions, medical doctors are doing God's Will; whereas by opposing them, orthodox theologians are violating it. An even stranger consequence is that abortionists may be more closely united with God's Will when they perform abortions than God's very own Power is united with His Will when it creates new life. Such a theology is not only irreverent but sacrilegious!

By removing the guidance of nature and installing private choice in its place, the pro-choice position becomes merely that, a choice without regard to the object chosen. It is an error concerning the will which is the counterpart to the Cartesian error concerning the mind. Descartes seized thinking as if it were an object in itself, not as an activity by which one becomes conscious of something. Similarly, the pro-choice advocate seizes choice as if it were an object in itself and not an activity by which one chooses something. But just as the Cartesian error leaves one imprisoned in what Ralph Barton Perry has called the "egocentric predicament," the pro-choice error leaves one abandoned to a moral darkness where neither reason nor goodness have any significance. Under such limiting circumstances, one really cannot choose at all since he has neither a basis on which he could make a choice or a motivation that would allow him to select one thing rather than another.

The absolutization of choice was clearly articulated immediately after the *Roe v. Wade* decision in 1973 when Joseph Fletcher, an Episcopalian ethicist, stated that the mere "freedom to get an abortion—and the exercise of that freedom—represents an advance in social ethics."[7] This whole-hearted endorsement of freedom, apart from its relationship to reason or good, was later adopted by *Catholics for a Free Choice*, an organization that is funded largely by secular institutions.

Lost in the excitement over the absolutization of freedom is the crucial distinction between freedom of autonomy and freedom of choice. Freedom of autonomy refers to a freedom of fulfillment, that which characterizes the free man who governs his own life without suffering undue constraint from any external cause.[8] Freedom of choice,

---

[7]*Time*, January 29, 1973, p. 37.
[8]Jacques Maritain, *Freedom in the Modern World* (New York: Gordian

on the other hand, is not a terminal value, or an end in itself. Rather, it is directed toward acquiring those goods that are needed in order to bring about the state of freedom of autonomy. Freedom of choice is not independent, but subordinate. And it is the function of reason to ensure that freedom of choice is directed to a person's autonomy and not misused as a mere exercise in gratuitousness. The central error of the pro-choice contingency is to make the highest form of freedom consist in freedom of choice. But if freedom of choice is the highest form of freedom, then one becomes eternally trapped in choosing again and again without his choosing furnishing him with the goods he needs in order to escape from an endless and meaningless cycle of choices to achieve freedom of autonomy. If freedom of choice is uprooted from reason it tends merely to dissipate in indefiniteness. Maritain argues that such dissipation erodes one's personality and one's capacity for love—"For love is always a bond."[9]

The formal constituent of freedom of choice as a moral action is not that it is isolated from reason, but that it is consonant with reason. It is not *from* but *through* reason that we are liberated. Freedom of choice must be anchored in reason to ensure that it is used to promote freedom of autonomy. In other words, freedom of choice is not for itself but for something higher—freedom of autonomy. By absolutizing freedom of choice, or by regarding it as the highest freedom, one becomes unmoved or indifferent to the goods of life that one must choose. Psychoanalytic humanist Erich Fromm enunciated this point when he declared that: "If man becomes indifferent to life there is no longer any hope that he can choose the good."[10] But if man is indifferent to life, he will also be indifferent to his higher freedom. And if he is indifferent to his higher freedom, he cannot be enthusiastic about his freedom of choice.

The freedom of choice rhetoric, then, is a strategy designed to promote abortion and not to enhance freedom. It follows the same short-sightedness exemplified by the rhetoric of compassion. It is not enlarging or humanizing. Compassion and freedom of choice are not only important, but indispensable for the moral life. But they cannot be elevated to a complete moral norm without doing violence to a host of other factors that are also indispensable for a life that is truly moral and humane.

The freedom of choice rhetoric suffers from another defect. Pro-choice advocates fail to distinguish between choice and wish. Indeed, it

---

Press, 1971), p. 30.
   [9]*Ibid.*, p. 32.
   [10]Erich Fromm, *The Heart of Man* (New York: Harper & Row, 1968), p. 150.

would appear that what they usually mean by choice *is* wish. Women with problem pregnancies are routinely told that by having an abortion, it will be as though they never were pregnant. This is a wish, not a choice, since choice must always be realistic, whereas it is not realistic to believe that a pregnancy which did exist also did not exist. Here we observe the falsification of fact by the introduction of wish.

A professor at North Carolina State University offers a case in point. A student of his explained to him why she had missed more than six weeks of his freshman composition class. She had an abortion. The counseling service at the university had recommended it. "It will be as if it never happened," she was told. "You needn't miss a class."[11] What really happened, of course, was that she underwent an abortion and not the retroactive abolition of her pregnancy. She wished that she had never gotten pregnant, but she chose an abortion. Reality is always more concrete than rhetoric. As a result of her real abortion, she suffered real consequences of that experience, in particular, shame and guilt. Now she was faced with the prospect of going home and explaining to her family how a "non-event" led to her failing all her classes.

"Pro-choice" promoters commonly choose to bury their head in the sand concerning abortion's primary victim—the fetus. Examples abound. "It may be biologically human, but it's not human to me," exclaims a student nurse.[12] A woman who eventually became disenchanted with the emptiness of "pro-choice" rhetoric reflects about her former attitude: "Somehow I was pretending that once an abortion took place that other life had never really existed at all."[13] "It's not a life," a husband advised his wife shortly before she underwent an abortion, "it's a bunch of cells smaller than my fingernail."[14]

In commenting on Aristotle's *Ethics*, Aquinas states, simply and frankly, that "choice is not said to apply to impossible things, because it

---

[11]R. V. Young, "Taking Choice Seriously," *The Human Life Review*, Vol. VIII, No. 3, Summer 1982, p. 87.

[12]*Ibid.*, p. 86.

[13]Ruth Rolander Cernera, "Abortion: Another View," *The Lutheran*, May 2, 1984, p. 14.

[14]Linda Bird Francke, *The Ambivalence of Abortion* (New York: Random House, 1978), p. 5. The woman mentioned in the text is Mrs. Francke who wrote about her abortion experience under the pseudonym Jane Doe. The *New York Times* published her account on its op-ed page which produced celebrity status for the author virtually overnight. Interestingly, moments before her abortion, she hoped that her husband would come to her rescue: "I waited for my husband to burst through the door and yell 'stop,' but of course he didn't." (p.6).

has reference to our own action. If a person said that he was choosing something impossible, he would appear to be stupid."[15] It is undoubtedly foolish to spend one's life wishing for millionaire status or wishing for eternal youth while neglecting the life and all its real possibilities that one has before oneself. It is also foolish to believe that abortion is merely a "choice," having no bearing on the fetus, one's own self-esteem, or one's reproductive system.

A pregnant woman may wish that she was never pregnant, just as anyone may wish not to die. We can wish for things that are impossible, but we must choose within the limitations set for us by reality. Choice always involves something that is within our power. It is not only intensely realistic, but is the only way we can become more fully realized as human beings. Through choice we become ourselves. By giving wish supremacy over choice, one is encouraging the adoption of a life that is essentially hopeless, one that takes people out of the realm of what is possible and places them in the fictitious realm of what is not possible. Such a view of wish has implications that are destructive of personal integrity and freedom in its highest and most realistic sense.

The endlessly repeated claims that abortion advocates are "compassionate" and "pro-choice" inevitably convey the implication that those who protest abortion lack compassion and oppose choice. Realistically speaking, however, compassion without moral illumination is woefully inadequate, and choice that pretends to be absolute and is confused with wish is actually an enemy of human freedom and moral integrity. The rhetoric of compassion and the rhetoric of choice are contrived and feeble attempts to conceal what is fundamentally an advocacy for abortion. At the same time, they are attempts to discredit "pro-life" supporters by making them seem one-dimensional. Yet "pro-life" advocates have demonstrated remarkable versatility and variety in offering a comprehensive range of services including care and counseling for women who suffer from the aftermath of abortion. By contrast, the same cannot be said for abortion promoters. From time to time their facade of cultural respectability falls away exposing a rather crass and decidedly uncompassionate demand for abortion at any cost. The New York Times Service reports the following incident that took place in Spain:

> Nearly 3,000 feminists gathered at a national convention in Barcelona
> ... , a group of their leaders announced that they had taken two preg-

---

[15]*Exposition of Aristotle's Ethics*, III, Lect. 5, nn. 443-446. Transl. V. J. Bourke. See also *Summa Theologica* I-II, 13, 5: "Our choice is always possible to us. Therefore we must needs say that choice is only of possible things."

nant young women into an adjoining conference room and that medical technicians had aborted both pregnancies. Two fetuses were presented in bottles. The hall rocked with cheers, and almost all the convention-eers signed confessions of responsibility. . . . [16]

Pro-life advocates acknowledge the importance of compassion and exemplify it in their life. They also recognize and affirm the immense significance of human freedom. But they understand well how compassion and freedom must be complemented by light and wisdom. Then, too, they know that a crucial issue such as abortion demands lightness as well as light, warmth as well as wisdom. One must have both the facts *and* the phosphorescence. Any moral problem calls for solutions that flow from the whole of man and not just from one specific virtue. Specialization is more appropriate for science and technology than it is for morality. Abortion is a great problem not because the issues are complex and confusing, but because the solutions are difficult and demanding. Indeed, they tax all the positive resources a culture has available. We do not move a step closer to a solution through hollow rhetoric and unfounded accusations. Our task is enormous. It demands that we be compassionate to everyone and contemptuous of no one, conscientious in everything we do and congenial to everyone we meet. It demands that we be convivial in the deepest sense, that is, to concelebrate our life with everyone.

---

[16]"Feminists Challenge Abortion Law," *The Toronto Globe and Mail*, Monday, November 11, 1985, A-1.

PART II

Bioethics and Church Teaching

We learn in freshman logic that by changing the quality and negating the predicate we can *obvert* propositions to demonstrate that affirmative and negative statements are equivalent to each other. Thus, "All men are good" is equivalent to "No men are not-good" (or "I am present" is equivalent to "I am not absent"). This is an important point to bear in mind before criticizing a position for being "negative." Since a "negative" proposition may be nothing more or less than an affirmative proposition obverted and therefore substantially the same thing, it is crass and simplistic to criticize something because its propositions happen to be cast in a negative form (as are most of the Ten Commandments).

It is commonplace for many critics to exclaim that Church teaching on the subject of bioethics is nothing more than an unbroken series of 'noes' to many biotechnological innovations that, presumably, stand to provide immeasurable benefits for countless human beings. This view of Church teaching as basically negative (and even anti-humanistic) is indeed crass and simplistic. Though many of its statements appear in a negative form, the Church's mind is fundamentally positive, affirming the inherent, created good of the human being.

The Church says "no" to biotechnological interventions that exploit man, only because she has already given her "yes" to the inherent good of man. Thus, her statements that man should not be harmed are rooted in her recognition that he should be affirmed. The obversion of the proposition "All men are worthy of being protected" is "No men are unworthy of being protected." It is myopic to dismiss the latter proposition for being negative because in doing so, one ignores the more relevant and fundamental fact that the Church perceives man to be good. The Church does not hold that all forms of bio-technology are bad, but only those that violate the good of man.

A more valid criticism may be leveled against these very critics of Church teaching themselves who are more enthusiastic about what contemporary scientists produce than about what original man needs. What is merely novel in biotechnology often has a hypnotic charm that can easily cause people to lose sight of what is original in the human being. And as a result of this infatuation with novelty, the potential harm to human beings that certain biotechnological innovations pose is either ignored or minimized.

But the Church has not forgotten the original constitution of man, nor has it forsaken its responsibility to protect that fundamental and original good. Church teaching on bioethics is based on a clear understanding of this good, and an equally clear realization of the moral principles that must be applied in order to safeguard that good. "Good" and "moral principles," therefore, are correlative terms, for the latter exists in order to insure that the former preserves its essential quality. At the same time, it is useful to clarify the meanings of these basic terms.

The substantive notion of "good," in the sense that the human being is entitatively "good," is based on the scriptural notion that man is created in the image of God. Man is good inasmuch as he participates in or is a reflection of the deity who is good in an absolute sense. God is all-good and as such invests goodness in everything He creates. A fundamental affinity therefore exists between God and creation such that goodness inheres in everything that He creates.

With respect to the human being, we may understand his good in a general way and speak of a general principle which safeguards that good. Accordingly, Pope John Paul II states that "since, in the order of medical values, life is man's supreme and most radical good, there is need for a fundamental principle: First prevent any damage, then seek and pursue the good."[1]

On the other hand, it is possible to understand the good of man in more particular ways. Hence, we may speak of man's *dignity, unity, integrity, identity,* and *spirituality*:

1)*Dignity*: By dignity, we refer to the fact that man is an intrinsic good and as such is an end in himself and therefore not a means to another good or another end. Man has dignity because he is not subordinated to any other creature. Dignity is the regal quality in man whereby his good shines as an end in itself.

2)*Unity*: Man is naturally constituted as a single, unified being. He is not to be regarded as so many parts or as certain parts dominating

---

[1]Pope John Paul II, "Address to members of the World Medical Association," *L'Osservatore Romano*, English edition, December 5, 1983, pp. 10-11.

other parts. He is a unified wholeness. This wholeness is a good inasmuch as it is a natural affirmation of his reality as one being.

3)*Integrity*: Man is more than a natural unity; he is also a moral unity. His crowning moral good is achieved when his life is in harmony with his nature, when his moral "ought" is in agreement with his natural "is." Through will and effort, man achieves an integration of life and nature, freedom and destiny. His integrity is a good that results from a harmonious synthesis of what he is by nature and what he becomes through choice.

4)*Identity*: Man has a specific identity as a member of the human species and as an individual person. These identities are good in themselves. One should not renounce either identity in quest of a different one. Identity is a specific good that distinguishes one good, either as a species or as an individual, from other like goods.

5)*Spirituality*: Spirituality belongs to man as a good that accords with his origin (as created by a spiritual God), his life (as sharing God's Life), and his destiny (as being with God). Man is not merely a material being and is not reducible to a collection of material parts. His spirituality is a good that proclaims his kinship with his Creator.

Each of these particular goods calls out for moral principles that are their natural and logical correlatives. A good and its correlative moral principle may be analogously compared with "value" and "protective policy." A man owns a automobile or a house which are said to have a certain market value. A insurance policy is routinely drawn up as a way of protecting these values. People readily understand that wherever there is a good or something of value, there should also exist some principle or policy to protect it. Just as an insurance policy protects an owner from losing the value he invested in his automobile or his home, so too, moral principles are designed to protect and safeguard the fundamental good of man.

Particular moral principles relate to particular goods. With respect to the five particular goods we have just enumerated, the moral principles are described as follows:

1) Since man has dignity, he should always be respected as an inviolable end and never used as a means.

2) Since man has unity, he should be honored as a whole, and none of his parts should be treated in isolation from that whole.

3) Since man has integrity, his moral good should be upheld, and his morality should never be divorced from his nature.

4) Since man has identity both as a member of the human race and as a unique person, these identities should be valued and allowed to develop and no attempt should be made to modify or radically alter

them.

5) Since man has spirituality, that quality should be affirmed, and no attempt should be made to reduce him to his material components or to limit him to what is merely natural.

Without the benefits that man stands to gain through the application of these moral principles, there exists the imminent danger of his falling victim to five forms of dissolution: 1) exploitation, 2) fragmentation, 3) disintegration, 4) dehumanization, 5) despiritualization.

Thus, Church teaching on bioethics has both a positive as well as a negative function. It is positive in that it seeks to affirm and cultivate the substantive good of man. In its negative role it seeks to protect man from the real dangers that certain uses of biotechnology represent. It might also be said that Church teaching is highly realistic. Not only is it based on a profound vision of man as he is originally constituted as a creature of God, but it is equally cognizant of specific threats that beset man in the present age. There can be no argument raised against the claim that modern biotechnology poses real threats to man in the way it can exploit, fragment, disintegrate, dehumanize, and despiritualize him. We need only think of a few biotechnologies in order to be assured of the reasonableness of this claim: using the human fetus as an experimental object or as an organ-farm for organ transplants (exploitation); employing abortion, contraception, and sterilization to divorce procreation from sexual intercourse (fragmentation); the attempt to perfect man through psycho-surgery and genetic manipulation (disintegration); attempts to produce mutants, cyborgs, super-men, hybrids, etc. which radically alter the identity of man (dehumanization); and attempts to program the behavior of man through various forms of genetic engineering, including genetic surgery and cloning, that regard man as merely material (despiritualization).

The following excerpts from recent declarations of popes and bishops exemplify how Church teaching on bioethics is aimed at defending and promoting the particular goods of the human being:

1) Concerning man's *dignity*:

On the subject of *in vitro* fertilization, the bishops of Victoria, Australia, where the most advanced experiments in this field have taken place, have stated:

> We, the Catholic bishops of Victoria, believe in the human dignity and the human rights of every human being without exception. We insist especially on the dignity and rights of those who have no one to speak out or lobby for them.
>
> We therefore categorically condemn any *using* of a human embryo, or of any other human being, as a mere means to others' ends and

purposes, however admirable—e.g., for scientific experiment or as therapeutic source material.[2]

Pope Pius XII had denounced the notion that a married couple (or anyone, for that matter) had a "right" to have a child. The basic right involved in marriage, as the Church has consistently taught, is the right to acts apt by their nature to the generation of children. To claim that a couple has a "right" to have a child implies that one human being (the child) is to be radically subordinated to another human being. Such radical subordination is contrary to human dignity which demands that one person not be treated as an object, or as a means to an end, even if this end be the fulfillment of the married couple. Thus, Pius condemns artificial insemination arguing that "The matrimonial contract does not give this right, because it has for its object not the "child," but the "natural acts" which are capable of engendering new life and are destined to this end."[3]

Pope John Paul II comdemns experimentations on human embryos for the same reason, namely, that all human beings, because they have their own intrinsic dignity, are unexploitable. He writes:

> I condemn, in the most explicit and formal way, experimental manipulations of the human embryo, since the human being, from conception to death, cannot be exploited for any purpose whatsoever. Indeed, as the Second Vatican Council teaches, man is "the only creature on earth which God willed for itself."[4]

2) Concerning man's *unity*:

The Church has always taught that man is a unification of body and soul. He is "*corpore et anima unus*," as Vatican II teaches.[5] Man is an "embodied spirit" or a "unity in multiplicity." The Incarnation, which is the fusion of the Word with human flesh, and the Holy Trinity, which presents God as one, yet triune, offer fundamental images of unity which are central to the Church's moral teaching. Thus, the Holy Father writes:

---

[2]"Letter of the bishops of Victoria, Australia to 'In Vitro' Fertilization Committee, Melbourne, 1984," *L'Osservatore Romano*, May 14, 1984, p. 19.

[3]Pope Pius XII, "Address to the Second World Congress on Fertility and Sterility," May 19, 1956.

[4]Pope John Paul II, "Address delivered by Pope John Paul II to the participants in the Week of Study sponsored by the Pontifical Academy of Sciences," *L'Osservatore Romano*, November 18, 1982, pp. 2-5.

[5]Constitution *Gaudium et Spes*, n. 14, par. 1. "Man, though made of body and soul, is a unity."

> The substantial unity between spirit and body, and indirectly with the cosmos, is so essential that every human activity, even the most spiritual one, is in some way permeated and colored by the bodily condition; at the same time the body must in turn be directed and guided to its final end by the spirit. There is no doubt that the spiritual activities of the human person proceed from the personal center of the individual, who is predisposed by the body to which the spirit is substantially united.[6]

But man's unity is twofold. Not only is there unity between body and spirit, but there is also an organismic unity within the body which is characterized by a harmony of all bodily parts and functions. With this twofold unity in mind, Pope John Paul II writes:

> It is important not to isolate the technical problem posed by treatment of a certain illness from the attention given to the person of the patient in all his dimensions. . . . You must at least try continually to consider the profound unity of the human being in the evident interaction existing among all his bodily functions, but also the unity of his bodily, affective, intellectual and spiritual functions.[7]

3) Concerning man's *integrity*:

The very mission of the Church, as Pope John Paul II points out, is to restore man "to his spiritual and moral integrity, to lead him toward his integral development. . . ."[8] One aspect of this integrity that the Church has regarded with special concern involves the marital act. Accordingly, the Church teaches that conjugal union should be an integration of body, emotions, and love that is both spiritual and unselfish. Pope Pius XII writes:

> The child is the fruit of the conjugal union when that union finds full expression by bringing into play the organic functions, the associated sensible emotions, and the spiritual and disinterested love which animates the union. . . . Never is it permitted to separate these various aspects to the positive exclusion either of the procreative intention or of the conjugal relationship.[9]

Pope Paul VI confirms this integration of the physical and spiritual in the marital act when he speaks of "the inseparable connection,

---

[6] Pope John Paul II, 1982.
[7] Pope John Paul II, 1983, pp. 10-11.
[8] Pope John Paul II, 1983.
[9] Pope Pius XII, May 19, 1956.

willed by God and unable to be broken by man on his own initiative, between the two meanings of the conjugal act: the unitive meaning and the procreative meaning."[10] This integration of *meanings*, of course does not mean that every act of intercourse should result in fertilization. But it does signify that procreation should never be regarded as a mere biological function, and that the unitive aspect of sexual intercourse should never be viewed as a mere expression of affection. The integration of the bodily and the spiritual, the procreative and the unitive is the very "nuptial meaning" of our bodies, as Pope John Paul II explains.[11]

4) Concerning man's *identity*:

The Church has always taken pains to affirm the unique identity of each person. The "conjugal act," for example, as Pope Pius XII asserts, "in its natural structure is a personal action, a natural self-giving which, in the words of Holy Scripture, effects the union "in one flesh."[12] The marital act is so profoundly personal, so resonant in its affinity between person and person, that it can effect an interpenetration of personal identities that results in two being united as one. Love is man's most personal act and flows essentially from his unique identity as a person.

Through the body man may be personally united with another. At the same time, the body is an inseparable part of his identity as a person. For this reason, Pope John Paul II warns against genetic manipulations aimed at altering man's identity, those "adventuresome endeavors," as he describes them, "aimed at promoting I know not what kind of superman."[13] In addition, certain genetic manipulations can alter the identity of one's offspring, the offspring of their offspring, and so on, through countless generations. Given this anthropological vision, the Pope asserts that "The biological nature of each person is untouchable, in the sense that it is constitutive of the personal identity of the individual throughout the whole course of history."[14]

Man's identity as a person, a lover, and as a generator is a good and should not be placed at risk by non-therapeutic biotechnological interventions.

---

[10]Pope Paul VI, *Humanae Vitae*, n. 12.

[11]Pope John Paul II, "Address on the Nuptial Meaning of the Body," January 9, 1980.

[12]Pope Pius XII, "Apostolate of the Midwives: An Address by His Holiness to the Italian Catholic Union of Midwives," October 29, 1951.

[13]Pope John Paul II, 1983.

[14]*Ibid.*

5) Concerning man's *spirituality*:

Pope Pius XII denounced artificial insemination because it reduced the conjugal act to a mere organic function, and converted the "domestic hearth" into "nothing more than a biological laboratory."[15] More recently, the Catholic Bishops of England denounced *in vitro* fertilization for similar reasons since, in their opinion, this procedure treated the embryonic human being as if it were a product rather than a person.[16] Concerning genetic manipulation, Pope John Paul II avers that it "becomes arbitrary and unjust when it reduces life to an object."[17]

Church teaching on this point is based on the understanding that man is more than a mere biological phenomenon or even a mere product of culture, and the consequent realization that it is a grave injustice to man to try to enclose him in a material world or to imprison him in a secular one. From the very beginning of his life man is a spiritual being, a person who transcends materiality. This is evident from the fact that he is generated by agents who are themselves personal and spiritual beings. Thus, as Pope John Paul II writes, human fertility "is directed to the generation of a human being, and so by its nature it surpasses the purely biological order and involves a whole series of personal values."[18] The process by which parents beget new life is essentially personal and involves an intimate communication between spiritual, personal beings, including a personal, creative God.

The Church is progressive in that it encourages man to gain dominion over the visible world. But it is progressive in an ethical way and denounces the misuse of the technological power that man has at his disposal, what one theologian has repudiated as the "anthropology of domination."[19] The difference between "dominion" and "domination" in this matter lies precisely in the difference between an inclusion and an exclusion of a bioethics founded on the original, constitutive good of the human being. In his encyclical *Redemptor Hominis*, Pope John Paul II places the true progressive spirit of the Church, that is, one which unites progress with ethical principles, in perspective when he states that the essential meaning of this "dominion" of "man over the visible world, which the Creator himself gave man for his task, consists in the

---

[15]Pope Pius XII, 1951.

[16]*Catholic Bishops' Joint Committee on Bio-Ethical Issues to the Warnock Committee on Human Fertilisation and Embryology*, para. 20.

[17]Pope John Paul II, 1983.

[18]Pope John Paul II, *Familiaris Consortio*, n. 11.

[19]Johann Metz, *The Emergent Church* (New York: Crossroad, 1981, p. 35.

priority of ethics over technology, in the primacy of the person over things, and in the superiority of spirit over matter."[20]

---

[20]Pope John Paul II, *Redemptor Hominis*, n. 16.

Bioethics and Theology

The unprecedented progress in recent years in man's technological capabilities to modify, reshape, or re-engineer himself evokes a sense of uneasiness and awakens the memory of Eden. Eat of the forbidden fruit, God warns, and you are surely doomed to die. Eat, promises the serpent; you certainly will not die, you will be like God. The temptation to be like God is at the root of the ethical dilemmas that contemporary biotechnology poses, particularly that branch of biotechnology that has the power to alter man in a radical way. Should science re-create man? Will *Homo futurus* resemble the superman of the Nietzschean or Shavian dream? Will re-created man be, as the serpent promised, more like God? Because such questions as these are raised, which surely carry the discussion beyond science and into the domain of theology, many social critics perceive a profound antagonism between certain bio-technological projects and Biblical Theology. "The most alarming features in the biotechnology revolution," writes author Wes Granberg-Michaelson, "are not its scientific advances but its theological assumptions."[1]

Ethicist Paul Ramsey has enlarged upon modern biotechnology's dubious aspiration to Godhood in his book, *Fabricated Man*. So familiar are we with "techno-theologians," he contends, that many of us believe they actually are theologians and that in their writings they are using theological concepts and are doing religious ethics.[2] These techno-theologians, in fact, are the shaman of an age in which cultic praise of bio-engineering is virtually the only form of prophecy that has social respectability.

---

[1] Wes Granberg-Michaelson, "The Authorship of Life," *Sojourners*, June-July, 1983, p. 20.

[2] Paul Ramsey, *Fabricated Man* (New Haven and London: Yale University Press, 1970), p. 138.

The Roman Catholic theologian, Karl Rahner, in an article titled "Experiment Man," probes the question of what, if anything, a theologian may say about present schemes for man's indefinite self-modification. Rahner argues that man has no alternative but to change himself if he wants a world population of billions to survive. In order to bring about this change, Christians must oppose what he calls "bourgeois conservatism." "Man," he argues, "is essentially a freedom event," a person who is subject to himself and capable of freely determining his own final condition. His "self-determination" is so complete, Rahner continues, "that he can ultimately and absolutely become what he wants to be."[3]

Rahner's argument can easily be interpreted as offering a *carte blanche* for unlimited human self-modification, for he states, optimistically, that "there is really nothing possible for man that he ought not do."[4] Nonetheless, he is still aware of contradictory and destructive forms of self-creation man might engineer on a large-scale that could have "irreversible, irreparable consequences in the future which future manipulation will be unable to undo." Ramsey finds Rahner's thinking on this point (and the thinking of Protestant theologians of secular, historical "hope") to be so vague and lacking in moral guidelines that would safeguard man in his own proper nature, as to obliterate the distinction between *being men* and being *God*.[5]

Ramsey is not developing but merely alluding to a distinction of fundamental importance, one that separates two competing theological perspectives in which we may say that man seeks to become either more *like God* or more *Godlike*. The linguistic distinction here is somewhat artificial, but since the blurring of these two ethical perspectives is at the heart of the essential ethical dilemma posed by current biotechnology, it is important to attempt to distinguish them clearly and to elaborate upon each in some detail.

The Promethean Perspective:

The fundamental assumption of the Promethean perspective is that man and God (gods) are essentially antagonistic to each other. Man needs something to fulfill his destiny—fire, light, knowledge, freedom, courage, and so on—that God withholds. In order for man to acquire what he needs, he must *take* it, as Prometheus stole the fire. A theology becomes Promethean, then, whenever it assumes that man's

---

[3]Karl Rahner, "Experiment Man," *Theology Digest* 16 (February 1968) p. 61; "Experiment Mensch: Theologisches über die Selbstmanipulation des Menschen," *Schriften für Theologie* 8 (Einsiedeln, 1967): 260-85.

[4]Rahner, p. 64.

[5]Ramsey, p. 142.

supreme perfection is something God wants to prevent him from attaining. But in seizing from God what God wants to keep for himself, the radical distinction between man and God dissolves and man becomes more 'like God'. At the same time, as explained by Promethean philosophers from Feuerbach to Sartre, God ceases to be.

Feuerbach argues in his book, *The Essence of Christianity*, that "the distinction between the human and the divine is illusory."[6] Man, according to Feuerbach, is radically unfulfilled because he alienates the best part of himself in the name of an imaginary God. The task of philosophy, therefore, is to convince men that the God to whom they attribute qualities of perfection and transcendence is really the alienated better part of themselves they have projected upon a non-existent being. Feuerbach simply transfers attributes of God to man and enjoins man to be like God. "Man with man, the unity of me and you: this is God! The love between men must be elevated to the rank of divinity."[7]

Marx, who was Promethean by temperament, later adopted Feuerbach's rational formulations of alienation and the illusory nature of God. In his earlier writings, Marx wrote about Prometheus chained to his rock and expressing contempt for the gods with lyrical enthusiasm and admiration. He saw in Prometheus a symbol of man denying the gods and assuming responsibility for his own creation. "I would much rather be bound to a rock," he exclaimed, "than be the docile valet of Zeus the Father"

We find a similar Promethean strain running through the thought of Nietzsche and other disciples of the "God is Dead" movement. "God is dead," Nietzsche announces, "now it is your will that Superman shall live."[8] Emil Bergmann proclaimed in words that anticipated some of today's techno-theologians, that "it is possible to breed not only animals but the man-God." As Henri de Lubac, S.J. has pointed out in his study, *The Drama of Atheist Humanism*, such thinkers trace their descent from Prometheus, whom they acclaim to be "the first of the martyrs."[9]

In Sartre's *Les mouches* and in Dostoevsky's character Raskolnikov of *Crime and Punishment* we find important landmarks in modern literature referring to man's attempt to rise above himself through his own heroism and claim the Godhead for himself. The Promethean themes of heroism and taking control are amply presented in modern

---

[6]See also an elaboration of this point in Ignace Lepp, *Atheism in Our Time* (New York: Macmillan, 1966), pp. 57-72.

[7]Quoted by Lepp, p. 63.

[8]Friedrich Nietzsche, *Also Sprach Zarathustra*, Part IV.

[9]Henri de Lubac, S.J., *The Drama of Atheist Humanism* (Cleveland: World Publishing Co., 1963), p. 28.

thought and application to the ethics of bio-engineering is clearly evident.

Ethicist Joseph Fletcher, who is also an ordained Protestant clergyman, is perhaps the most outspoken of today's Promethean techno-theologians. "To be men," he expostulates, "we must be in control. That is the first and last ethical word."[10] Fletcher regards it as a sacred duty for modern man to take control of his own heredity. Yet he advocates more than that and even welcomes the opportunity "to bio-engineer or bio-design para-humans of 'modified men.'"[11]

The Promethean perspective is not only anti-theistic but anti-humanistic as well. Man's nature, given its mortality and finitude, must be transcended. And since God, or the idea of God, resists this transcendence, God cannot be an object of hope. Thus, man must attempt the heroic (perhaps the impossible) and try to become God himself, a man-God, or a self created being who is like God.

Gerald Feinberg, a physicist at Columbia University, is the author of *The Prometheus Project*. In this work, Feinberg urges mankind to press on to "transcendent goals" which "require the creation or achievement of something qualitatively new." Since man, as Feinberg reasons, despairs at the recognition of his own finitude—a recognition which prevents him from achieving abiding contentment—we must inaugurate "a transformation of man into something very different from what he is now . . ."[12]

It should be clear that projects such as those proposed by Fletcher, Feinberg, and others, are rooted in a despair over man as he is. This despair is the natural and inevitable reaction to the human condition which is mortal and finite and the awareness that man can find neither satisfaction nor hope in his limited and fallible human nature. The Promethean call invites man to attempt a quantum leap beyond mere humanness into the realm of the gods. Such a call summons heroic courage. But in the end, after rejecting both God and human nature, man is left with no place to find rest, no place to stand. At the same time, in the spirit exemplified by Malraux and Camus, it may be that the struggle itself is enough to satisfy the mind and heart of the Promethean figure. Yet the techno-theologians have more ambitious hopes.

Humanistic psychoanalyst Erich Fromm, in *The Sane Society*, re-

---

[10]Joseph Fletcher, "Ethical Aspects of Genetic Controls," *New England Journal of Medicine*, Sept. 30, 1971, p. 782.

[11]*Ibid.*, p. 776.

[12]Gerald Feinberg, *The Prometheus Project* (Garden City, New York: Doubleday, 1968), pp. 50-1.

marked that life is so burdensome that it is truly surprising more people are not insane.[13] A few years later he wrote a book bearing the title *You Shall Be As Gods*, affirming the promise of the serpent.[14] We are left to wonder how Fromm can place any credence in such a quantum leap, or whether he envisages a race of gods verging on insanity.

The Biblical Perspective:

At the heart of the Biblical perspective is the conviction that man and God are friends. In fact, this friendship (or sonship with God) is such that it constitutes a world of grace. To put it another way, grace is testimony to the harmonious continuity between God and man. Accordingly, nature is the soil of grace and through nature man is able to return to God. Grace means that there is no opposition between man and God, and that man is able to be sufficiently united within himself (not alienated) to live without opposition to God. If there is an infinite abyss that separates God from man, there can be no grace and finite man is thus left to his own natural resources to achieve his ultimate perfection.

God in no way is resentful of man's innermost natural needs. Everything that God creates is good ("There are no dustbins in the house of the Lord," as G. K. Chesterton says). He "hates nothing that He has made." He does not oblige man either to save his soul by a Promethean *tour de force*, or come crawling towards Him on his stomach. God creates man in such a way that he makes it possible for man to participate in His own Divine life, that is to say, to become more Godlike. Because the world of human nature and the world of God are united by grace, man, by becoming more Godlike, not only fulfills his human nature but surpasses it, satisfying his deeper longings for the eternal and infinite which mere nature itself cannot fulfill.[15]

The philosophical-theological vision of Thomas Aquinas is in perfect accord with this notion of the harmony and continuity between nature and God. Etienne Gilson, the well known Thomist and historian of philosophy, has remarked that "The central intuition which governs the whole philosophical and theological undertaking of Saint Thomas is that it is impossible to do justice to God without doing justice to nature, and that doing justice to nature is at the same time the surest way of

---

[13]Erich Fromm, *The Sane Society* (New York: Fawcett, 1955), p. 34.

[14]Erich Fromm, *You Shall Be As God* (New York: Fawcett, 1966), p. 53: "The Serpent who said *eritis sicut dei* ('You shall be like [as] gods') had been right."

[15]Francis Thompson addresses this paradox in his poem "The Hound of Heaven" when he writes: "All which I took from thee I did but take,/ Not for thy harms,/ But just that thou might'st seek it in my arms."

doing justice to God."[16]

In the Promethean perspective the assumption is made that man comes into possession and entitlement of what he needs through conquest. According to the Biblical perspective, God offers man what he needs as a gift that needs only to be accepted. Here, salvation belongs to the order of love and acceptance, rather than to the order of resentment and conquest. Man becomes more Godlike as he freely accepts the gift of God that exists within his own soul. Something belongs to man, then, not because he has taken it through power, but because he has received it through love.

Genesis 1:26 reads: "Let us make mankind in our image and likeness." First, man is created in God's image. This "image" is in the structure of man's soul, whether he is aware of it or not. But this "image" becomes a "likeness" of God when the intelligence is enlightened in a spiritual understanding of God and when the will raises the whole soul in love for God. The "likeness" of God (being Godlike) is the perfection, through knowledge and love, of God's "image" in man. According to St. Augustine, "In this image (which is the soul) *the resemblance of* God will be perfect when the vision of God is perfect.[17] Aquinas adds that likeness, which is a kind of unity, "signifies a certain perfection of image."[18] It is not enough for man to recognize the "image" of God within himself which makes him potentially Godlike; he must actualize this potential through knowledge and love.

In the Promethean approach, man raises himself up by his own powers. This represents merely, an intensification of powers that are already present in human nature. According to the Biblical perspective, on the other hand, man is raised up by supernatural gifts for which his nature has a passive and obediential potency.

The Promethean approach is intensely humanistic in that it calls man to realize his full potential as a human. Nonetheless, it is anti-humanistic in that it demands that man go beyond his human nature, re-creating himself according to a pattern that is not human. Because the Promethean approach requires extraordinary courage and heroism, its fundamental appeal is to the individual. Indeed, for the Promethean individual, everything converges upon the self. According to Biblical theology, however, the self is fulfilled by selfless love for other persons. The notion of biogenetic perfection that is discussed among techno-theologians is one that devolves upon man in his material individuality

---

[16]Étienne Gilson, "Nature and God. St. Thomas Aquinas, *"Proceedings of the British Academy,* Vol. XXI (London: Oxford Press, 1935), pp. 29-45.

[17]St. Augustine, *De Trinitate,* XIV c. 15 n. 23.

[18]St. Thomas Aquinas, *S.T.,* I, Q. 93, a.9.

alone, for such spiritual realities as fellowship in God, love of others, and faithfulness to God are not subjects for biotechnical operations. At the same time, it is important to acknowledge the courage the Biblical perspective demands. Whereas Promethean courage is needed for the individual to stand alone and accept his struggle, the Biblical approach demands a sterner and yet more humble courage to accept the human condition with all its painful finitude *and* to accept the reality that we cannot be like God. Here the virtues of humility and faith complement courage and protect it from degenerating into fanaticism. The Promethean seems pre-eminently heroic only because all of his strength is concentrated into a single virtue—courage. Realistically, however, he is prone to a host of disabling vices, including intemperance, pride, and arrogance.

Thomas Merton offers a summary distinction between the Promethean and Biblical (Christian) perspectives in describing *The New Man* that emerges as more Godlike rather than more like God:

> The union of the Christian with God is the exact opposite of a Promethean exploit, because the Christian is not trying to steal something from God that God does not want him to have. On the contrary, he is striving with his whole heart to fulfill the will of God and lay hands upon that which God created him to receive. And what is that? It is nothing else but a participation in the life, and wisdom, and joy and peace of God Himself.[19]

The radical limitations of the Promethean perspective are many. We draw attention to but four. The first represents a virtual rejection of religion, at least traditional Biblical religion. The Promethean perspective does not justify this rejection, it merely assumes that no justification is necessary. But in rejecting religion, it accepts excommunication from a possibly real and loving God who confers vital benefits upon his creatures. It also disavows the type of ultimate meaning that only a religious framework can provide. André Malraux, whose life dramatically illustrates the Promethean attitude, writes in *The Human Condition* that it takes sixty years of incredible suffering and effort to make a unique individual, and then he is good only for dying. The Promethean

---

[19]Thomas Merton, *The New Man* (New York: New American Library, 1963), pp. 34-5. Granberg-Michaelson *op. cit.*, draws a distinction between trying "to be like God," orienting life around self-chosen purposes apart from God, wanting to decide "autonomously the intentions for life and creation, and then attempt to carry out that rule by its own power and for its own ends," and being "the image of God," in "serving as the representative of God's rule and purpose in the creation . . ."

attitude, which begins in despair must also end in despair. Marx's defiant revolutionary phrase, "I am nothing and should be everything," is a perfect articulation of this despair.

Secondly, the Promethean perspective focuses narrowly on man as a material individual and fails to recognize his whole nature that is spiritual as well as material, free as well as determined. Thus, it neglects the importance of the moral values that serve to safeguard this wholeness. These values are not amenable to biotechnological control; they presuppose man's freedom and autonomy. In addition, to live morally demands a rectitude of will, that is to say, a will that chooses what is good. Such a well-ordered will, however, requires wisdom, another acquisition that biotechnology cannot provide. Renowned author and ethicist Dr. Leon Kass reminds us that in the absence of a moral wisdom that directs us toward our proper destiny, we simply do not know where we are going, no matter how sophisticated the technology is that we have at our disposal. He writes:

> Let us not fail to note a painful irony: our conquest of nature has made us the slaves of blind chance. We triumph over nature's unpredictabilities only to subject ourselves to the still greater unpredictability of our capricious wills and our fickle opinions. That we have a method is no proof against our madness. Thus, engineering the engineer as well as the engine, we race our train we know not where.[20]

In addition, the Promethean approach is incapable in principle of overcoming the more radical weakness of the human being—his mortality and finitude, including the unannullable facts that he is not God, not his own creator, and not the object of his own beatitude. Ernest Becker concludes his Pulitzer Prize winning work, *The Denial of Death*, by asserting that "a project as grand as the scientific-mythical construction of victory over human limitation is not something that can be programmed by science."[21] Concerning the ineradicable limitations that the Promethean spirit is wont to deny, he writes: "There is no strength that can overcome guilt unless it be the strength of God; and there is no way to overcome creature anxiety unless one is a god and not a creature."[22]

The fourth limitation is perhaps the most significant and has to do

---

[20]Leon R. Kass, "The New Biology: What Price Relieving Man's Estate?" *Bio-ethics*, ed. Thomas A. Shannon (Ramsey, N.J.: Paulist Press, 1981), p. 397.

[21]Ernest Becker, *The Denial of Death* (New York: Free Press, 1975), p. 285.

[22]Becker, p. 261.

with the fact that the Promethean perspective, rooted as it is in despair over the human condition, is essentially anti-humanistic. Thus, it is a perspective that is not so much interested in serving the needs of human nature, as in responding to needs that transcend human nature. An exaggerated interest in what Paul Ramsey calls "questionable aspirations to Godhood"[23] can easily displace a normal interest in the human role of medicine and science as a human enterprise that serves human beings. Human nature, limited as it is, is a good. Moreover, the immediate and common universal needs of man which biotechnology can remedy are health needs.

The vast array of health remedies that biotechnology possesses and promises—from gene therapy to the regeneration of organs—provides a great service as well as a great hope for mankind. Perhaps the greatest danger to biotechnology's realizing its great potential is the abiding belief that biotechnology has a more important function to play in re-creating man.

The Biblical perspective does not see the world's humanization as first dependent on technical progress.[24] At the same time, this perspective demands the full employment of bio-technology in the interest of restoring men to health. Because human nature is regarded as a good created by God, and, through grace, harmoniously united with Him, bio-technology serves a vital function in coming to its aid. Medical technology is good only because human health is good.

At the close of their book, *Who Should Play God?*, authors Howard and Rifkin express the fear that biotechnology will be applied contrary to the good of human nature. "The very knowledge that we can now be replaced," they write, "should provide a stimulus for us to prove that we are worthy of being preserved."[25] Yet how do we "prove" that human nature is a good worthy of being preserved? Such a proof, involving, as it does, a metaphysical valuation, cannot be made by science. Is not the whole moral force of the Biblical perspective nothing other than conveying the truth that man is good (and worthy of being preserved) because he is the creation of a God who Himself is all good? Paul Ramsey makes the point in these words:

---

[23]Ramsey, p. 138.

[24]See Ulrich Eibach, "Genetic Research and a Responsible Ethic," *Theology Digest* (Vol. 29, No. 2, Summer 1981); "Leben als Schöpfung aus Menschenhand? Ethische Aspekte genetischer Forshung und Technik," *Zeitschrift für Evangelische Ethik* 24:2 (April, 1980), 111-30.

[25]Ted Howard and Jeremy Rifkin, *Who Shall Play God?* (New York: Dell, 1977), pp. 229-30.

> We ought rather to live with charity amid the limits of a biologi-
> cal and historical existence which God created for the good and simple
> reason that, for all its corruption, it is now—and for the temporal future
> will be—the good realm in which man and his welfare are to be found
> and served.[26]

All men by nature seek God. In practice they either seek to be
God or to be with God. In either case, they need a transforming force
that allows them to advance toward their ultimate destinies. This force
is either a natural power that exists within man, or a super-natural love
by which man participates in the life of God. These two distinct approaches—one Promethean, the other Biblical—are irreconcilable. In
the former case man seeks to be like God (equivalent to God); in the
latter, he seeks to be Godlike (participating in the life of God). The
current discussion concerning modifying man through bio-technology
includes a theological dimension which stands to be greatly clarified by
distinguishing between the Promethean and Biblical perspectives.
Paradoxically, it is the latter perspective which ostensively is concerned
with man's relationship with God, that is also concerned with man as a
good that is worthy of the kind of salutary help biotechnology can offer
him. The Promethean perspective, on the other hand, in stressing the
importance of man transcending his nature through his own effort, presents the twofold danger of failing in its intent and deflecting interest
away from man's basic health needs that are grounded in his reality as
an imperfect and limited human being.

---

[26]Ramsey, p. 149.

Genetic Engineering

The expression 'genetic engineering' is one that many scientists dislike intensely. For many of them, it conjures up the inappropriate image of amoral technicians who are driven by some unnamed Fury while engaged in trying to alter the basic structure of man himself. We are being led into "wild country," *"terra incognita,"* writes one critic of genetic engineering, "that is full of threats to the increasingly tentative belief that all human life is of value and should be treated reverently."[1] Nonetheless, the expression has great rhetorical force and has become an established part of the current language we use in discussing bioethical issues.

Since 'genetic engineering' is a journalistic creation, it is not surprising that it lacks scientific precision. In the broad sense, according to Daniel Callahan, it refers to a wide range of possible and actual biotechnical breakthroughs from *in vitro* fertilization to genetic manipulation and recombinant DNA, and the development of new forms of human life.[2] For some other thinkers, 'genetic engineering' covers "anything having to do with manipulation of the gametes or the foetus, for whatever purpose, from conception by other than sexual union, or the treatment of disease *in utero*, to the ultimate manufacture of a human being to exact specifications."[3] In the stricter interpretation that we will employ here, it refers to various direct attempts to change genes to correct or eliminate gene disorders, or add new traits with a view of

---

[1]George Will, "Irreverent Test Tubes," reprinted in *The Human Life Review*, Fall 1978, p. 74.

[2]Daniel Callahan, "The Moral Career of Genetic Engineering," *Hastings Center Report*, April 1979, Vol. 9, No. 2. See also Thomas Shannon, "Ethical Implications of Developments in Genetics," *Linacre*, November 1980, p. 347.

[3]*Journal of the American Medical Association*, Vol. 220 (1972), p. 1356.

engineering a more desirable or more desired human being.[4] In this sense, it is contrasted with *eugenic engineering*[5] which involves controlling genotype by directed control of conception, and *euphenic engineering* which is the effort to compensate for a genetic defect by controlling the phenotype rather than the genotype, such as a diabetic taking insulin as a compensatory measure.[6]

The central issue regarding genetic engineering involves its relationship with gene therapy, a branch of genetic medicine that treats "hereditary diseases by influencing genes directly."[7] Genetic engineering is, at this state, largely a theoretical science; nonetheless, its absence of occasions for practical application has been more than compensated for by imaginative speculation. Some scientists envision genetic engineering as controlling the very process of evolution. Uses of genetic engineering that are truly therapeutic are part of gene therapy and come under the traditional canons of medicine. Other possible uses of genetic engineering are either questionably therapeutic or clearly not therapeutic.

The repairing, replacing, or suppression of a defective gene through various techniques of genetic surgery could be unquestionably moral, as long as there are no disproportionate risks involved. Depending on the defect, genetic surgery before or even after birth could prevent abnormality, and insure that it was not passed on to subsequent generations. Bernard Häring applauds such basic remedial intervention as "corrective foresight."

The DNA contained in genes carries messages that direct calls to carry out certain chemical operations, for example to produce a particular enzyme or protein that is essential for the normal functioning of the body. Where there is a 'wrong' message being conveyed by DNA that is harmful to the body, it is theoretically possible to introduce by genetic manipulation the 'correct' message so that the body can be restored to health. For example, corrective DNA could be introduced in people suffering from phenylketonuria to direct the body to convert the phenylanaline in their food to tyrosine.[8] This treatment could be done

---

[4]Bernard Häring, *Ethics of Manipulation* (New York: Seabury Press, 1975), p. 180.

[5]Harmon Smith, "Genetics and Ethics: Reaffirming the Tragic Vision," *Linacre* August 1973, p. 160.

[6]LeRoy Walters, "Technology Assessment and Genetics," *Theological Studies*, 33 (1972), p. 677.

[7]W. French Anderson, "Genetic Therapy," in Michael Hamilton, ed., *The New Genetics and the Future of Man* (Grand Rapids: Eerdmans, 1972), p. 109.

[8]William May, *Human Existence, Medicine and Ethics* (Chicago: Francis-

in two different ways: 1) through *transformation* in which pure DNA carrying the desired gene is introduced into a cell; 2) *transduction* in which the desired gene is attached to a nonpathogenic virus particle which then carries the gene into the cell where it is incorporated into the cell's genetic pool.[9]

Two important questions arise in conjunction with this form of gene therapy, however. If the subject of the genetic manipulation is not a human organism but a gamete or a pre-cursor to a gamete, are we really treating a patient? Paul Ramsey strongly opposes such a practice. If there is a child already conceived requiring genetic surgery, according to Ramsey, a parent can consent to investigational surgery in his behalf. But, he adds, a parent cannot legitimately submit a child to the same treatment and the same potential hazards "who is as yet a hypothetical nothing."[10]

The second question is a methodological one involving how we can determine the safety of genetic surgery before we use it on human subjects for the first time. Some scientists point out that we may have the ability to manipulate genes long before we know whether it is safe to do so.[11] Ramsey points out the problem, perhaps invincible, of the first trial. How do we know that in removing one deleterious gene through genetic surgery what gene will replace it, or the side effects, genetic or otherwise, that will be produced at the same time.[12]

William May argues that, "in the future, after sufficient experimentation has been done on higher mammals, such genetic surgery may be justifiable when *positively induced* damage by the surgery on the child-to-be can be *reasonably* excluded."[13]

Some scientists believe that the first successful genetic engineering will be done with the patient's own cells, for example, liver cells grown in culture. In this procedure, a desired new gene is introduced into a cell which is then allowed to grow in a mass culture. When re-implanted in the patient's liver, these normal cells re-program the liver so that it functions normally.[14]

Genetic engineering can be genuinely moral. However, it may be

---

can Herald Press, 1977), pp. 114-115.

[9]Anderson, p. 117.

[10]Paul Ramsey, *Fabricated Man* (New Haven and London: Yale University Press, 1970), p. 134.

[11]Anderson, p. 117.

[12]"Problems with Genetic Manipulation," in Preston Williams, ed., *Ethical Issues in Biology and Medicine* (Cambridge, Mass.: Schenkman, 1973), pp. 249-50.

[13]May, p. 116.

[14]Gerald Leach, *The Biocrats* (Baltimore: Penguin, 1972), p. 157.

exceedingly difficult, in most cases, because of its technical subtlety and complexity, for therapists to be reasonably assured that its deployment can be justified on moral grounds.

The fundamental justification of a medical intervention of any kind is the reasonable prospect of restoring a person to *health*, or as the etymology of that word suggests, *wholeness*. Therapeutic medicine is justified primarily because it is good for man to be healthy or whole.

The 17th century German philosopher Gottfried Leibniz asserted that the limitation necessary in every created being is a privation by which a thing is less than God, who is unlimited or infinite. Leibniz called this privation a "metaphysical evil."[15] The idea that not being God is an evil in any sense has a somewhat blasphemous implication when looked at from the opposite view that God can create only evil things.

Nonetheless, this Leibnizian notion has, in some way or another, always been part of man's historical consciousness. And its application to genetic engineering is irresistible. If it is evil to be limited, as human beings are inasmuch as they are not God, can we not justify the intervention of genetic medicine in the interest of making man less limited and more like God? Can genetic engineering be therapeutic in that it cures us, to whatever small degree, of our limitedness, our finitude? This question carries us into the domain of theology, yet it has more often been raised in recent years by scientists than theologians. Can science make man more like God? Do scientists have a collective obligation to make the attempt?

In his provocative book, *Come, Let Us Play God*, Leroy Augenstein states:

> We can be reasonably sure that initially we will use transforming viruses only to avoid and correct certain kinds of defects. However, once such a technique is perfected at all—considering the pressures that exist in our world—very quickly we'll go to somebody's definition of the ideal man or woman.[16]

But what is the ideal man or woman that could be genetically engineered? Is it better for a particular human to embody this ideal rather than be what he would have been had he not been a subject of this kind of genetic engineering? Paul Ramsey sees a dangerous aspiration to God-hood on the part of some scientists, what he calls a "messianic

---

[15] Gottfried Leibniz, *Theodicy*, tr. by E. M. Huggard (New Haven: 1952).

[16] Leroy Augenstein, *Come, Let Us Play God* (New York: Harper & Row, 1969), pp. 29-30.

positivism" that is essentially incompatible with true humanism.[17] "Men ought not to play God," he advises, "before they learn to be men, and after they have learned to be men they will not play God."[18]

A *Time* magazine article called "The New Genetics: Man into Superman" glibly states: "DNA can be created in the laboratory. Soon, man will be able to create man—and even superman."[19] Yet, current predictions about the appearance of re-engineered man are singularly uninspiring. We have already noted visions of legless astronauts, an increased number of brain cells in larger heads, extra thumbs and protruding eyes. Moreover, these projected modifications of man are obviously not therapeutic. They are not aimed at restoring man to human wholeness. They operate from the assumption that human nature is not quite good enough, perhaps, as Leibniz reasoned, stained by the metaphysical evil of not being God.

"Man is becoming his own creation,"[20] writes Karl Rahner who urges man to "make future self-creation a project worthy of man's absolute future—God himself."[21] Robert Francoeur displays a similar enthusiasm for genetic engineering when he writes:

> Why, then, should we be shocked today to learn that we can now or soon will be able to create the man of the future? Why should we be horrified and denounce the scientist or physician for daring to 'play God'?[22]

And yet the basis of this enthusiasm for radical human change cannot be genetic engineering, which has done virtually nothing to this point to re-design or re-create man, as much as a disaffection with man as he is. Moreover, as many argue, man is not improved so much by genetic modification as through his own free expressions of love.

The enthusiasm for genetically engineering *Homo novus* or *Homo futurus* betrays a profound misconception of genetics. Man is infinitely more than his genotype. Genetic engineering can do very little to improve him as a human being. Yet the hope of better humans through bio-technology persists. One quality that enthusiasts of genetic engi-

---

[17]Ramsey, pp. 138-151.

[18]Ramsey, pp. 138 and 151.

[19]*Time*, April 19, 1971, p. 43.

[20]Karl Rahner, "Christianity and the 'New Man'," *Theological Investigations*, V (Baltimore: Helicon Press), pp. 135 ff.

[21]Karl Rahner, "Experiment: Man," *Theology Digest* 16 (February 1968), pp. 57-69.

[22]Robert T. Francoeur, "We Can—We Must: Reflections on the Technological Imperative," *Theological Studies*, September 1972, p. 429.

neering consistently single out as an appropriate subject for genetic improvement is intelligence. This may be due to the fact that intelligence is presently the most easily measured of the human characteristics that seem important in the life of man. We may ask, however, whether purely technical intelligence is the same kind of intelligence we are in greatest need of having increased. An increase of this kind of intelligence may mean a decrease in wisdom.

Nonetheless, the relationship between genetics and intelligence is extraordinarily complex. Intelligence is a *polygenic* trait, that is, one that involves the peculiar cooperation of many genes. Secondly, many of the genes relatable to intelligence are *polymorphic*, capable of existing in a wide variety of alternate forms. Finally, the function of genes is dependent on their *interaction* with a host of changing environmental factors.[23] Geneticists estimate that man probably has tens of thousands of genes contributing to polygenic traits, compared with only a few hundred recognizable through monogenic traits.

Harvard biochemist John Edsall advises that we not concentrate too heavily on intelligence as a quality to be promoted through genetic medicine. "Kindheartedness and generosity of spirit," he states, "are at least as important for a good world."[24] And another biochemist, Leon Kass writes:

> It is probably as indisputable as it is ignored that the world suffers more from the morally and spiritually defective than from the genetically defective. Thus, it is sad that our best minds are busy fighting our genetic shortcomings while our more serious vices are allowed to multiply unmolested.[25]

Life would seem to have a nearly infinite capacity for variation and flexibility. The philosopher Bergson remarks that "the role of life is to insert some *indetermination* into matter." Between the genotype, the genetic inheritance, and the phenotype, the expression of the living organism, is a vast reservoir of indeterminism. Geneticist Theodosius Dobzhansky speaks of man's high degree of "phenotypic plasticity." Human behavior is, in the main, genetically unfixed;[26] it is largely the

---

[23]Bernard Davis, "Threat and Promise in Genetic Engineering," in Preston Williams, ed., *Ethical Issues in Biology and Medicine*, pp. 19-20.

[24]John Edsall, "Biology and Human Values," in Walter Ong, ed., *Knowledge and the Future of Man* (New York: Simon & Schuster, 1968), p. 171.

[25]Leon Kass, "Making Babies: The New Biology and the 'Old' Morality," *The Public Interest*, November 26, Winter, 1972, p. 21.

[26]Theodosius Dobzhansky, *The Biological Basis of Human Freedom* (New York: Columbia University Press, 1960), p. 130.

result of environment, socialization, education, personal freedom, and perhaps even grace. To a degree more significant than many intellectuals realize, the moral controversy surrounding genetic engineering involves the eternal tension between grace and gravity. The basic structure of the organism is set by the genes, but the direction and extent of development are, for the most part, evinced through non-genetic factors.

The presupposition concerning man that underlies thoughts about his genetic re-design is that he is a complete entity unto himself, perfectible as an individual. But man is more than an individual, he is a person, that is, a rational being who needs loving relationships with other people in order to complete himself as a man. In thinking about those qualities that would be desirable in designing one's descendants, philosopher Alasdair MacIntyre includes the following: the ability to live with uncertainty, an understanding of one's past which provides a sense of identity, the ability to engage in non-manipulative (loving) relations, finding a vocation in one's work, accepting one's death, and developing the virtue of hope.[27] Here MacIntyre emphasizes those non-genetic qualities by which we understand ourselves in the context of man's continuing history, relate lovingly to others, contribute positively to society, and face the transcendent. These are broader qualities than those associated with individual man such as intelligence, rationality, strength, and physical health. They are qualities that appear to make persons more human.

Paul Ramsey makes the comment that "when geneticists begin to describe those human qualities to be selected and bred into the race, they write remarkably as if they were describing the attributes of mind and of character that would make a good geneticist, or at least a good community of scientists."[28] This comment may be unfair to geneticists since there is no doubt that many of them recognize the more primary value of being a good man. And yet if one were to think of engineering a perfect man, one would be irresistibly drawn to thinking of him not as a person, but as an individual subject. The problem is in trying to envision a perfect man in the first place. The paradox of the person is that he needs to recognize his imperfections in order to grow in human perfection. Thus, imperfections or faults are not a categorical evil for a person, but the normal condition that affords him the possibility of moral growth. For Aristotle, the hero's *agon* or struggle for a new identity is made possible by a "tragic flaw" or defect. As Charles Olson ex-

---

[27]Alasdair MacIntyre, "Seven Traits for the Future," *The Hastings Center Report*, February 1979, pp. 5ff.
[28]Ramsey, p. 22.

plains in his book *Proprioception*: "The fault can be a simple one . . . but if he has no fault he cannot change for the better, but only for the worse . . . he must pass through an experience which opens his eyes to an error of his own."[29]

The difference between genotype and phenotype is so broad that it is commensurable with life itself. This is a notion that is more often a conviction of the artist than the rational scientist. A remarkable example of a scientist identifying human life with genetic substance appears in a statement by a British sociobiologist:

> [Genes] swarm in huge colonies, safe inside gigantic lumbering robots, sealed off from the outside world, manipulating it by remote control. They are in you and me; they created us body and mind; and their preservation is the ultimate rationale for our existence . . . we are their survival machines.[30]

On the other hand, Boris Pasternak, as an artist, expresses the broader view that life can be transfigured only through life itself. He writes:

> Reshaping life! People who can say that have never understood a thing about life—they have never felt its breath, its heartbeat—however much they have seen or done. They look on it as a lump of raw material that needs to be processed by them, to be ennobled by their touch. But life is never a material, a substance to be molded. If you want to know, life is the principle of self-renewal, it is constantly renewing and remaking and changing and transfiguring itself, it is infinitely beyond your or my obtuse theories about it.[31]

When man becomes reconciled with himself and the human condition, he will lose his enthusiasm for engineering a new man. The restlessness and disatisfaction with self that drives him to want to re-design himself is ample testimony to his own imperfection and finitude. Man is ambiguous. He has the capacity to negate or accept himself. Science itself offers no clue as to which alternative he should choose. As the great mathematician Poincare once noted, science speaks in the indicative, not the imperative. Science will do its job as science and will leave to non-science the responsibility of enlightening men's consciences. Science without conscience is not a human enterprise and rightly evokes

---

[29]Charles Olson, *Proprioception* (Berkeley, Calif.: Four Seasons, 1965).

[30]Richard Dawkins quoted in "Why You Do What You Do, Sociobiology: A New Theory of Behavior," *Time*, August 1, 1977, p. 36.

[31]Boris Pasternak, *Doctor Zhivago* (New York: The New American Library, 1960), p. 282.

disturbing images in which progress, as one writer expresses it, is a runaway locomotive with "demons at the switch."[32] And let us not forget the appropriateness of the word "demon". The legendary Faust, obsessed with the desire to master the "germinal forces" of life, had a foreboding premonition when confronted with his own demon, which inspired him to utter the following words:

> I, image of the deity, deeming myself already close to the mirror of eternal truth, exulting in the thought of myself amid heavenly glory and light, having sloughed off the son of earth; I, more than heavenly cherub, whose untrammeled forced already dared presume that it flowed through the veins of Nature and by creative action enjoyed the Haelife of gods, what punishment now is mine![33]

[32]Ralph E. Lapp, *The New Priesthood: The Scientific Elite and the Uses of Power* (New York: Harper & Row, 1965), p. 29.

[33]Johann Wolfgang von Goethe, *Faust* (New York: The Library of Liberal Arts, 1954), p. 18.

Fetal Experimentation

To rationalize abortion as something other than the killing of un-born humans, its advocates have regularly employed sub-human terms to describe the "fetus" (itself a word far less human than, say, "preborn child"). "It" was mere "gametic materials" (Joseph Fletcher), or "protoplasmic rubbish" (Philip Wylie), or even likened to "marmalade" (William Baird). But now that abortion is legally secured, many of the same people have made a rhetorical about-face. Now, the purpose is to justify research and experimentation on the unborn. So the *humanness* of the "fetus" is again stressed: new scientific knowledge of human subjects will have unique and beneficial application to the needs of other humans, inside or outside the womb.

A few years ago, Reuters News Agency reported the story of a Lebanese man who was impotent, and had a testicle transplant from a fetus aborted at six months.[1] Clearly, the transplanted organ was deemed not only a human part of a human being, but one capable of in-fusing the impotent beneficiary with a masculine power that his own human physiology had failed to provide. Wordsworth, who viewed the child as "the father of the man," could not have known that the child in the womb could provide the manhood of the father. Whether the oper-ation proved successful is beside the point. What is pertinent here is the belief demonstrated by the patient and the surgical team that the hu-man fetus is indeed human and in fact can supply human parts for its homologue who lacks them.

Another case, reported in the *Hastings Center Report*, concerns a 28-year old engineer who found life on a dialysis machine intolerably restricting.[2] Since he had been adopted as an infant and did not know

---

[1]Nick Thimmesch, "Strange Tales of Fetal Life and Death," *Human Life Issues*, January 1983, Vol. 9, No. 1, p. 4.

[2]"Can the Fetus be an Organ Farm?", *The Hastings Center Report*, Oc-

his natural family, an ordinary kidney transplant had been ruled out. The novel solution was agreed upon: the man's wife would get pregnant and, after five or six months, have an abortion. The kidneys from their own pre-born child would then be transplanted to the husband. Here again, the point is that the fetus, being human, offers real hope (sometimes the only hope) for other humans who suffer from some physiological dysfunction. But it raises the prospect of using the uterus as an organ farm, and the fetus as an organ bank. While based on the recognition that the fetus is human, it denies the right of unborn children not to be exploited as a means for some other human's end.

In Australia, serious consideration is being given to deliberately growing human embryos to provide organs for transplantation in children. Mr. Justice Kirby, chairman of Australia's Law Reform Commission, has expressed his belief that a majority of the populace might see this as better than simply burying the aborted fetuses.[3] The inequity of allowing some fetuses to live and consigning others to an arbitrary and premature death does not disturb some people as much as the "waste" involved in not using aborted human fetuses to improve the health of other human beings. As a spokesman for the medical faculty at Adelaide University puts it: "In Adelaide alone there are over 4,000 foetuses a year. It seems a waste if they are not going to be used."

In 1980, the U. S. Food and Drug Administration announced its approval of the use of fetal lung tissues in a vaccine against human rabies. Even people who find this to be an acceptable use of parts of aborted fetuses may not be so accepting toward less medically-justifiable cosmetic uses. Two years ago a reputable French legal journal, *Gazette du Palais*, reported the interception by customs officials of a truck loaded with frozen human fetuses at the Swiss-French border. The fetuses were destined for French cosmetic laboratories, where they could become ingredients for "beauty products used in rejuvenating the skin," a high-price item in France.[4] One seller, Madame Renée Ibry's, advertises the claim that her beauty products are "absolutely natural"—a rather grotesque compliment to the unborn human fetus. The commercial trafficking in human fetuses is precisely what inaugurated the public debate on fetal research and experimentation in Great Britain in 1970, when Norman St. John-Stevas, M.P., shocked the English-speaking world by reporting to Parliament the commercial sale in England of human fetuses for research purposes. His report caused

---

tober 1975, Vol. 8, No. 5, pp. 23-25.

[3]Quoted from the *Australian* in *The Human*, April 1982, p. 4.

[4]Claude Jacquinot, *Gazette du Palais*, Nos. 98, 99; Wednesday 8th, Thursday 9th, April 1981.

the appointment of an advisory committee, under the chairmanship of Sir John Peel, to draft regulations. In May, 1972, The Peel Report on "The Use of Fetuses and Fetal Material for Research" was issued.[5]

The British guidelines were drawn not only to end the scandal of commercial sale of fetuses to researchers, but also to end what virtually everyone agreed was the worst abuse—keeping them *alive* for up to three or four days.[6] Another central concern of the Peel commission was to offer equal protection for wanted fetuses and those scheduled for abortion. The Report states:

> In our view it is unethical for a medical practitioner to administer drugs or carry out any procedures on the mother with the deliberate intent of ascertaining the harm that these might do to the fetus, notwithstanding that arrangements may have been made to terminate the pregnancy and even if the mother is willing to consent to such an experiment.

A parallel situation soon followed in the United States. The *New England Journal of Medicine* reported (May 18, 1972) a study to determine whether or not rubella-vaccine viruses administered to the mother are capable of causing infection of the fetus. In this study, "most of the samples, obtained by hysterotomy, were delivered to the laboratory still surrounded by intact membranes."[7] In March of that same year, Wilhamine Dick, testifying at Pennsylvania's Shapp Abortion Law Commission Hearing, said that Pittsburgh's Magee Women's Hospital packed aborted fetuses in ice while they still showed signs of movement and shipped them to experimental laboratories. On the same date in the following year, Connecticut's Attorney General presented an affidavit to the U. S. Supreme Court regarding a Yale-New Haven experiment in which a baby boy was dissected without anesthesia before he died. The next month (April 15, 1973), the Washington *Post* reported that Dr. Gerald Gaull, chief of pediatrics at New York State Institute of Basic Research in Mental Retardation, "injects radioactive chemicals into umbilical cords of fetuses . . . While the heart is still beating he removes their brains, lungs, liver and kidneys for study."[8] Also in 1973, a

---

[5]"The Uses of Fetuses and Fetal Material for Research," Department of Health and Social Security, Scottish Home and Health department, Welsh Office. London: Her Majesty's Stationery Office, 1972.

[6]The Washington *Post*, April 10, 1973.

[7]Vaheri, Anttis; Vesikari, Timo *et al.*, "Isolation of Attenuated Rubella-Vaccine Virus From Human Products of Conception and Uterine Cervix," *New England Journal of Medicine*, May 18, 1972, Vol. 286, No. 20, pp. 1071-1074.

[8]Joan Wester Anderson, "Beyond Abortion—Fetal Experimentation,

medical journal reported experiments carried out on live-born fetuses who were decapitated in order that their heads could be perfused to study carbohydrate metabolism.[9]

In 1974 the Federal Drug Administration approved a prostaglandin known as Prostin F2 Alpha for use in second trimester abortions. The important feature of this abortion-inducing substance is that it often results in the delivery of a live, intact baby—a highly suitable subject for research purposes. Dr. Kurt Hirshhorn of New York's Mt. Sinai Hospital has stated that "with prostaglandins, you can arrange the whole abortion . . . so [the fetus] comes out viable in the sense that it can survive hours, or a day."[10] According to Hirschhorn, since "it is not possible to make this fetus into a child, therefore we can consider it as nothing more than a piece of tissue." Of course, if the "fetus" were *not* aborted, it *could* be "made" into a child. But the thinking here seems to be that prospective viability is the only characteristic which could warrant protecting the "abortus," while the lack of prospect for viability is sufficient to justify experimentation. The late Dr. Andre (then director of the Kennedy Institute for the Study of Human Reproduction and Bioethics) opposed this in the strongest terms: "[that means] If it's going to die, you might as well use it." If that is not "the British approach," said Hellegers, "it was certainly that of the Nazi doctors."[11]

Because of the abuses going on in fetal research and experimentation, and the conspicuous absence of ethical thinking on the matter, some concerned Americans expressed indignation which evoked an immediate response from the National Institutes of Health (NIH) in 1973 in the form of a "status" position indicating its strong opposition to work on *live* aborted fetuses.[12] Later that year the NIH published its proposed guidelines, titled "Protection of Human Subjects: Policies and Procedures," a document which Paul Ramsey has called "the finest product to date—whatever its defects—to come from our medical bureaucracies."[13] However, in 1974—after very little public

---

New Upjohn Drug Delivers Perfect Fetus For Laboratory Use," *Our Sunday Visitor*, April 13, 1975, p. 1.

[9]Adam PAJ, Ratha N., Rohiala E., *et al*; "Cerebral oxidation of glucose and D-beta hydroxy, butyrate in the isolated perfused human head." *Trans Am Pediatr Soc.* 309:81, 1973.

[10]*National Observer*, April 21, 1973.

[11]Andre Hellegers, "Issues in Draft Policy Debated in Council," *Ob-Gyn News*, April 15, 1973.

[12]"Fetal Research," *Scientists for Life Newsletter*, October 1, 1975, p. 3.

[13]Paul Ramsey, *The Ethics of Fetal Research* (New Haven and London: Yale University Press, 1975), p. 11.

dialogue—NIH published revised guidelines which offered the "abortus" much less protection, particularly from harmful experimentation.

In the interim between NIH's proposed and revised guidelines, an important congressional action took place which cut across the rule-making by the health departments. In July of 1974, Congress passed the National Research Act establishing the National Commission for the Protection of Human Subjects of Biomedical and Behavioral Research. The Commission was charged to investigate the extent of research involving the human fetus, and to recommend to the secretary of HEW (then the Dept. of Health, Education, and Welfare, now HHS—Health and Human Services) the circumstances, if any, under which research should be conducted and supported by that department.

The eleven-man commission completed its report on May 21, 1975.[14] It made 16 recommendations, ten of them non-controversial, which were passed unanimously. (They concerned such things as therapeutic research directed toward the mother, non-therapeutic research directed toward the fetus *in utero* or the possibly viable infant, informed consent, a "conscience clause," etc.)

The Commission's most controversial conclusion (and the main area of controversy in the field of fetal research in general)[15] involved *non-therapeutic* research on a pre-viable abortus. This issue is not only controversial, but highly complex, involving six distinct levels of significant ethical analysis: 1) the nature of the research subject; 2) the notion of pre-viability; 3) the principle of equality; 4) the problem of consent; 5) the principle of "do no harm"; 6) the relevance of abortion to fetal research. In fact, careful assessment of this one issue provides an understanding of the ethics of fetal research and experimentation in general. Therefore, we will discuss each of these six levels separately.

1) The Nature of the Research Subject

The National commission refers to the human embryo and fetus, in or outside the uterus, developing or aborted, in the specific context of "human subjects" which it seeks to protect. This expression has the merit of being neutral, but the disadvantage of being too broad and consequently vague. The expressions "abortus" and "fetus *ex-utero*" are problematic. "Abortus" does not describe what the subject is, but merely what happened to it, namely that it was aborted. "Fetus *ex-utero*" may be contradictory. Pediatrician Eugene Diamond maintains

---

[14]The *Federal Register*, August 8, 1975.

[15]See Tabitha Powledge, "Fetal Experimentation: Trying to Sort Out the Issues," *Hastings Center Report*, April 1975.

that a fetus *ex-utero* is an infant.[16] The late David Louisell, then a professor of law at the University of California at Berkeley, stated that the non-viable fetus *ex-utero* has been known up to then by law and by society in general as an *infant*, however premature.[17] But HEW restricted the term "premature infant" to the viable fetus *ex-utero*.[18] "Embryonic human being," "fetal human being," "abortus human being," "infant human being," "neonatal or newborn human being" represent reasonably well the nature of the research subjects. According to these terms, the state of development is properly placed in an adjectival, not substantive, position.[19] Moreover, the subjects are given an intrinsic denomination, rather than a merely extrinsic one. These are more accurate terms, and consequently, since we are dealing with human beings, more *just* than other frequently-used terms such as "fetal material" or "product of abortion." Therefore, when we speak of a non-viable fetus *ex-utero*, we are speaking of a premature infant human being, though "fetal human being " may be acceptable for some people.

2) *The Notion of Pre-Viability*

The distinction between viable and pre-viable (non-viable) is a somewhat artificial one. The fetus, of course, is viable at all stages unless it is removed from its natural environment. Pre-viable then, often describes a natural response to a lethal situation. In this sense, we could all be rendered "pre-viable" easily and quickly. Thus pre-viability is usually an induced condition. In addition, the development of artificial wombs could make the distinction between viable and pre-viable obsolete.

Dr. Hirschhorn, as we have seen, describes a fetus outside the womb as "viable" in the even more artificial sense of promising to live long enough for it to be a useful subject for experimentation. But critics point out that a pre-viable fetus is *not* one that has already died; it deserves to be respected like any other living fetal or infant human being.[20] Since *Roe v. Wade*, viability has been functioning as a legal standard of personhood—a very arbitrary and vague standard which has lead to the erroneous (if understandable) belief that a fetus which is "not viable" according to the Supreme Court is either not living or not

---

[16]Eugene Diamond, "Redefining the Issues in Fetal Experimentation," *Linacre*, May 1977.

[17]David Louisell, "Fetal Research: Response to the Recommendations," *Hastings Center Report*, October 1975, p. 10.

[18]"The HEW Regulations," *Scientists for Life Newsletter*, October 1, 1975, p. 9.

[19]Ramsey, *op. cit.*, p. xx.

[20]Semour Siegal, "A Bias for Life," *Hastings Center Report*, June 1975.

deserving of any protection.

It is also important to recognize that a fetus is judged pre-viable by *prognosis*. In a given case of a fetus who is on the borderline of "legal" viability, this judgement could quite often be inaccurate. Surely ethics demands that efforts should be made to save the lives of fetuses (or infants or neonates) in such borderline cases. In this way—by trying to save the lives of some—"salvage" techniques will be developed that will enable physicians to save the lives of many others. In short, ethics and progress in fetal life-saving techniques are not incompatible.

3) The Principle of Equality

The National Commission recommended different standards of care for the non-viable fetus *ex-utero* (or abortus) who is the subject of non-therapeutic research, compared with his counterpart who is judged viable. The former receives but a single protection: that research and experimentation not alter the duration of his life.[21] But the viable fetus receives a much broader protection. In his interest, the Commission recommends that "No additional risk to the well-being of the infant be imposed by the research."[22] This unequal protection for two artificially-distinguished classes of fetuses exposes the non-viable fetus to any kind and degree of harm that does not alter the duration of his life. Only one of the Commission members, David Louisell, strongly dissented from this recommendation, appealing to "the essential equality of all human beings," and expressing the fear that American society is at risk of "losing its dedication 'to the proposition that all men are created equal.'"[23] He stated:

> Although the Commission uses adroit language to minimize the appearance of violating standard norms, no facile verbal formula can avoid the reality that under these Recommendations the fetus and non-viable infant will be subjected to non-therapeutic research from which other humans are protected.[24]

Louisell went on to complain that the unequal protection given to the non-viable fetus *ex-utero* as well as the fetus *in-utero* gives the researcher a vested interest in the actual effectuation of a particular abortion, and society a vested interest in permissive abortion in general.

More recently (in late 1982) the U. S. House of Representatives

---

[21]"Deliverations and Recommendations of the National Commission for the Protection of Human Subjects," *Hastings Center Report*, June 1975.

[22]*Ibid.*

[23]Louisell, *op. cit.*, pp.9 and 11.

[24]*Ibid*, p. 9.

renewed its dedication to the proposition that all men are created equal when it voted 260-140 to ban the National Institutes of Health from funding experimentation on unborn or aborted fetal or infant human beings. The pertinent passage in the bill, introduced by Congressman William Dannemeyer (R., Calif.), states that:

> [NIH] shall not conduct or support research or experimentation in the United States or abroad on a living human fetus or infant, whether before or after induced abortion, unless such research or experimentation is done for the purpose of insuring the survival of that fetus or infant.[25]

However, subsequent legislative processes reflected a less noble proposition. Congressman Henry Waxman (D., Calif.) opposed Dannemeyer's amendment as an "ideological statement" which would imperil important research, even though earlier Waxman supported an amendment to protect laboratory animals (the amendment prohibits "more than momentary minor pain or discomfort, or any procedure except where the animal is anesthetized throughout the entire course of that procedure")[26]—which would clearly provide better treatment for laboratory animals than aborted human fetuses, a point Congressman Mark Siliander (R., Mich.) noted when he protested that "The fetus was not injected with an anesthetic when doctors sliced open his stomach."[27]

After Senator Robert Packwood (R., Ore.) successfully blocked a Senate vote on the Dannemeyer amendment, a House sub-committee voted for a much weaker restriction prepared by its chairman, the same Henry Waxman, which would permit experimentation posing "minimal risk" to the fetus intended for abortion and authorized the Secretary of HHS to wave any restrictions under certain circumstances.[28] In May, the full House Energy and Commerce Committee also rejected the Dannemeyer amendment in favor of Waxman's. Thus, at this writing, the prospect of applying a uniform principle of research and experimentation to all human fetuses is not encouraging.

---

[25]"House Votes to Ban Funds for Fetal Experimentation," *Lifegram*, Romeoville, Illinois, Fall 1982. The amendment is attached to HR 6457, a bill authorizing research on cancer and other diseases and was introduced on the floor by Rep. Bill Dannemeyer (R-CA).

[26]Quoted by Paul Fisher, "House Bans Fetal Experimentation," *The Wanderer*, October 14, 1982, p. 1.

[27]*Ibid*, p. 6.

[28]Douglas Johnson, "Waxman Subcommittee Rejects Ban on Fetal Experimentation Funding," *NRL News*, March 24, 1983, p. 1.

4) The Problem of Consent

Consent is required for non-therapeutic experimentation on a fetus *ex-utero*. The Commission initially recommended the mother's consent, the father not objecting, and later modified its position to request paternal consent as well (this was the Commission's only major modification.) The immediate problem that arises in the case of an aborted human being is the moral validity of its mother's consent. Can a mother who has already consented to abort her own baby be the appropriate person to grant consent for fetal experimentation on the same child?[29] (Some have suggested that a guardian be appointed who might better represent the interest of the fetal subject of experimentation.[30])

Another problem involves the effect that consent has upon the woman who might change her mind about going through with an abortion. If she consents to possible harmful fetal experimentation prior to abortion, her liberty to change her mind about abortion is impaired. "Even if she had an arbitrary liberty to abort," as Paul Ramsey points out, "we would not say she has an arbitrary liberty to injure and then to change her mind about abortion."[31] Few people (if any) would argue that a woman has a right to expose the child she is going to bring into the world to medically-unwarranted experimentation she knows may seriously injure him. Consent to non-therapeutic experimentation here would seem highly unethical and clearly contrary to established and respected norms concerning proxy consent.

5) The Principle of "Do No Harm"

The fundamental problem with non-therapeutic experimentation involving any risk whatsoever to the subject is that it violates the minimal "do no harm" principle. With this in mind, Rabbi Seymour Siegal, Professor of Theology and Ethics at the Jewish Theological Seminary in New York, writes:

> Research and experimentation on fetuses should be limited to procedures which will present no harm or which have as their aim the enhancement of the life systems of the subjects.[32]

Some moralists have suggested that all members of society owe certain minimal debts to society, and these debts may include children, as well as fetal subjects, taking part in low-risk biomedical and behav-

---

[29]Diamond, *op. cit.*
[30]Ramsey, *op. cit.*, p. 97.
[31]*Ibid*, p. 57.
[32]Seymour Siegal, *op. cit.*, p. 25.

ioral research. They see this involvement in the perspective of social justice.[33] At the same time, it is important to understand clearly what is meant by minimal risk to a fetal subject. In the case of the "pre-viable" human, some argue that minimal risk loses much of its relevance since as such the subject cannot be "injured for life." In addition, one must distinguish between the statistical chance of injury and the nature of an injury. A small chance of great harm may be unacceptable, whereas even a great chance of a small harm might not. A one-to-two percent chance of contracting Down's Syndrome is too high a risk, but a much greater chance of contracting a minor infection may be regarded as a low risk.[34]

Wilfred Gaylin and Marc Lappé have argued the case for non-therapeutic experimentation on the pre-viable fetus *ex-utero* in the context of *philantropic* experimentation.[35] Since the aborted fetus is going to die anyhow, they would like to see its death ennobled by serving those more fortunate. They regard a pre-viable infant's exposure to the rubella vaccine to determine its effect, for example, a small indignity compared with what happens to it during an abortion. "The medical ethic 'do no harm' would, of course, be violated," they admit, "but we already violated that principle when we accepted the concept of abortion."[36]

But Gaylin and Lappé mount their case on the untenable premise that an established *great* harm justifies the introduction of a *lesser* harm, something Paul Ramsey has termed a "slip-back-up-the-moral-slope" argument.[37] Quite aside from the morality of abortion, this is a premise that has no logical or moral validity. Nor does the contention that a subject "going to die anyway" should suffer non-therapeutic experimentation in the interest of the good of others (besides, it argues for too much—we are all going to die anyway). The class of humans who are "going to die anyway," and soon, also includes those who are terminally ill. Accepted ethical norms do not permit harmful research on these subjects.

What Hans Jonas says against "using" the unconscious, terminally ill patient applies with equal force to the fetus:

---

[33]Richard McCormick, "Fetal Research, Morality, and Public Policy," *Hastings Center Report*, June 1975, p. 27.

[34]Karen Lebacqz, "Fetal Research: Response to Recommendations," *Hastings Center Report*, October 1975, p. 11.

[35]Wilfred Gaylin and Marc Lappé, "Fetal Politics: The debate on experimenting with the unborn," *Atlantic*, May 1975, pp. 66-71.

[36]*Ibid.*, p. 70.

[37]Ramsey, *op. cit.*, p. 41.

Drafting him for non-therapeutic experiments is simply and unquali-
fiedly not permissible; progress or not, he must never be used, on the
inflexible principle that utter helplessness demands utter protection.[38]

6) The Relevance of Abortion to Fetal Research

The U. S. Supreme Court's 1973 abortion decisions granted a
woman the right to abort on the basis of what it said was her "right to
privacy." Once the mother and her baby are separated, however, the
"right to privacy" ruling is no longer pertinent. As Eugene Diamond
points out, "surely the infant cannot be construed as part of the mother,
with its rights in conflict with hers, if the mother is in a recovery room
and the infant is in an incubator in the nursery."[39] David Louisell said
much the same thing when he wrote: "If an infant survives the abortion,
there is hardly an additional right of privacy to then have him or her
killed or harmed in any way, including harm by experimentation impermissible under standard norms."[40]

In fact, the principles that bear upon abortion and fetal experimentation are largely different. This is a fact that is often overlooked.
The Society for Developmental Biology, for example, unanimously
passed a resolution supporting the "continued use of human tissues at
all stages of development, embryonic and fetal, within the framework of
the *Doe v. Bolton* ruling of the U. S. Supreme Court.[41]

The attempt to reason from the legal "is" to the moral "ought"
represents the fallacy of legal positivism. The legal "is" may very well
be a moral wrong. An attitude of legal positivism, therefore, promotes
the vice of removing the initiative to redress the legalized moral wrong.
It represents an unconscionable moral complacency. Rather than assume that the abortion rulings have settled the ethics of fetal research,
it may be that the ethics of fetal research will unsettle the ethical
thinking behind the abortion rulings.

Marc Lappé has remarked that "once we have incurred the costs
of doing abortion, the moral universe in which we have to operate is *in
fact* changed, and we acquire new moral duties."[42] Lappé makes the assumption that it is the "moral universe" that we have changed. What we
have changed is law, policy, and practice. The "moral universe" is safely

---

[38]Hans Jonas, *Philosophical Essays: From Ancient Creed to Technological
Man* (Englewood Cliffs, N.J.: 1974), p. 126.

[39]Diamond, *op. cit.*, p. 151.

[40]Louisell, *op. cit.*, p. 10.

[41]*Pediatric News*, September 1975, p. 5.

[42]Marc Lappé, "Abortion and Research," *Hastings Center Report*, June
1975.

beyond our meagre powers to change. In fact, our ethical obligation is to understand and serve the "moral universe," rather than try to collapse it into law, policy, or practice which may reflect the very antithesis of morality.

The following statement by American Citizens for Life, Inc. (presented before the Senate sub-committee on constitutional amendments in 1974) provides a concise summary of many of the main ethical issues of fetal research and experimentation:

> Proper concern for the rights of the unborn child need not bring medical research to a halt. New therapeutic techniques can be used with the hope of improving them superior to traditional methods of treatment, after adequate theoretical work and animal experimentation has been carried out. Parents can give consent for experimental therapeutic treatment of the unborn if there is valid reason to believe that such treatment is in the best interests of the child. In addition, organs may be transplanted from the dead fetus, and tissue may be developed from fetuses which are clinically judged to be dead according to the same criteria which would be used for a·born child or adult. We recommend careful retrospective clinical and statistical study of defective babies for identification for teratogenic drugs. However, this is not the same thing as purposefully introducing known or suspected harmful substances for research purposes into the live child or his mother which could cross the placental barrier. Systematic benefit should not be derived from systematic induced abortion. We do not approve of experiments which would be judged "cruel" or "senseless" by the average sensitive layman. And parents cannot consent to non-therapeutic research on unborn children who are being purposefully aborted.

Such a statement is grounded in established medical ethics and recognizes the role of the intelligent layman in the formulation of ethical public policy. While it may be improvable, it is a good place to begin. It has two outstanding merits that deserve special mention: it provides equal protection to all human fetuses, whether intended for birth or abortion, a protection that current legislation does not provide; it reflects a consistent recognition of the dignity and humanity of the unborn, in striking contrast with the semantic acrobatics that have been used to de-humanize, re-humanize, and then de-humanize again, the defenseless child in the womb.

In Vitro Fertilization

The world's first *in vitro* fertilization child, Louise Brown, was born on July 25, 1978, a date that has the added and ironic distinction of marking the tenth anniversary of *Humanae Vitae*, Pope Paul VI's encyclical on marriage and human generation. Within six years after that historic birth, some 700 "test tube" babies were born, and approximately 200 IVF clinics have been established around the world. Within ten years the number of IVF babies swelled to more than 2,000. Some inside observers foresee an accelerated growth of the IVF industry in the coming years. Clifford Stratton, director of an *in-vitro* lab in Reno, Nevada, for example, predicts that by 1989 there will be a successful IVF clinic in every city in the United States[1]

Despite its spectacular growth throughout the world, however, *in vitro* fertilization remains intensely controversial. It is indeed far more than "a tempest in a test tube," as one journalist adroitly describes it. IVF involves the integrity of marriage and the family, the integrity of the sex act, the moral obligation of parents and society to protect the well being of their offspring, and concerns that transcend the present human community and touch upon the future of the species.

The following discussion describes the technique of *in vitro* fertilization, assesses its need, and explores the procedural and substantive problems that are at the core of the controversy.

The first step in the process of IVF is to obtain a fertilizable egg from the body of the woman. This is accomplished by a technique called laparoscopy, a delicate operation performed under general anesthesia. In the more commonly employed method used by Steptoe and Edwards, a laparoscope—a long, jointed metal microscope about one-

---

[1]Claudia Wallis, "The New Origins of Life," *Time*, September 10, 1984, p. 40. The number of IVF babies born by early 1987 was 1,992 according to *Time*, March 23, 1987, p. 58

third inch in diameter with a miniature flash light which serves as a viewing device—is inserted in the woman's body through a small incision in the navel. This allows the doctor to locate an egg that is about to be released from a ripe follicle. Through another incision, an aide holds the ovary in place with forceps while the doctor inserts a hollow needle with his other hand and extracts the egg and draws it through an attached aspirator tube. Dr. Steptoe is able to accomplish this entire process in about 80 seconds. Some clinics are beginning to use ultrasound imaging instead of a laparoscope to guide the needle into the follicles. This procedure can be done in a doctor's office under local anesthesia; it is less expensive than laparoscopy, but may be less reliable.

Following removal from the body, the egg is placed in a petri dish in a nutrient solution and subsequently exposed for about 12 hours to a few concentrated drops of spermatozoa, after which it is transferred to fresh media. If fertilization takes place, the embryo is monitored for a normal growth curve in culture. If the embryo is judged to be growing normally, it is then considered suitable for transfer to the woman's uterus. At the eight-cell (3rd day) or the sixteen-cell stage (4th day), the embryo is placed in the uterus through a catheter or tube inserted through the cervix. If implantation takes place, the fetus begins to progress in the normal manner.[2]

While the success rates in extracting and fertilizing eggs is roughly between 80 to 90 per cent, the chance of any one fertilized egg or embryo, attaching itself to the lining of the uterus is considerably lower. In their report to the Royal College of Obstetricians and Gynecologists, Steptoe and Edwards reported that, as of January 1979, they had attempted 32 such implants. Four had been successful but two aborted spontaneously, one at 11 weeks gestation (reported to be abnormal), the other 20 weeks (reported normal except for prematurity). In addition to Louise Brown, Alastair Montgomery, born in January of 1979, gave the procedure a 6.25% success rate in terms of embryos that were placed in the uterus who were brought to term. If the success rate, however, is computed in terms of the percentage of *in vitro* fertilized

---

[2]There are many detailed descriptions of this technique. See Albert S. Moraczewski, O.P., "In Vitro Fertilization and Christian Marriage," *Linacre*, November 1979 (Fr. Moraczewski's description is based largely on notes prepared for the DHEW's Ethical Advisory Board by Prof. R.V. Short, Medical Research Council, Unit of Reproductive Biology, from a presentation made by Dr. P.C. Steptoe and Dr. R.G. Edwards at the Royal College of Obstetricians, January 16, 1979). See also Eugene Diamond, "A Call for a Moratorium on In Vitro Fertilization," *Linacre*, November, 1979; Anne Taylor Fleming, "New Frontiers in Conception: Medical Breakthroughs and Moral Dilemmas," *The New York Times Magazine*, July 20, 1980.

eggs brought to term, it drops appreciably. It has been estimated that Steptoe and Edwards discarded 99.5% of all fertilized ova produced in their laboratory over a period of 12 years because of various problems including obvious abnormality and development beyond the optimum stage for implantation.[3] The members of the IVF team at the Norfolk, Virginia clinic admitted that they expected a success rate of 25% at best, although they have not achieved that high figure.

All things considered, given the present state of the art, the most likely eventuality for a childless couple that seeks to have a child through IVF is that they will remain childless.

Infertility now affects approximately one in six North Americans. According to a study by the National Center for Health Statistics, the incidence of infertility among married women ages 20 to 24, normally the most fertile age group, jumped 177% between 1965 and 1982. Dr. Alvin Goldfarb, president of the American Fertility Foundation, estimates that there are 650,000 married women in the United States who are infertile because of a tubal pathology. Corrective surgery could result in full term pregnancies for, at the very least, 30% of these women. Thus, apart from financial considerations and the presence of a desire to have children, about 455,000 infertile women might envision IVF as their only way of having children of their own. However, not all these women will be suitable candidates for IVF since many who have blocked oviducts also have associated disordered ovaries which make it impossible for a doctor to obtain eggs from them. In Canada, David Armstrong of the University of Western Ontario, who has convened a conference on IVF, estimates that there are 25,000 Canadian women who might benefit from IVF.

These figures, despite continuing progress in microsurgery and, more recently, laser surgery, to repair blocked oviducts, will probably increase, rather than decrease, because of certain developments in current society. Among these developments would include: 1) the pandemic of venereal disease with its attendant increase in pelvic inflammatory disease; 2) the increase of late childbearing; 3)tubal disease related to the widespread use intra-uterine devices; 4) the large number of tubal ligations performed as a method of sterilization, only a small fraction of which can be reversed through surgery; 5) sterility associated with induced abortion.[4]

At the same time infertility is increasing, factors other than infertility itself are causing the number of babies available for adoption to decrease. At Catholic Charities, for example, couples must now wait

---

[3]Diamond, p. 296.
[4]Diamond, p. 296-7.

seven years to adopt a child. Part of the explanation for the dearth of adoptable babies is the high incidence of abortion together with the growing acceptance of single motherhood.

An indication of the extent to which there is a felt need for IVF services may be found in the fact that in 1980, the Norfolk clinic received requests from 5,000 women seeking IVF despite the fact that the clinic had been open for only a few months, had not reported a single success, and charged a minimum of $4,000 for the first IVF attempt.

The felt need for IVF raises two important ethical questions: 1) does an infertile married couple, or anyone for that matter, have a *right* to have a child?; 2) in responding to a woman's or couple's request for IVF, is the medical profession responding to a *disease* or a *desire*?

An individual person does not have a right to have a child since having a child involves the cooperation of two people. One individual does not have the right to expropriate from another what is needed in order to produce a child. Society generally condemns the type of action exhibited by an unmarried Los Angeles woman who impregnated herself with a computer scientist's sperm she took, under false pretenses, from a California sperm bank that calls itself The Repository for Germinal Choice.[5]

At the same time, it is dangerous to argue that even a married couple has a *right*, in the strict sense of the term, to have a child. A child is a person and no person has a right to another person. We do not want to reduce certain people—children in this case—to objects. Asserting a right to have another person implies this reduction.[6] Psychotherapist Rollo May states that in our contraceptive culture "no longer does 'God' decide we are going to have children; we do. And who has begun to comprehend the meaning of that tremendous fact?" May speaks of the nameless, pervasive guilt parents have about their chosen, planned children that is attached to the calculated way in which they had them, and the tremendous psychic weight these children must carry.[7]

Children are neither objects, slaves, property, nor extensions of their parents. They are gifts conceived in a moment of intimate self-sur-

---

[5] AP wire service story in the Kitchener-Waterloo *Record*, July 20, 1982. See Cornelia Morrison Friedman, "Making Abortion Consultation Therapeudic," *The American Journal of Psychiatry*, November 1973, Vol. 130, No. 11, p. 260. The author speaks of "The highly narcissistic rather grandiose young woman who decides to have a baby just because she wants one and is not in the least embarrassed to describe her motivation in this way."

[6] Moraczewski, p. 314.

[7] Rollo May, *Love and Will* (New York: W.W. Norton, 1969), p. 120.

render between husband and wife. IVF, given the great amount of control and calculation and separation that is required, is in sharp conflict with intimacy, self-surrender, and gift. Leon Kass has expressed it this way:

> Ultimately, to consider infertility (or even procreation) solely from the perspective of individual rights can only undermine—in thought and in practice—the bond between childbearing and the covenant of marriage.[8]

Kass goes on to express other concerns associated with the notion that there is a right to have children, including the exploitation of women and their bodies, as well as the practice of child buying and selling.[9]

The fundamental problem of how to have children without a "right" to have them is solved, so to speak, by nature through the marital act of sexual intercourse. Husband and wife do have a right to engage in intercourse with each other.[10] This act, however, both physiologically and psychologically, is ordered to a final, climactic expression that clearly enunciates the surrender of self and the relinquishing of individual control.

The essential dynamism of sexual intercourse leads husband and wife toward an experience of ecstasy that is indistinguishable from their renunciation of control. The union of two lovers, which sexual intercourse profoundly symbolizes, is thus inseparable from its equally profound demand that the partners forego something of their exclusive individualities. Sexual intercourse, therefore, is ideally suited to provide the perfect context in which husband and wife *invoke* new life. This act of invocation describes the disposition of the partners as being prepared to receive new life if it is given to them. It is an act which in no way suggests a subordination of one human being to another which is the case when one claims that he has a "right" to have children, and

---

[8]Leon Kass, "Making Babies—the New Biology and the 'Old' Morality," *The Public Interest,* November 26, Winter 1972, p. 20.

[9]Kass, p. 37.

[10]Cf. T. Brinkerman, "John Paul II's Theology of the Human Person and Technological Parenting," A. Moraczewski *et al.* (eds.) *Technological Powers and the Person* (St. Louis: Pope John XXIII Medical-Moral Research and Education Center, 1983), p. 375: The author speaks of a married couple having "a direct right to acts apt for procreation and hence only an indirect right to a child." See also Christopher Derrick, *Ibid.*, p. 18 and F. Morrissey, *Ibid.*, p. 449: "The law of the Church is very clear saying that there can be no right to children. The basic right involved in marriage is the right to acts apt by their nature to the generation of children.

even the right to determine the the kind of children he will have.

There are rights, to be sure. But on the part of the parents it is the right to have intercourse which, by its very nature, invokes new life, and the right to raise and educate their offspring. On the part of the child-to be, it is the right to be called into existence in such a way that his independent and unsubordinated humanhood is fully recognized and respected. The Rev. Donald McCarthy of the Pope John XXIII Medical-Moral Research and Education Center in St. Louis has specified a set of rights for the new child which include the right not to be frozen, a right not to be experimented on, a right not to be destroyed, and a right to be procreated as a consequence of "personal self-giving and conjugal love."[11] A child has a right to the status of radical equality with his parents, a right which is threatened when his parents seek to exercise non-medical modes of control over him which includes even the attempt to control his sex. And to borrow from ethicist Paul Ramsey, a baby has one more right, "the right to be a *surprise*."[12]

If people do not have a right to *have* another person, a child, then a doctor has no moral justification to produce one for them. Nonetheless, a doctor is morally justified in treating a diseased condition in order to help render the body more capable of begetting children. In this case the doctor's concern is a proper one, the integrity of the body, and not an improper one in which he responds not to a disease, but to a desire.[13]

Several years ago a particular woman became the center of controversy when she had a healthy breast removed surgically because it interfered with her golf swing.[14] The pertinent issue here is not whether what she did was censurable, but whether what her surgeon did was medicine. Was he treating a disease or a desire? Most people would agree that in this case, the surgeon was treating a desire.

Similarly, when a married couple requests IVF, is the doctor asked to treat a disease or a desire? If, for example, the doctor uses a laser technique to repair a blocked oviduct, he is treating a diseased condition with the aim of restoring it to its normal function. On the

---

[11]Otto Friedrich, "A Legal, Moral, Social Nightmare," *Time*, Sept 10, 1984, p. 53.

[12]Paul Ramsey,, "On In Vitro Fertilization," *An Educational Publication of Americans United for Life*, Inc. No. 3, n.d., p. 15.

[13]For discussions on the difference between desire and disease see Harmon L. Smith, "Genetics and Ethics: Reaffirming the Tragic Vision," *Linacre*, August 1973; Kass; George Will, "Abortion as Commodity, Not Medicine," reprinted in *The Human Life Review*, Fall 1978, pp. 73-4.

[14]Will, p. 73.

other hand, if he employs an IVF technique on the same woman, even if he is successful, he does not restore the woman's diseased condition to a state of health. She is still infertile; she still has a blocked oviduct. In this instance, the doctor is not practicing medicine as much as he is gratifying a desire. And the woman is not so much patient as she is a consumer. The doctor is treating not the cause of her problem, the blocked oviduct, but its *effect*—her childlessness. Moreover, he is using a child as a *means* to produce and an end which is the gratification of her desire to have a child. His surgical intervention is not in the interest of health, that is to say, it is not therapeutic. It does not conform to any of the essential types of therapeutic treatment; it is neither diagnostic, curative, alleviatory, or preventative. Nor does it fall under the general category of cosmetic surgery.

The advocate for IVF finds himself in a moral dilemma. If he recognizes that IVF is treating a desire, he finds himself in conflict with traditional medical ethics. On the other hand, if he believes it is treating a disease, he must depersonalize the child involved. When Paul Ramsey asks whether the IVF child is "a prosthesis for his mother's condition?," he is alluding to this dilemma.[15] The only way to legitimize IVF therapeutically, from the point of view of the patient's health, entails the reduction of the child conceived to the status of a possession or property.

Traditional medical ethics has taught that the goal of medicine is health. As Leon Kass has pointed out, when medicine's powers were fewer, its goals were clearer. From the fact that only a surgeon is allowed to practice surgery, it does not follow that every surgical procedure is medically justified. Surgery is medically justified when it takes place in the interest of a patient's health. IVF is not medically justified because it operates independently of a goal of health.

The desire to have a child is one of the profoundest and most worthy desires human beings can have. Nonetheless, this desire should not be construed as a right nor can it legitimize medical intervention. There is a crucial distinction between treating an infertile woman and treating a woman for her infertility. The medical profession cannot be expected to assume the task of making people happy. At the same time, medicine can make great technical advances within the context of traditional, health-oriented ethics.

According to Beverly Freeman, executive director of Resolve, a national infertility-counselling organization, micro-surgery can restore fertility in 70% of woman with minor scarring around their tubes.[16] Dr.

---

[15] Paul Ramsey, "Shall We Reproduce?", *Journal of the American Medical Association*, 220:10 (June 5, 1972).

[16] Wallis, p. 40. See also Fay Orr, "Test-Tube Babies," *Alberta Report*,

Joseph Ballina, head of the Laser Research Institute of New Orleans, has reported to the International Congress of Gynecological Laser Surgery an 80% success rate in repairing blocked Fallopian tubes. Of 65% women having blocked tubes, 80% became pregnant following tubal surgery by Dr. Ballina's new laser technique.[17]

What are the moral premises that are generally persuasive today? Daniel Callahan, director of the Institute of Society, Ethics and the Life Sciences, asked this question while reflecting on the moral discussion contained in the first ten years of his institute's journal—*The Hastings Center Report*. There are three, Callahan finds: 1)individual liberty (as long as no harm is done to another); 2)the application of a risk-benefit analysis in matters of uncertainty; 3) the principle that it is better to attempt to do good than to try to avoid harm.[18]

These premises taken together, according to Callahan, provide a perspective that is severely limiting, one that prevents us from posing larger questions about the future of human happiness, the most appropriate direction for science to take, and the best ends to which human freedom should be directed. They foreclose the possibility of attempting to integrate wider questions into the analysis. At the same time, however, Callahan dismisses the broad ethical perspectives of Leon Kass and Paul Ramsey, whom he regards as the most articulate opponents of the broad sweep of genetic engineering of which IVF is but one example. "They are talking in an unfortunately dead and unintelligible language," writes Callahan.[19] For Callahan, then, one side of the procedural dilemma is inadequate, while the other is unintelligible.

William May of Catholic University also recognizes the reality of this procedural dilemma. He sees one side, represented by Robert Francoeur and Joseph Fletcher, arguing for a form of rational, biotechnical advance that threatens the sanctity of life. Yet the other side, represented by Kass and Ramsey, is identified (though unfairly, in May's estimation) as "ante-diluvian," the querulous and worrisome fruit of a "mystical" or "metaphysical" frame of mind.[20]

The root of the problem may lie in the fact that the advances of the rational-technical approach tend to evaluate everything from the

---

April 10, 1984, p. 31.

[17]"In Vitro Lab Approved," *National Right to Life News*, January 1980, Vol. 7, No. 1, p. 23.

[18]Daniel Callahan, "The Moral Career of Genetic Engineering," *Hastings Center Report*, April 1979, Vol. 9, No. 2.

[19]Callahan, p. 9.

[20]William May, *Human Existence, Medicine and Ethics* (Chicago: Franciscan Herald Press, 1971), p. 58.

standpoint of applied reason producing a better product. On the other hand, the more traditional-metaphysical position goes beyond reason to include transrational dispositions such as love and faith, and beyond a concern for a human product to include a concern for the integrity of a human activity such as the sexual act which is the natural way of invoking new life. Hence, those who support the traditional-metaphysical view may seem unintelligible to the rational-technologists simply because a purely rational perspective cannot understand what it cannot see.

Apart from the procedural problems, there are the concrete, substantive problems that affect the embryo and the subsequent child, the parents, the family, and society. Nonetheless, these substantive problems are not entirely separate from the procedural, theoretical problems.

For example, nature provides its own way of selecting the best oöcyte to mature and the best sperm to reach the mature egg and effect fertilization. According to British scientists, the eggs taken after superovulation of the female may not be those that would normally develop.[21] But it is much more clearly evident that the sperm apt to fertilize an egg through IVF are simply those that, by chance, happen to be placed in close proximity to the egg, rather than the strongest and healthiest sperm which is likely to be the case when fertilization is effected through sexual intercourse.

> Up to 15 or 20 per cent of the sperm production of a normal healthy man is abnormal and one way of regarding the female reproductive tract is as a series of hurdles designed to eliminate unhealthy sperm. The cervix hangs down into the top of the vagina—the opposite design to the one that any intelligent plumber would make—and the tube leaves the uterine cavity by the smallest of openings; so of the hundreds of millions of sperm deposited in the vagina, only a few hundred make it as far as the egg. It is reasonable to believe that the abnormal sperm are screened out in the process.[22]

The percentage of morphologically abnormal sperm in human semen is notoriously high, often in excess of 40%, whereas the other primates (except the gorilla) have remarkably uniform sperm.[23] Just as nature provides a means by which the strongest drone mates with the

---

[21]Ramsey, n.d., p. 8.

[22]Malcolm Potts and Peter Selman, *Society and Fertility* (London 1979), pp. 19-20.

[23]R.V. Short, "The evolution of human reproduction," *Proceedings of the Royal Society of London*, 8, Vol. 195 (1976).

queen bee in her nuptial flight, so too, natural human intercourse provides a means by which only the hardiest of sperm can reach the vicinity of the fertilizable egg. IVF effectively does away with this screening. In fact, it may even have the opposite effect.[24]

Further, IVF involves a high rate of "wastage," that is, destruction of human embryos. In 1975, Steptoe and Edwards published a report on their early IVF research, admitting that they had failed in at least 200 attempts to effect embryo transfer.[25] While techniques have improved since 1975, it is inevitable that there will continue to be "wastage." Moreover, some researchers argue that laboratory experimentation (and its attendant "wastage") is necessary in order to improve the technique of embryo transfer. Dr. René Soupart of the Vanderbilt School of Medicine received permission and funding from the United States government to begin a three year experimental project that would involve fertilizing about 450 eggs, studying them for about a week, and then destroying them.[26] Dr. Soupart died in 1981, however, and never began the project.

In Britain, a 16-member committee established by Parliament and chaired by Mary Warnock, recommended that experimentation on living embryos be permitted, but only for the first 14 days of the embryo's life, and only if each experiment is carefully reviewed and licensed.[27] Scientists opposing the Warnock recommendation have pointed out that abortion already allows disposal of embryos more than 100 days old, and that an arbitrary 14-day limit for embryos outside the body constitutes a double standard.

At the heart of the "wastage" controversy is the question of the nature of the human embryo. The human that is conceived in a petri dish is just as human as one that is conceived in its mother's body. There can be no question that the human embryo is a member of the human species. Thus, Paul Ramsey declares that we "must regard experiments in *in vitro* fertilization as *ab initio* inherently immoral, because the physician must be willing to discard mishaps at any point in that span of time which do not come up to the standards of an acceptable human being."[28] On the other hand, R. G. Edwards argues for the

---

[24]*Ibid.*. See also Walter Sullivan, "Successful Laboratory Conception Intensifies Debate over Procedures," *The New York Times*, July 27, 1978.

[25]*The New Biology: In Vitro Fertilization* (Toronto: The Right to Life Association, 1980), p.3.

[26]*Ibid.*, p. 16. See also Fleming, pp. 48-9.

[27]"U.K. panel test-tube embryo experiments," Washington *Post*, in the Kitchener-Waterloo *Record*, Aug. 17, 1984.

[28]Ramsey, 1972, p. 1347.

liceity of such experimentation from rather dubious premises: 1) because "fertilization is only incidental to the beginning of life" (though, we must add, crucial to the beginning of *individual* life); 2) because "nuclei can potentially sustain the development of an embryo" (here Edwards ignores the salient fact that the nucleus of a somatic cell and a human embryo are different *in essence*); 3) because many persons implicitly accept the abortion of early embryos since IUD's almost certainly expel unimplanted embryos from the uterus; 4) because of the prevalence of eugenic abortion (these last two points are illustrations of the fallacy that an action is really good simply because it is done).[29]

Bernard Häring reflects a more temperate judgment when he writes:

> The very probability that we may be faced with a human person in the full sense constitutes, in my opinion, an absolute veto against this type of experimentation.[30]

André Hellegers and Richard McCormick concur with this judgment and suggest that embryo wastage is really a form of abortion. They write:

> The evaluation of nascent life in these early days is indeed a problem. But that does not mean that the problem can be decreed out of existence by simply going ahead. Where human life is at stake and we have doubts about its evaluation, does not prudence dictate that as a general rule life enjoys the benefit of our doubts.[31]

As the child develops, the number of manipulations in an unnatural surrounding that is involved in the processes of IVF and embryo transfer present real, though unknown hazards to the developing human. This fact must be rigorously considered in terms of compatibility with the minimal principle of medical ethics, "Do no harm." We recall that, aware of the real possibility of something going wrong in the development of the world's first IVF child, Louise Brown, Dr. Steptoe required her parents to promise they would abort their baby if there was even a suspicion that it was deformed.

Mindful of such dangers, Nobel Laureate James Watson has sug-

---

[29]R.G. Edwards, "Fertilization of Human Eggs In Vitro: Morals, Ethics and the Law," *Quarterly Review of Biology*, March 1974, Vol. 49, No. 1, pp. 13-4.

[30]Bernard Häring, *Ethics of Manipulation* (New York: Seabury Press, 1975), pp. 198-9.

[31]André Hellegers and Richard McCormick, "Unanswered Questions on Test Tube Life," *America*, August 12-19, 1978, Vol. 139, No. 4 p. 76.

gested that the physician attending the birth of what he calls a "product of IVF" should have "the right to terminate [the] baby's life should it come out grossly abnormal."[32] Bernard Häring draws the conclusion that IVF must be opposed chiefly because it is "manipulation . . . of the embryo itself, with no safety and with numerous hazards imposed on another being, the child-to-be."[33]

We do know that manipulating animal embryos seems to present a slight risk. Animal studies suggest that 3% additional risk of abnormality at birth is to be expected in pregnancies initiated by IVF and embryo transfer.[34] But it is well to keep in mind what Dr. Richard J. Blandau, a reproductive biologist at the University of Washington School of Medicine points out: "Who would be concerned over any deficiency in creative ability in a cow or sheep."[35] However, research with animal models may not tell us what we need to know in order to insure the safety of humans subjected to the same kind of manipulation. University of Pennsylvania biologist Luigi Mastroiani advises that "although animal models are useful in establishing important basic knowledge, one cannot confidently make inferences from the laboratory animal to *Homo sapiens*. There are substantial differences in fertilization even among closely selected laboratory species."[36]

One well known risk to the IVF child is prematurity, and prematurity is the major cause of mental and motor retardation in infants. Dr. Victor Gomel, who heads an IVF team at the University of British Columbia, has remarked that for some unknown reason, it is not uncommon for IVF babies to be born prematurely.[37] His remark was particularly applicable to his own success—Canada's first infant conceived in Canada outside the mother's womb—who arrived two months prematurely and weighed but two pounds, two ounces.

Prematurity in IVF babies is an inevitable side-effect of multiple conceptions. Of the world's first 700 IVF babies, there have been an unnaturally high proportion of multiple births: 56 pairs of twins, 8 sets

---

[32]James Watson, "Child from the Laboratory," *Prism* (AMA) May 1973, Vol. 1, No. 2, p. 13.

[33]Häring, p. 200.

[34]William Marshner, "A Review of the Report of the Ethics Advisory Board," *Family Policy Division, Free Congress Research and Educational Foundation*, Washington, D.C., 1979, p. 8.

[35]Fleming, p. 48.

[36]Luigi Mastroiani, Jr., "Reproductive Technologies: IV. In Vitro Fertilization," in Warren Reich, ed., *Encyclopedia of Bioethics* (4 vols.: New York: Free Press-Macmillian, 1978), IV, p. 1449.

[37]"All-Canadian test-tube baby doing well," Vancouver (CP), in Kitchener-Waterloo *Record*, Feb. 11, 1984.

of triplets, and two sets of quadruplets.

Finally, IVF presents a host of serious problems for the parents, especially the mother. Drugs, such as Clomid and Pergonal, are used to stimulate the development of more than one egg at a time. Laparoscopic surgery is used along with the administration of anesthesia. Dr. Kurt Semm has reported one death in Germany during laparoscopy, and another death has been reported of a Latin American woman who died during the anesthesia stage of IVF.[38] In addition, a woman may be exposed to the inevitable problems associated with multiple pregnancies. Finally, with multiple pregnancies and a higher rate of prematurely, there is a greater need for delivery by Caesarean section.

Collectively, these problems are of such magnitude that a strong incentive exists to provide safer ways of producing children for infertile woman. One alternative is the surrogate woman who conceives a child that she gestates for the infertile woman who will raise the child. The legal problems associated with surrogate mothers, however, are formidable enough to discourage the practice in many instances. As a means of avoiding these legal problems—such as laws that prohibit accepting money for a child, and laws that allow the surrogate to change her mind and keep the child—some people have seriously suggested that a cow be used to gestate a human being.[39]

Another alternative that has been proposed is Embryo Transfer. In this technique, a volunteer female is impregnated, usually through artificial insemination, with sperm from the husband of the infertile woman. Five days after conception, the newly formed embryo is washed out (a process called "lavage") and transferred to the uterus of the infertile woman. Nonetheless, this procedure is also fraught with serious problems, not the least of which is the accidental abortion of the embryo and the persisting pregnancy which may occasion a deliberate abortion on the part of the volunteer who conceived the child.[40]

The problems are more than psychological however. Leon Kass sees IVF as a "degradation of parenthood";[41] Paul Ramsey goes one step further, regarding it as the "destruction of parenthood."[42] What we

---

[38]Lori B. Andrews, "Embryo Technology," *Parents* , May 1981, p. 66.

[39]*Ibid.*, 66-7.

[40]Harris Brotman, "Human Embryo Transplants," *New York Times Magazine*, Jan. 8, 1984.

[41]Kass, p. 49. See also William Smith, "The Test Tube Baby," *The Human Life Review*, Fall 1978, Vol. IV, No. 4.

[42]Paul Ramsey, *Fabricated Man* (New Haven & London: Yale University Press, 1970), p. 130.

do know is that with IVF the natural process of begetting[43] a child is shifted toward an artificial process of manufacturing a product. This shift inevitably introduces factors that depersonalize and mechanize human procreation, on the one hand, and sunder and violate the two-in-one-flesh intimacy of the married couple, on the other. In addition, it trivializes a process that, in its natural mode, is one of the most profound and awesome mysteries of human existence.

Catherine Rankin is the first Canadian woman to have children through IVF, although the procedure was carried out in England at Dr. Steptoe's clinic. On March 25, 1982 she gave birth to fraternal twins. More recently, in explaining the procedure to a Grade 13 class, she was pleased to hear a boy state, "That's it? That's all there is to it?" Comments Mrs. Rankin, "When you explain it to people it really is ho-hum. It's a big deal because it's not accessible."[44]

Leon Kass warns that "mastery drives out mystery."[45] It is important to note that he does not use the word "mystery" as a cover for our ignorance, but to denote an aspect of reality that is not reducible to rational analysis. To drive out mystery, then, is to drive out reality. This same thought was expressed by C. S. Lewis several years earlier in *The Abolition of Man*: "Analytic understanding must always be a basilisk which kills what it sees and only sees by killing."[46] We destroy the mystery, the dignity, the sacredness of things so that we can see things more clearly, rationally, and scientifically. Thus, human procreation must become "ho-hum" and along with it, human parenthood. We must ask, however, whether such scientific progress should not be better understood as moral regress. In choosing to treat our most sacred and most human activities as mere raw material, do we not take a perilous step closer to becoming raw material ourselves?

Already, we liken ourselves too much to machines. Consider how readily young woman submit to abortions, fully confident that their reproductive machinery will remain intact to service them whenever they want to have a child later on. "The entire rationalization of procreation," writes Paul Ramsey, "can only mean the abolition of man's embodied personhood."[47] IVF demands sundering flesh from spirit in an

---

[43]William May, "'Begotten, Not Made': Reflections on Laboratory Generation of Human Life," *Perspectives in Bioethics*, Vol. 1, ed. F. Lescoe & D. Liptak, Pope John Paul II Bioethics Center, Cromwell, Connecticut.

[44]Margaret Cannon, "The Continuing Act of Love," *Maclean's*, November 15, 1982, p. 59.

[45]Kass, p. 51.

[46]C.S. Lewis, *The Abolition of Man* (New York: Macmillan, 1965), p. 90.

[47]Ramsey, 1970, p. 89.

area where the integrity of parenthood demands they be one, and sundering that flesh to the manipulation of technicians. Inevitably, something important, though unseen, stands to be harmed in the process. And what stands to be harmed is human parenthood. IVF exteriorizes a process that is meant to be an intimate and inseparable part of a profoundly personal expression of love. "Is there possibly some wisdom in that mystery of nature," asks Leon Kass, "which joins the pleasure of sex, the communication of love, and the desire for children in the very activity by which we continue the chain of human existence?"[48]

By removing the child from the personal context of conjugal love, as IVF does, a decisive step is taken which necessarily depreciates that love. Love that is thus "debodified,"[49] to borrow Richard McCormick's expression, is lacking in what we might call the full weight of human love, all that love can be. To exclude the bodily aspect of human love is to weaken love to some degree. And to weaken this love which is the essential bonding act of the family—uniting parents with children and children with their parents, as well as each one to each other—is to weaken the family. And since the family is the basic unit of society, what weakens the family also weakens society. To compromise the family in any way is to undermine that natural arrangement which offers ordinary people that best opportunity for growing and developing as human beings.

In a more specific vein, the developing technique of freezing embryos for long periods of time before implanting them into the uterus offers the possibility of drastically altering the normal age span that exists between family members, and creating compound relationships in which someone could be both a sister and a mother, or an aunt and a mother to the same child. Alan Trounson and Carl Wood at Monash University in Melbourne have been freezing embryos fertilized *in vitro* in liquid nitrogen at -196C. By May of 1984, they had 250 of such embryos stored at Queen Victoria Hospital in Melbourne.[50] These embryos are available for women who want to try again to have a child through IVF, and mothers who want additional children through the same means.[51]

Theoretically, many years can elapse before a frozen embryo is

---

[48]Kass, p. 49.

[49]Richard McCormick, "Genetic Medicine: Notes on the Moral Literature," *Theological Studies*, September 1972, Vol. 33, No. 3, p. 551.

[50]Robyn Rowland, "Social Implications of Reproductive Technology," *IRNFP*, Fall 1984, p. 196.

[51]Clifford Grobstein, "The Moral Uses of 'Spare' Embryos," *Hastings Center Report*, June 1982, Vol. 12, No. 3.

thawed and implanted, thus creating the possibility of a daughter carrying her mother's child and giving birth to her own brother or sister. As another example, a woman might wish to donate her embryo to her infertile sister who would give birth to her own niece or nephew. Confusing family relationships in this way invites phychological chaos. Leon Kass warns that "confusion and conflict would seem to be almost inevitable."[52]

The first child to be conceived through IVF, frozen, thawed, implanted, and born is Zoe Leyland. Zoe was born in Melbourne on March 28, 1984. Her mother, when superovulated, had produced a prodigious number of eggs—eleven! Ten of these eggs were fertilized and three were lost as a result of unsuccessful implantation. The remaining seven were frozen. Of these, six were suitable. Four of the seven, however, did not survive the freezing process. The final two were implanted: one survived and came to be known as Zoe Leyland.[53] Critics of this method of generating human life in which wastage is inevitable maintain that for a doctor deliberately to create a situation in which he has more patients than he can save is outrageous.[54]

An even more problematic episode involving frozen embryos concerns the late Mario and Elsa Rios of Los Angeles. In 1981, Mrs. Rios had several of her eggs fertilized with sperm from an anonymous donor. Some were implanted in Mrs. Rios and two were frozen. "You must keep them for me," she said. The implants failed, and the couple later died in a plane crash in Chile. Australian laws grant no "rights" to the two frozen embryos, although local officials believe they have the "right" to destroy them. The orphaned embryos seem orphaned from the human race, entirely without a protector who can act in their behalf.

The threats that IVF represents in terms of dislocating parenthood, confusing family relationships, abandoning the fate of orphaned embryos to committee decisions, and so on, shed additional light on the meaning and morality of IVF.

The desire on the part of science to control matter, and the desire on the part of infertile couples to have children—no matter how valid and laudable—are subject to moral limits.[55] These limits must be rec-

---

[52]Kass, p. 36.

[53]Wallis, p. 42; Jo Wiles, "The Gift of Life," *Star World*, April 24, 1984, pp. 24-6.

[54]Marshner, p. 14.

[55]See Sean O'Reilly, *Bioethics and the Limits of Science* (Front Royal, Virginia: Christendom College Press, 1980).

ognized if we are to treat each other justly and protect ourselves from exploitation, degradation, and undue harm. The evidence indicates that *in vitro* fertilization is: 1) exploitive of another human—the child-to-be—since its mechanism tends to treat that child not as a gift but as a product; 2) degrading the two-in-one-flesh unity of parents by deflating the importance of the flesh as a vehicle of love in the formation of new life; 3) dangerous to the child since it imposes undue hazards (on an unconsenting human being) through a series of manipulations in an unnatural surrounding.

People do not have a *right* to have a child, since no one has a right to another person. In marital conjugal intercourse, new life is invoked in a moment of mutual self-giving and self-surrender on the part of husband and wife who are prepared to accept the responsibilities that attend the reception of this new life. New human life, therefore, should be regarded as a gift which is the incarnation of marital love.

Finally, scientific and rational control are severely limited as a means of fulfilling man and ensuring his well being. Man is the sum of all of his parts which include, in addition to reason: love, emotions, faith, freedom, and flesh. The attempt to define human activity solely in terms of rational activity is one of the curiosities of our time, a case of science usurping the place of a broader, more inclusive philosophy of man. We find the writings of Joseph Fletcher a particularly clear example of this attempt to scientize man. His enthusiasm for rationalizing the process of human procreation is without equal. He writes:

> Laboratory reproduction is radically human compared to conception by ordinary heterosexual intercourse. It is willed, chosen, purposed and controlled, and surely these are among the traits that distinguish *Homo sapiens* from others in the animal genus, from the primates down. Coital reproduction is, therefore, less human than laboratory reproduction....[56]

Rational control does not make man moral. Man may employ reason for immoral ends, as human history has plainly shown. A human act is not the same as a moral act. What makes a human act a immoral one is not its degree of rationality, but the fact that it promotes the good of man. Considering the evidence, it would appear that *in vitro* fertilization does not promote the good of man, and therefore does not qualify as a truly moral activity.

---

[56] Joseph Fletcher, "Ethical Implications of Genetic Controls," *New England Journal of Medicine* 285 (1971), p. 781.

Sex-Preselection

Three years ago, Corinne Parpalaix, 22, a secretary in the Marseille police department, sued a sperm bank in an attempt to recover sperm which her late husband had deposited. A great deal of international publicity was given to the ensuing trial, and the arguments for and against releasing the sperm raised an intrigueing assortment of opinions concerning the status of this last living vestige of Monsieur Parpalaix. Was the sperm to be construed as an organ transplant? An inheritable piece of property? The bank's attorney argued that the sperm was part of the deceased's body and his right to "physical intergrity" demanded that it should not be given over to another person. The Court, however, ruled in favor of the widow, maintaining that the deposited sperm implied a "contract" and that this "secretion containing the seeds of life" be given to Mrs. Parpalaix. Pleased with her victory, Parpalaix made an announcement concerning her prospective infant: "I'll call him Thomas. He'll be a pianist. That's what his father wanted."[1]

This young woman's remark, made so casually and with such an air of confidence, superbly mirrors the prevalent attitude in today's world that any scientific method aimed at gaining greater control over reproduction belongs to people as their rights. And contraception, abortion, artificial insemination, *in vitro* fertilization, and now sex-preselection are presumed to be rightful options for no other reason than the fact that people want them. Novel and unreliable as sex-preselection techniques are at the current moment, newspapers are already printing glowing testimonials from satisfied customers, and social psychologists are reporting the high percentage of people who are ready to use the technique if it were available to them.[2] It is as natural as

---

[1]Otto Friedrich, "A Legal, Moral, Social Nightmare," *Time*, Sept. 10, 1984.

[2]Richard D. Lyons, "New Technique Increases Chance of Having a

breathing for people raised in today's culture to assume that determining the sex and even talents of one's offspring is fully in accord with progress. Society finds it easy to regard the Parpalaix case as having a happy ending, while at the same time quietly pays homage to science for preserving a dead man's sperm and salvaging the procreative potential of the marital act through a medical technique that, in addition to bestowing life, might even procure the child's desired sex. A clear victory, it would seem, of science over fate. Thanks to science, death will not rob husband and wife of the son they both wanted. It is the thoroughly modern way of having a baby, and no one should raise any objections.

How to effect the gender of one's choice has always been one of nature's most coveted secrets. Folklore contains a fascinating variety of amusing and bizarre suggestions on how this might be accomplished. Medieval alchemists, for example, prescribed for those who desired a son, a precoital drink of lion's blood. This prescription, like so many others, clearly illustrates the triumph of credulity over credibility, while exposing a tendency in frail human nature that we are well advised not to take lightly. A moment's reflection could have enlightened even the most credulous of medieval clients, for the lion himself, full to the brim as he is with pure grade lion's blood, produces as many female offspring as male.

Already, in the '80s, journalists confidently relegate to the realm of superstition and pseudoscience "scientific" claims for sex-preselection that were made in the '70s.[3] The thesis put forward by Landrum Shettles recommending a baking soda douche for a son and vinegar for a daughter exemplifies how rapidly the assertions of serious scientists can pass into folklore. Even now, people are saying of the Ericsson-Glass method of sex-selection as found in their book, *Getting Pregnant in the 1980s*, that "This could be Landrum Shettles all over again."[4] Separating scientific statements from expressions of hope is not always an easy thing to do; but it is especially difficult when strong emotions are involved such as desire for control over offspring on the part of parents and desire for fame and fortune on the part of medical personnel.

The present combination of public eagerness and scientific imprecision provides an ideal climate for exploitation. With regard to sex-

---

Child of Desired Gender," *The New York Times*, May 29, 1984, p. 19.

[3]Joan Beck, "What if you chose child's sex?" *Chicago Tribune*, June 5, 1983.

[4]Claudia Wallis, "Can Science Pick a Child's Sex?" *Time*, August 27, 1984, p. 59.

preselection, there are currently two approaches scientists are working on, neither of which could be considered, by any objective standard, as being reliable. The first involves an attempt to separate X and Y chromosones—the factors in the male gametes that determine the sex of the child—and then, through artificial insemination, infuse the gamete that will effect the desired sex. Ronald Ericsson, founder of Gametric Ltd. of Sausalito, California, claims a success rate of 77% using this method with 146 women to produce males. However, independent researchers who tested this method found it to be less than encouraging.[5] Producing females involves even less precise methods. The Philadelphia Fertility Institute, in attempting to isolate the X-carrying female gametes in order to produce females, found success in seven of eleven pregnancies, with one set of male-female twins occurring.

The second method involves timing the moment of intercourse in relation to the occurrence of ovulation. It is believed that since the Y spermatazoon is about three percent lighter than its X counterpart, it is more motile and can reach the ovum more easily. Thus, it seems reasonable to assume that intercourse close to the moment of ovulation is apt to produce a higher incidence of male offspring. This thesis has been supported by Kleegman, Shettles, Vear and others who report varying degrees of confirmatory results in their own studies. Shettles claims a success rate of 85% in a study involving 41 pregnancies.[6] At the same time, other researchers have reported contrary findings. France, Guerrero,[7] and James,[8] for example, report the occurrence of significant numbers of male conceptions from sperm surviving 3 to 5 days (though not significant enough to establish the counter thesis).

The France study[9] is of particular interest in that it shows rather decisively how extremely difficult it is to pinpoint the time of ovulation. Three indicators of the time of ovulation were used—the rise in luteinizing hormone, the peak cervical mucus symptom, and the shift in basal body temperature—and each indicated a different time of ovula-

---

[5]*Ibid.*, p. 60, referring to testing done at Chicago's Michael Reese Hospital.

[6]Landrum B. Shettles, "Factors influencing sex ratios," *Int Journal Gynaec Obstet*, 8: 643, 1970.

[7]R. Guerrero, "Association of the type and time of insemination within the menstrual cycle with the human sex ratio at birth," *N Eng J Med* 291: 1056, 1974.

[8]W. H. James, "Time of fertilization of sex of infants," *Lancet*, 1: 1124, 1980.

[9]J. France *et al.*, "A prospective study of the preselection of the sex of offspring by timing intercourse relative to ovulation," *Fertility and Sterility*, Vol. 41, No. 6, June 1984, 894.

tion while bearing distinct correlations with the resulting sex ratios. The implication here is that truly confirmatory results will not be achieved one way or another with regard to theories concerning the effect that the timing of intercourse has on sex ratios until the moment of ovulation can be more accurately and reliably predicted. In the meantime, France *et al.* emphasize caution in concluding that the sex of offspring can be predetermined by appropriately timing intercourse.[10]

John Kerin has pointed out as a result of a literature search of no less than 70 articles on the subject that at least 30 variables have been associated with variations in sex ratio. He concludes, therefore, that it is impossible to draw any clear conclusion about the importance of any one particular variable.[11] In addition, the fact that about half of all fraternal twins are male-female combinations[12] may indicate that the reliability of sex-preselection methods based on the appropriate timing of intercourse is subject to severe natural limitations. One would plausibly assume that because fraternal twins are often conceived within a relatively short time span that considerably more than half of such twins would be of the same sex. Yet, approximately 50% of all fraternal twins are binomial.

Given the fact that the present methods of sex-preselection only slightly improve the chances of producing the desired sex (Kerin states that at best, they alter the sex ratio by a factor of less than 10%), it would seem that there is insufficient reason, on a purely practical level, to encourage or counsel people to employ them. In many cases, chance alone may prove a more reliable method than the best "scientific" method that is available. Moreover, sex-preselection is probably wholly irrelevant to couples who want several children and are not particularly fussy about the order in which their sons and daughters arrive.

But beyond the practical realm of getting the sex of one's choice, there is a range of psychological and sociological problems that sex-preselection may introduce. The couple that is highly motivated, for example, may experience sharp disappointment when its sex-selection method fails. This disappointment could be compounded by rejection, guilt, and remorse. Besides, the couple may fail to achieve pregnancy. Even where the sex-selection method does not appear to fail (one never really knows whether the desired sex was brought about by the method or by chance), the child, nonetheless, may carry through life the

[10]*Ibid.*, pp. 899-900.

[11]John Kerin, M.D., M.R.O.C.G., F. Aust. C.O.G., *Australian Council of Natural Family Planning, Inc. Newsletter*, January 1983.

[12]Vincent & Margaret Gaddis, *The Curious World of Twins* (New York: Hawthorne, 1972), p. 22.

burden of his parents' desires and expectations that are attached to his sex.[13]

The sociological implications would come into focus if sex-preselection were widely practiced and highly reliable. Paradoxically, sex-preselection is uncommendable because it has a high failure rate, but it would be even more uncommendable if it had a high success rate. Social psychologist Roberta Steinbacher reports that among a group of people who expressed a willingness to use a sex-preselection method, 91% of the women and 94% of the men indicated that they would prefer their firstborn to be a boy.[14] Ms. Steinbacher fears that the overwhelming preferences for firstborn males would, if widely carried out, institutionalize a second-class status for women because of their ranking in the birth order. "We would become a nation of big brothers and little sisters," she says.[15] Moreover, sex-preselection techniques would inevitably be unaffordable by the poor, thus contributing to a socioeconomic split between the sexes, producing disproportionate numbers of sons born to rich parents while the proportion of daughters born to poor people would remain unchanged. Dr. Robyn Rowland goes as far as to predict that the disadvantages to women brought about by widespread sex-preselection would occasion an escalation of female suicide rates.[16] Another social researcher summarizes her fear of how women might be victimized by sex-preselection when she writes:

> Sex preference can mean that a child is disadvantaged before it is even born. In extreme cases, sex preference may lead to selective abortion or infanticide; more often, it involves child neglect.[17]

Apart from the practical, psychological, and sociological objections to sex-choice technology, there are some fundamental philosophical objections which warrant discussion. These objections more firmly establish the moral dimension of sex-preselection, placing it on a level

---

[13]Robyn Rowland, "Social Implications of Reproductive Technology," *IRNFP*, Fall 1984, p. 200.

[14]Richard Lyons, *op. cit.*. Roberta Steinbacher, "Futuristic Implications of Sex Preselection," in Holmes *et al.*, (eds.), *The Custom-made Child? Women-centered Perspectives* (New Jersey: Human Press, 1981).

[15]Quoted in Joan Beck, *op. cit.*. Cf. L. Fidell *et al.*, "Some Social Implications of Sex-choice Technology," *Psychology of Women Quarterly*, 1979, 4, (1), 32-42.

[16]Rowland, *op. cit.*, p. 200. Cf. "Parents Still Prefer Boys," *Psychology Today*, 1984, 19-30.

[17]Nancy E. Williamson, Ph.D., "Sex Preference and its Effect on Family Size and Child Welfare," *Draper Fund Report*, 1982.

of discussion that cannot be superannuated by a mere improvement in technique. It is theoretically possible that practical objections to sex-preselection would disappear with the development of a more reliable technique. Proper advice and psychological counselling could very well mitigate many of the psychological problems. Dr. Robert G. Edwards of Cambridge University offered a remedy for the possible upset of the sex ratio brought about by sex-preselection as early as 1974 when he stated, though perhaps naively, that "Imbalance of the sexes could probably be prevented by recording the sex of the newborn child, and adjusting the choice open to parents."[18] Edwards is suggesting that a discriminating use of sex-choice technology could prevent certain adverse sociological consequences, although by adopting a method of adjustment that would withhold the use of sex-preselection techniques from many couples who happened to desire the "wrong" sex.

Three philosophical objections, in particular, warrant discussion: 1) that desire alone is a morally inadequate basis on which to justify medical intervention; 2) that sex-preselection is inseparable from the subjectivization of a human being's value; 3) that parents do not have the *right* to determine the sex of their offspring.

First, in order to become aware of the moral dimension of a human act, one must take into account more than the presence of a desire and the expected consequence connected with that desire. One must also consider the essential character of the act itself together with other consequences that are also likely to flow from the act. It may seem morally innocuous to desire a son or daughter and employ a method which fulfills that desire, but the relevant moral dimension does not come into focus until all the pertinent factors are brought together. In experiencing their opposition to *in vitro* fertilization, the Catholic Bishops of England underscored this point when they wrote:

> Choices are not mere isolated events, but take up a stance towards human goods, and mould the chooser's character which may last into eternity and which also tends to find expression in socially significant acts and attitudes.[19]

Sex-preselection, involving as it does, medical intervention, does not conform to any of the traditional categories of medical practice. It is relatable neither to diagnostic, preventative, alleviatory, or curative

---

[18]R. G. Edwards, "Fertilization of Human Eggs in Vitro: Morals, Ethics and the Law," *The Quarterly Review of Biology*, 49:1 (March 1974), pp. 3-26.

[19]*Catholic Bishops' Joint Committee on Bio-Ethical Issues to the Warnock Committee on human fertilisation and embryology*, para. 20. See also John Finnis, "IVF and the Catholic tradition," *The Month*, February 1984, p. 55.

medicine. Nor is it relatable even to cosmetic medicine. To engage the medical profession in an activity which is essentially non-medical is to ignore the framework of medical ethics which exists in order to ensure that a particular medical intervention is indeed morally justifiable. The practices of amputating a healthy toe so that a patient may avoid the military draft, or extracting teeth that are perfectly sound so that a patient can register a better insurance claim, are not medically justifiable because they do not treat a genuinely medical problem. Moreover, such acts as these are morally indefensible because they treat something good (healthy parts of the body) as if they were not good (or pathological). Complicity in such procedures on the part of the patient is also morally indefensible since he is treating healthy parts of his own body as if they were diseased.

Medical intervention is morally justified in the context of promoting health and opposing disease. This justification is based on the objective philosophical principle that health is good for the body and disease, in working against health, is bad. In other words, health is consonant with the wholeness of one's being, whereas disease connotes some form of privation and a disintegrating tendency that moves in the opposite direction, away from wholeness and health. But with regard to sex-preselection, there is no objective basis for the employment of these distinctions between good and bad, health and disease, wholeness and privation. It is not unhealthy to be a female or a male in and of itself. Neither is it good in a particular instance for a person to be a male and not good to have been a female, or vice versa. It is not contrary to health or goodness or wholeness to be a nonmale or nonfemale, any more than it would be to be a nonpianist. Logically, the opposition between male and female is one of contrariety and not privation.

Since medical intervention is justified only in the context of health, its involvement in sex-preselection as the fulfillment of a mere desire to produce a male or female child would seem to be outside of the parameters of medical ethics and therefore morally unacceptable. Whenever medical practice violates medical ethics, the inevitable implication is that something which is good or healthy is treated *as if* it were bad or diseased. It was inevitable that defenders of the practice of aborting healthy unborn babies, for example, would argue (as some have argued) that an "unwanted" child represents a "pathology," a "diseased condition," and even a "venereal disease." Some doctors have gone so far as to state that from a strict medical viewpoint, "every pregnancy should be aborted."[20]

---

[20]Quoted by Andrew Scholberg "The Abortionists and Planned Parenthood: Family Bedfellows," *IRNFP*, Vol. LV, No. 4.

Thus, one of the undesirable additional consequences of sex-pre-selection involves the irremovable tendency (which inevitably will have its expression in actuality) of regarding certain males and fe-males—whose sex represents a frustration of their parents' desires—as being bad in some way simply because they are males or females. In ad-dition, we must also be concerned about the integrity/prostitution of the medical profession. Prostitution, by definition, puts some carnal in-terest, such as money ahead of personal or professional integrity; it puts *wrongs* ahead of *rights*. The medical profession, acting in its professional capacity, does not have the *right* to sell services that are essentially non-medical, any more than a woman has a *right* to treat her body as a saleable commodity.

On the other hand, the purpose of sex-preselection methods may be genuinely medical. In such an instance, a male or female is desired or undesired not for reasons of sex (a reality that has nothing to do with medicine), but in order to prevent the occurrence of a disease that is associated with a particular sex. Families with a history of certain hereditary diseases could have a morally acceptable reason for sex se-lection that is truly medical since some genetic disorders, including hemophilia and a devastating form of muscular dystrophy, primarily af-fect one sex and not the other. In this instance preventative medicine is practiced not to avoid a male, but to prevent a serious disease that would, in all likelihood, not be present in a female. It is more a case a disease-prevention than sex-selection. This is not to say that any type of sex-selection technique is morally justifiable simply because a medical motive is present. Other questions must still be asked concerning the type of method used (does it involve artificial insemination), whether an abortion is planned if the unborn is the "wrong" sex, and so on. But it is to say that there can be a medical purpose associated with sex-preselection and that this procedure could also be morally acceptable. Sex-preselection, however merely to satisfy a desire, is neither a medi-cal nor a moral procedure.

A second philosophical objection is that the fundamental value of a human being is not derived from another human being, nor is it de-pendent on how other people happen to view him. A human being's value is inseparable from his substance; it is intrinsic and inalienable, belonging to him as an attribute of his fundamental reality as a human being. Thus, a person has value primarily because he *is* rather that for what he *does* or how he *acts*. This is not to disvalue what people do or how they act, but to recognize that in the natural order of things, *being* precedes *doing*.

The difference between justice and authoritarian power is relatable to the difference between regarding a human as having a right to be because he *is* and not having a right to be because of something he has failed to *do* or someone he has failed to *become*. Now that biotechnology has given us certain powers over the next generation, the temptation to disregard another person's objective right to be when, subjectively, he has the "wrong" sex, is proving irresistible for many people. In two countries in particular, China and India, where there is much pressure on parents to desire male firstborn, amniocentesis followed by abortion of the female is not uncommon. In these cases, the female unborn child is disvalued because she is not a male. In other words, the objective, human value of the female child is not recognized because the basis for her value is the subjective preference of the parents. In California, a gynecologist by the name of Ferdinand Beernink—whose method of sex-preselection involves segregating X and Y sperm—gives his patients 75% odds of having a baby in the sex of their choice. Where tests taken during pregnancy show that the child is the "wrong" sex, Beernink will arrange an abortion. If the contentious term "sexism" ever conveyed moral significance, it would have to be in this instance where a child in the womb is destroyed specifically because of its sex. Such acts as these where the value of life is radically subjectivized are essentially incompatible with justice.

Justice demands that people respond to the rights of a person because he *is*; authoritarian power confers rights to a person only if he conforms to certain subjective standards that exist in the minds of others. Sex-preselection is an extension of this subjective mentality, and one that has already proven itself to be extremely dangerous. The abortion phenomenon alone offers us an object lesson that is only too graphic. The unwanted child has prepared the way for the child of undesired sex, a trend that also places at risk the unneeded handicapped, the unappreciated indigent, and the unloved elderly. It is asking too much of human beings, if we understand the lessons of past and present experiences, to encourage them to want the "right" sex and at the same time expect them not to unwant the "wrong" sex to the point of unwanting the child of the "wrong" sex. Once they are given the power and the license to control the kind of offspring they want, it can hardly be surprising that they would unwant the offspring they did not control. A technological triumph does not ensure a corresponding victory for justice. In fact, justice demands that we resist controlling others, subjectivizing their intrinsic value, reducing them to objects of arbitrary preference, precisely so that we can recognize the value and good that human beings are in their own right. Sex-preselection represents a temptation we would be wise to avoid, one that inclines us to stigmatize those human beings who, through methodological failures, must inevitably be looked upon as the embodiments of our frustrated desires. But human beings do not exist to be fulfillments of their parents desires. They have their own destinies to fulfill, their own mysteries to explore.

Third, philosophical exception must be taken to the position of authors Pfeffer and Woollett, who have stressed that the "right" for infertile women to have children—through *in vitro* fertilization, for example—is as imperative a "right" as that of remaining childfree.[21] Such a notion of "right" is part of the "reproductive freedom" that some feminists consider essential to their "liberation." The panoply of rights implied by "reproductive freedom" would, by logical extension, include sex-preselection.

Establishing reproduction in the soil of an ideology of "reproductive freedom," however, creates a moral problem of the first magnitude. The human who is "reproduced" is, in reality, not a manifestation of someone else's rights or a tangible expression of feminist freedom, but a separate human entity with rights and dignity that are grounded in his own independent being. To regard the conception of a child as the fulfillment of a personal right is to fail to recognize the autonomy of that child and to subordinate one human being to another in the way a product is subordinated to its maker.[22] It is a strange irony that feminism, which gives primacy to equality between human beings, endorses an ideology of rights that demands a far greater degree of inequality between human beings than any against which feminism originally revolted.

At the same time, there are many men who also endorse sex-preselection and do so apart from any sympathy they might have for feminist ideology. Nonetheless, they also hold that parents have rights that extend beyond the right to have a child to include the right to determine that child's sex. If one grants, however, that one human being has a right to another human being, it is impossible to maintain a position of radical equality between them.

The principle of equality demands that no human being or group of human beings has a right to another human being. Deductively, a married couple does not have a right to have a child.[23] This particular expression of the more general principle may seem startling to many.

---

[21]N. Pfeffer and H. Woollett, *The Experience of Infertility* (London: Routledge & Kegan Paul, 1984).

[22]Catholic Bishops, *op. cit.*, para. 25.

[23]Albert Moraczewski, O.P., "In Vitro Fertlization and Christian Marriage," *Linacre*, November 1979, p. 314.

Yet, if it is true that humans do not have a right to other humans, husband and wife do not have the right to a child. This is not to imply, of course, that children should not be conceived. But it is to indicate that the particular relationship that obtains between parents and children is not one that can be understood in terms of *rights*.

The law of the Catholic Church is very clear in stating that there can be no right to children.[24] As we have seen, the basic right involved in marriage is the right to acts that are apt by their nature to the generation of children. A parent speaks of "my" child just as naturally as a married couple speaks of "our" children. But, ethically, these personal adjectives must be taken as partitive rather than as possessive genitives. Parents beget their children rather than produce them; they are stewards of their children, rather than possessors of them.

Again, the act of sexual intercourse offers a marvelously clear context within which the proper relationship between parent and child should be understood. Husband and wife have a right to express their love for each other through sexual intercourse. But the nature of this act leads both partners to an abdication of control. The climactic moment of orgasm—often described as ecstasy—is one of mutual self-surrender. At the same time, sexual intercourse is an invocation to new life. The only element of subordination lies in the willingness of the married couple to be disposed to accept God's creative will. The child is not subordinated to the parents' control or rights, nor are the parents subordinated to te child or to each other.

Christopher Derrick has expressed this delicate matter rather beautifully: "As a general rule, the only decent and Christian attitude towards one's actual or potential children is one that we can express by adapting some well-known words of Job: "The Lord may or may not give: the Lord may or may not take away: blessed be the name of the Lord!"[25] Sexual intercourse, properly respectful of God's will sets the tone for the continuing relationship parents have with their offspring as an existential preamble. The loving care husband and wife display for each other during intercourse, together with their abdication of control and renunciation of possessiveness profoundly symbolizes the kind of relationship they are to have with their children. Parenting is a natural extension of love-making. The act that makes them parents tells them a great deal about how they are to act as parents.

Pope John Paul II speaks of parents submitting their being to the

---

[24]Frank Morrissey, O.M.I., Moraczewski *et al.* (eds.) *Technological Powers and the Person* (St. Louis: Pope John XXIII Medical-Moral Research and Education Center, 1983), p. 449.

[25]Christopher Derrick, Moraczewski *et al.* (eds.), p. 18.

blessing of fertility.[26] The notion of "submitting" may cause many people who fancy themselves as "liberated" to react with indignation. But the Pope realizes that a reasonable submission is needed in order to avoid an unreasonable subordination. Implicit in the Pope's remark is his opposition to a radical inequality between human beings in which parents assume they have a right to have children that extends to their right to employ technological methods in order to manipulate them in accordance with their own private motives which are non-medical in nature. The Holy Father is advising that parents submit not to other human beings but to God—who uses fertility as a means through which he expresses his love for man—so they can properly dispose themselves to receive new life as a gift. He is also suggesting that this submission be with one's "being" and not merely some particular part of one's being (it is the humans who procreate, not their gametes). A corollary of this statement indicates that unless man submits to God, he will inevitably require other humans to submit to him.

The notion that life is a gift has two fundamentally different implications. First, it is a gift to the child, the receiver of life. Here, the gift is wholly undeserved and unsolicited, a gift in the fullest sense. Moreover, the gift is irrevocable, belonging permanently to the recipient. Secondly, life is a gift to the parents in the sense that the living child is given to them to love and care for. But the gift of life belongs primarily to the child. It is a substantial gift in that it gives the child its very substance. On the other hand, the marriage partners—who invoked new life in behalf of someone other than themselves—receive a gift that is essentially relational; their's is the irrevocable gift of parenthood.

Sex-preselection does not affect in any way the gift of parenthood. Whether they have a boy or a girl, husband and wife are parents in exactly the same way. However, from the viewpoint of the child, to be male or female means to be human in ways that are not the same. Language has no word to distinguish the parent who has a male child from the parent who has a female. Parents are simply "parents," whereas their children are either "sons" or "daughters."

Thus, it would seem, parents have no right to alter their child's own gift of life through attempting to determine its sex, because that gift belongs primarily and exclusively to the child. Moreover, the parents do not have such a right for a second reason, because it is fundamentally irrelevant to their own gift, which is the gift of parenthood. The attempt to determine the sex of one's child is incompatible with the

---

[26]Pope John Paul II, "Revelation and Discovery of the Nuptial Meaning of the Body," Address of January 9, 1980 in *L'Osservatore Romano*, English ed. N. 2(615) January 14, 1980.

reverence that is appropriate for the proper conferring and receiving of both of these gifts.

The third volume of C. S. Lewis' space-science trilogy, *That Hideous Strength*, is a fictional dramatization of what the author expressed in more philosophical terms in a previous book of his, *The Abolition of Man*. In this volume, the forces of technology, freed from any concern to conform the soul to reality, or to abide by Christian principles, are using science and magic "to subdue reality to the wishes of men."[27] The powers which are preparing the final assault upon humanity are concentrated in the National Institute for Coordinated Experimentation (N.I.C.E.). The acronym is intentional and offers, in a nutshell, an image and an argument that members of our own secular society find persuasive.

It would be *nice* if science could make it possible for children to be sexed to their parent's desires. It would be *nice* if technology could oblige infertile couples by producing babies for them. It would be *nice* if applied science could crown a consumer-society governed by the principle "I want," by gratifying all its wants. But in the final analysis, "nice" merely mirrors a private dream that is born of bare desire, one tat lacks the wisdom to unite itself with the needs of society, humanity, or even the deeper needs of the self. Those whose lives and hopes are fused by such desires inhabit a suffocatingly small universe, perhaps like the one Hamlet alluded to in which he could count himself "king of infinite space," though "bounded in a nut-shell."[28]

Illusions always seem larger and brighter than reality to those who use desire as their moral compass. It would be *nice* if every baby was wanted, every relationship meaningful, and every death painless. It would be *nice* if we were not mortal, finite, or defectible. It would be *nice*, but the reality of the situation is otherwise.

Morality obliges us to involve ourselves in a world of limitations and difficulties, a world that frustrates our will and shatters our dreams, but a world that broadens and purifies us so that the truth we come to know and the joy we finally experience is a fulfillment of our whole being. Morality exists to let us know that the best things in life are not *nice* only because they are more than nice: love is redemptive, marriage is sacramental, fertility is a blessing, children are a joy, and life is a great gift.

---

[27]C. L. Lewis, *The Abolition of Man* (New York: Macmillian, 1965), p. 88.

[28]Shakespeare, *Hamlet*, Act II, Scene 2.

Surrogate Motherhood

What does one call a woman who gets pregnant, carries her child to term, goes into labor, and gives birth to a new baby? If one answers, "a mother," he may be roundly criticized these days for committing the unpardonable error of viewing things in black and white. He may also be criticized for not being aware of the latest merchandising strategies connected with current modes of technological reproduction. Because of a specific contractual agreement she signs, the woman in question is not to be considered a mother but merely a "surrogate" mother. By implication, therefore, someone else is the "real" mother, usually the wife of the husband whose sperm artificially inseminated the "surrogate."

Commercial advertising has long believed that words have magical properties. It is what you *call* a thing that counts, not what it *is*. If jeans do not bear the name Levi, they are not jeans; an aspirin is not an aspirin unless you call it a Bayer aspirin. Now that procreation has been made a branch of private enterprise, it no longer follows that a certain natural, biological course of events establishes a woman's motherhood; rather it is determined by how her contract reads. Calling her a "surrogate" magically transforms her into something other than a real mother, and by the complementary, an infertile woman metamorphoses into a "mother."

A "surrogate mother" is very much the original mother, both genetically and gestationally. To refer to her as an adultress who rents her womb and gives up her child as soon as it is born, is obviously contrary to sound merchandising principles. The designation "surrogate" is created to appease the consumer, who is not only paying to have a baby, but to be known as the child's mother as well.

The prospect of using a "surrogate" arises when a married couple cannot have a child of its own, specifically when the wife is unable to

173

conceive or carry a pregnancy to term. An arrangement is made with another woman who agrees to be artificially inseminated with the sperm of the infertile wife's husband. The "surrogate" agrees to relinquish the child to the contracting couple once it is born. For her services, the surrogate is paid anywhere from $5,000 to $30,000. Hence, she is sometimes called a "mercenary mother."

We may express the same scenario in the following way: A woman cannot have a child of her own, so she hires a woman who can have one for her. But when the child arrives, she credits herself with being the mother and not the woman who bore the child. Traditionally this practice of passing off another person's accomplishments as if they were one's own is considered to be reprehensible. If an executive cannot type and hires a secretary to type for him, he does not claim that she is is a "surrogate" typist and he is the "real" one. A batter who is a poor hitter is replaced by a pinch hitter. But if the latter delivers a hit, it is he who is credited with it and not the batter he replaced.

In the movie version of Peter Shaffer's play, *Amadeus*, Antonio Salieri attempts to carry out a thoroughly despicable series of actions. He himself cannot write great music and therefore hires Mozart to do so in the form of a Requiem. He plans to assassinate the composer once the music is completed, and then claim authorship of the masterpiece. It is a plot calculated to make him appear magnanimous in the eyes of the populace because Salieri will dedicate the Requiem to his dear, departed friend and conduct its performance at Mozart's funeral Mass. The movie, in a sense, represents the converse of abortion. Instead of killing the offspring for the sake of the one who conceived it, one kills the one who conceived it for the sake of the offspring. Given the intense legal battles that are now being fought over custody rights between surrogates and their contracting parties, Salieri may one day become a role model for frustrated infertile women who are willing to take the law into their own hands. After all, the nub of Salieri's problem, in a certain sense, was that he was infertile.

Feminist Gena Corea, author of *The Mother Machine*, prefers to call surrogate mothers "breeders," though what this term gains in accuracy it loses its prestige. Women are being exploited and denied their motherhood. They are manipulated into believing they are mere "living incubators" or "oocyte donors." "We are *supposed* to be confused," states Ms. Corea rather angrily. "The confusion keeps us speechless and powerless. It is as a Native American friend once told me: Confusion is a tool of oppression."[1]

---

[1] Gena Corea, *The Mother Machine* (New York: Harper & Row, 1985), p. 236.

Annette Baran, co-author of *The Adoption Triangle*, comments on how women are subjected to conditioning processes at one particular surrogate clinic: "They recite in chorus, 'We're doing something great for somebody else. We're carrying somebody else's baby.' It's really a brainwashing affair."

This conditioning is reinforced by lawyers and members of the medical profession. In an article in the *Western Journal of Medicine*, for example, the authors refer to the surrogate as "the woman attached to the rented womb" and to her child as "her tenant."[2] The New York *Times* reflected a similar view in an editorial concerning one Denise Thrane, a surrogate contracted by James and Bjorna Noyes, who decided to keep her baby. According to the editor, Baby Thrane was "residing in a rented womb." Furthermore, "Mr. and Mrs. Noyes may have lost the lease on the womb; their lawyer seems something less than a crack real estate agent; and Mrs. Thrane is claiming her property."[3]

An interesting facet of the rhetoric that promotes surrogate transactions is how unconsciously it shifts from one cause to another. A main tenet in the pro-abortion rhetoric was the assertion that a woman had a right to control her own body and the fetus, after all, is merely a part of the woman's body. The new rhetoric that defends the interests of the contracting parties in the surrogate motherhood issue claims that the fetus is not a part of the woman's body or even related to her as her child. It is alleged to be a "tenant" or a "resident" in a rented womb.[4] In addition, the rhetoric that promotes embryo transfer and the interests of the gestating mother holds a third position, namely, that gestation is a sufficient factor in determining motherhood. Dr. John Buster, a pioneer in embryo transfer technology is adamant that the real mother of the child is "the woman who nurtures and shapes the child for nine months. If that isn't being a mother, what is?"[5] An advocate for surrogate motherhood would answer Buster's question by saying, "the infertile wife who contracts a woman to serve as a surrogate to gestate her husband's child on her behalf." A "pro-choice" enthusiast would make motherhood a matter of will, arguing that a woman is not a mother until she chooses to be one.

The propaganda shifts along several different fronts at the same time. One feminist complained that the notion of maternal instinct was

---

[2]Laurence E. Karp and Roger P. Donahue, "Preimplantation ectogenesis," *The Western Journal of Medicine*, 1976, 124 (4).

[3]"Love for Sale," *New York Times*, April 2, 1981.

[4]Karp and Donahue, 124 (4)

[5]*The Phil Donahue Show*, #08223.

drilled into women in every imaginable way. But when markets for surrogate motherhood opened up, the new view became: "Well, as long as you know it's not yours, you can give it up . . . They're conditioning women to say: 'It's not my baby. It's yours because you paid for it.' How fast they change! They switch propaganda on us to suit their needs."[6]

Underlying the shifting propaganda is a constant—the desire of the consumer. Those who are wary of moral absolutes associated with traditional norms with regard to procreation might be well advised to direct their antipathies to the absolutization of desire. It is appropriate, though still unorthodox, that Lori Andrews' recent book on the latest forms of technological reproduction is entitled: "A Consumer's Guide to the Newest Infertility Treatment."[7] Encouraging people to look upon motherhood as an object of their desire which technology and financial resources will help them to achieve, most assuredly cultivates an invidious consumer mentality. It adapts to human procreation the "have it your way" cafeteria approach to food items.

Noel Keane, who operates a surrogate clinic in New York City, refers to the child as an "investment." In his book, *The Surrogate Mother*, for example, he states: "How can the husband be sure he is indeed the father of his 'investment' short of isolating the surrogate from other male contacts."[8] Dr. Richard Levin of the Surrogate Parenting Association in Louisville explains that in his program paternity testing is done to ensure that the baby was fathered by the client and not the surrogate's husband.[9]

Noel Keane speaks of one client, Olive May, aged 60, who wanted to secure the services of a surrogate to provide a child for her husband who is 40. If a child was conceived under such circumstances, its "mother" would be 70 before the child turned 10! Harriet Blankfield, head of the National Center for Surrogate Parenting accepts single men as clients. Some programs provide surrogates for fertile women. One woman who already had two children prior to her hysterectomy, found a surrogate to provide her with a child for her second husband.

Despite its arbitrariness, however, surrogate motherhood propaganda is effective, though certainly not in all cases. *Time* magazine did a personal profile on one surrogate mother who said of the child she con-

---

[6]Corea, p. 238.

[7]Lori Andrews, *New Conceptions: A Consumer's Guide to the Newest Infertility Treatments, Including In Vitro Fertilization, Artificial Insemination, and Surrogate Motherhood* (New York: St. Martin's, 1984).

[8]Noel P. Keane with Dennis L. Breo, *The Surrogate Mother* (New York: Everest House, 1981), p. 265.

[9]*The Phil Donahue Show*, #04150.

ceived, carried, and delivered: "I feel like a loving aunt to her."[10] A Florida woman who carried a child for her sister stated: "To this day, I feel like a loving aunt. I was just babysitting."[11] An Illinois surrogate commented: "I think of myself as a human incubator."[12]

In Oak Ridge, Tennessee, a woman who already had a 10-year-old son served as a surrogate for her married sister who lived in New England. She presented her sister with a six-pound five-ounce baby girl. In this case the baby girl was separated from her half-brother to be raised by her aunt, while regarding her own mother as an aunt.[13] Even more vexing is the case involving a Michigan surrogate who presented her sister with a gift of triplets.[14]

Some of the surrogate applicants Michigan psychiatrist Philip Parker interviewed asserted that their babies belonged to the adoptive couples. They denied the possibility that they might feel any loss when they gave up their infants. Among the reasons they gave for not expecting any emotional bond to develop between themselves and their babies, according to Parker: "I'm only an incubator," and "I'd just be nest-watching."[15] Finally, one surrogate mother expressed her attitude as follows: "I never looked at the baby as *my* baby. It was *their* baby. I felt like I was doing like my chickens do. I was hatching it and all the other chickens would take care of it."[16]

A surrogate may be persuaded mentally or intellectually that the child she carries is not hers, but another force operates within her which can easily supplant her initial conviction brought about by the power of suggestion. This more existential force is the reality of her motherhood and the bond that develops between her and her child. The power of being is often a more persuasive force than the power of propaganda. By conceiving and carrying a child to term, women become mothers. This is a truth they grasp in a most immediate and profound way, and no form of ideological rhetoric can cause them to think otherwise. Despite the careful screening, the group therapy sessions, the promise to adhere to the contractual agreement, surrogates change

---

[10]Claudia Wallis, "A Surrogate's Story," *Time*, Sept. 10, 1984, p. 51.

[11]"Sisters Share the Joy of Birth," *The Buffalo News*, Nov. 8, 1985, C-1.

[12]Lori Andrews, p. 197.

[13]Elaine Markoutas, "Women Who have Babies for Other Women," *Good Housekeeping*, April 1981, p. 96.

[14]"Woman Presents Sister With Gift—of Triplets," *The Buffalo News*, June 26, A-10.

[15]Corea, p. 222.

[16]Philip J. Parker, "Motivation of surrogate mothers: Initial findings," *American Journal of Psychiatry*, 140 (1).

their minds and decide to keep their babies.

In England, an infertile couple engaged in a prostitute to serve as a surrogate mother. When the child was born, however, the prostitute changed her mind and decided to keep the child. The couple tried to entice the woman into surrendering the infant by offering her: first, money and a secondhand car; and then their house. In this case, the matter was settled in court. The judge granted custody to the prostitute, stating that he was unwilling to enforce what he deemed to be a pernicious agreement for the sale of a child.

In another case, a Columbus, Ohio surrogate who already had three daughters refused to relinquish the son she delivered so she could round out her family. A California surrogate refused to surrender the child she delivered despite the threat of a law suit. The trial was called off at the last minute when preliminary investigation revealed that the contractual mother was really a man who had previously undergone a sex-change operation.[17]

The most sensationalized and dramatic case in which a surrogate changed her mind and decided to keep her child is the Hackensack, New Jersey episode involving two married couples: the Sterns and the Whiteheads. William and Elizabeth Stern contracted with Mary Beth Whitehead early in 1985 for her to conceive Mr. Stern's child through artificial insemination and carry out the pregnancy in their behalf. Mrs. Whitehead already had two school-age children and claimed that she did not want any more children of her own. After signing the surrogate agreement, she promised not to "form or attempt to form a parent-child relationship" with the infant.[18]

Despite her declared intentions, something happened to Mrs. Whitehead that she had not anticipated. As she told the court, the experience of childbirth "overpowered" her. "Something took her over," she said, "I think it was just being a mother." After handing her child over to the Sterns, according to her husband Richard's testimony, Mary Beth cried hysterically, asking, "Oh God, what have I done?"

The Whiteheads took the child home with them after she was born. Three days later, the Sterns arrived and collected the baby. But the very next morning, Mrs. Whitehead came by the Stern's household and begged for temporary custody of the child. A two-hour emotional battle ensued which resulted in Mrs. Stern, who feared that Mary Beth was suicidal, giving in to her demand. Two weeks later, the Sterns attempted to regain custody of the child. The Whiteheads refused to cooperate. A month later, after obtaining a court order, the Sterns re-

---

[17]*Noyes v. Thrane*, California Superior Court, filed Feb. 20, 1981.

[18]Richard Lacayo, "Whose Child Is This? *Time*, Jan. 19, 1987, p. 61

turned with five policemen to get the child. In the ensuing confusion, Richard Whitehead escaped with the child through a bedroom window. The Whiteheads then fled to Florida with the infant. The Sterns countered by hiring a private detective to track down the Whiteheads. Authorities returned the child to New Jersey and a judge granted temporary custody to the Sterns.

On March 31, 1987, Judge Harvey Sorkow ruled that the Stern-Whitehead contract was legal and binding. In addition, he awarded full custody of the child to the Sterns. Four days after her first birthday, the child—whom the Whiteheads called Sara, the Sterns Melissa, and the Court identified as Baby M—was finally given a permanent home, a fixed address, and specific parents.

Even more catastrophic, however, is the situation that develops when no one wants the child. Just as a surrogate may renounce the contract and keep her child, the contracting party might change its mind and reject the child. The Malahoff-Stiver imbroglio is a case in point, and one whose catastrophic proportions would be difficult to surpass.

Alexander Malahoff, of Middle Village, New York, signed a contract with Mrs. Judy Stiver of Lansing, Michigan who agreed to act as a surrogate mother. Malahoff hoped that the baby so produced through the artificial insemination of Mrs. Stiver with his sperm, would be what he needed to convince his own estranged wife to return and resume their marriage. Malahoff promised to pay Mrs. Stiver $10,000 as soon as the baby was born. The child was born in January 1983 with a strep infection and microcephaly, a disorder indicating possible mental retardation. Malahoff decided that he did not want it and told the hospital to withhold treatment. Mrs. Stiver stated that she had not established a "maternal bond" with the child since she had not held him. According to Michigan legislator Richard Fitzgerald, "For weeks the baby was tossed back and forth like a football—with no one having responsibility".[19]

Then, as a macabre touch that Boston University health-law professor George Annas said makes the soap operas appear pallid, Malahoff and Mr. Stiver had blood tests to establish the child's paternity and went on the *Phil Donahue Show* to await the results. During the show, Donahue announced that Malahoff was not the father. The Stivers had intercourse shortly prior to the artificial insemination procedure; the child was genetically theirs.

Malahoff reacted by suing the Stivers for not producing the child he ordered. He also sought to recover the $30,000 he paid out in related expenses. The Stivers sued the doctor, lawyer, and psychiatrist of

---

[19]Andrews, p. 240.

the surrogate program for not properly advising them about the timing of sex. Apparently the Stivers had been told to abstain from intercourse for a month after the insemination but had not been told to abstain in the days immediately before the procedure. Incredibly, the Stivers, who agreed to appear on the *Donahue Show*, sued Malahoff for violating their privacy by making the whole affair public. And finally, the Stivers claimed that their child's illness was caused by a virus transmitted by Malahoff's sperm.

The idea of a third party suing a married couple (and for millions of dollars in the Malahoff-Stiver case) for privately engaging in sexual intercourse as husband and wife seems patently absurd. It seems equally absurd that the same third party could order a hospital to withhold treatment for a baby that is not his, or that a married couple could sue a lawyer and other professionals for not telling them when they should not have intercourse. Nonetheless, in the shuffling of gametes and sex partners brought about by technologized, consumer-oriented approaches to parenthood, the possibilities for such moral absurdities certainly exist and appear to be unlimited.

We have withstood the shocks of Watergate, Pearlygate and Irangate; but can we do the same for Surrogate?

Promoters of surrogate motherhood view it essentially as a way of offering a husband and his infertile wife a chance—perhaps their only chance—of having a baby that is at least partly their own. Therefore, they see this reproductive technology in positive terms, as humanistic and liberating. But their view is shortsighted and neglects the jarring fact that surrogate motherhood is inseparable from a consumer mentality that exploits women, and relegates the child to the status of a commodity. Far from enhancing human freedom, the whole moral climate that surrogate motherhood generates actually circumscribes freedom to the point where it is in conflict with human rights. Moreover, the impossibility of regulating the surrogate industry morally opens the door for no end of abuses, complications, and personal tragedies.

The standard contractual agreement with a surrogate does not grant her many rights, but it does put her under a good number of restraints. Generally, the woman agrees to abstain from intercourse, sometimes as long as a month before and a month after the artificial insemination procedure (and there may be several attempts to achieve insemination). She also agrees not to smoke or drink or use drugs, including aspirin, without her doctor's written permission. She is often required to be present for psychological counselling and is contractually bound to obey all medical instructions of the inseminating physician and the obstetrician. Some programs require surrogates to keep the staff apprised of their whereabouts at all times, to get a certain amount of sleep each night, and to refrain from specific kinds of work. Quite often the interest of the contracting clients is placed above that of the surrogate.

Most agreements forbid the surrogate woman to abort without the consent of the inseminating father. (Here, the agreement is more stringent than law. In the United States and Canada, a woman can secure an abortion without the consent of the father even when he is the husband. In fact, the father does not have the right to consultation or notification in this matter.) On the other hand, most agreements require a woman to undergo an abortion when amniocentesis reveals the presence of fetal abnormalities. (In this case, the agreement is in conflict with a woman's right not to abort.)

Secular society looks upon a commercial agreement between a male client and his surrogate woman as having more binding force than a marriage covenant between a husband and his wife. The popularization of such an attitude cannot help but trivialize the bond of matrimony. A father's sense of responsibility for the welfare of his unborn child is accorded far more respect in the business world of surrogate motherhood than it is in marriage. A man might even eschew marriage for a surrogate agreement because he sees in the latter a certain freedom and respectability he may not find in the former. He may also find a surrogate agreement more attractive for the unseemly and morally regressive reason that it promises him a degree of control that is not available to him in a marriage.

The surrogate woman is put in the unhappy and unnatural position of denying the *bonding* that is developing between herself and her child, while submitting to the *bondage* devised by the contracting party and its battery of professional cohorts. At the same time, the infertile wife is deprived of the bonding experience, a deprivation that should not be taken lightly. Medical research reports a correlation between incomplete mother-child bonding and child battering.[20]

The difference between *bond* and *bondage* provides a pertinent insight into the difference between traditional Judaeo-Christian norms that apply to marriage and the family, and the new approach associated with the surrogate industry. Bonds, between husband and wife, parents and children, help perfect interpersonal love by bringing nature and spirit, body and psyche into greater intimacy with each other. The road to achieving proficiency at being a mother or father is steep and arduous. To alter Charlie Brown's *bon mot*, "I need all the friends I can

---

[20]H. B. Valman, "The First Years of Life, Mother-Infant Bonding," *British Medical Journal*, Feb. 2, 1980.

get," we could say, "I need all the bonds I can get." Bonds serve the interest of friendship, love, intimacy, and even freedom. Without bonds, people are alienated from each other.

Bondage, on the other hand, always implies an inordinate subjugation to something that is below the plane of parenthood. It was a favorite word of the 17th century century philosopher Spinoza for whom bondage was the result of making desire absolute, or riveting one's desire to external circumstances. It was this notion of Spinoza that inspired Somerset Maughham's novel about the ruinous potentialities associated with pure sexual desire—*Of Human Bondage*.

To excel at the demanding vocation of motherhood or fatherhood requires husbands and wives to gather together the fullness of their being. They should welcome and affirm all the bonds belonging to the integrated pattern of friendship, love, passion, conjugal intimacy, conception, pregnancy, motherhood, fatherhood, and family life.

Surrogate motherhood, because it repudiates bonds, inevitably gravitates toward bondage. At its very foundation is a form of selfish desire that is more compatible with the objectives of a commercial world than with the needs of the family. Surrogate women are routinely exploited, their offspring are often reduced to the status of commodities, and the contracting parties assume a buyer-product relationship with the babies their surrogates provide for them. The surrogate industry, through carefully placed advertising (particularly in *People Magazine* and the *Phil Donahue Show*[21]), has been able to create an illusion of freedom, but no more than that. In reality, it strikes at humanity's most venerable notions of the integrity of the family and the bonds between husband and wife, mother and child. It is an attempt to disintegrate even further the unity that belongs to marriage, conjugal intimacy, motherhood and fatherhood.

---

[21]Corea, p. 216.

Conclusion:
Technologized Parenthood
and the Attenuation
of Motherhood and Fatherhood

In Robert Francoeur's book *Utopian Motherhood*, the author presents the following scenario: a barren woman receives an ovarian transplant from another woman. She conceives, but has difficulty in continuing her pregnancy and therefore arranges for a third woman to carry the child to term. Since this woman's husband is sterile, she had been fertilized artificially by another man, one who died eleven years ago but left his frozen sperm to posterity. Francoeur asks his readers to "puzzle out" who the parents are and how many there might be.[1] This hypothetical situation is by no means farfetched. By one count there are now 23 ways to have a baby. We have entered the era of "High-Tech Babymaking" and one of the central issues that has emerged involves the extent to which the intervention of technology in human procreation has attenuated our traditional understanding of motherhood and fatherhood. Gena Corea, author of *The Mother Machine*, expressed her concern at a conference on "High-Tech Babymaking" that women could become merely collections of body parts, divorced from their procreative power and left with a more tenuous sense of self. "If science can produce better babies than women can," she remarked, "it reinforces the expendability of women."[2]

---

[1] Robert Francoeur, *Utopian Motherhood*: *New Trends in Human Reproduction* (London: George Allen & Unwin, 1971), p. 112.

[2] "Hartford College for Women hosts first conference on implications of new reproductive technologies," *The Chronicle* (Hartford College for Women), Spring-Summer 1986, pp. 1-12.

Episcopalian theologian Joseph Fletcher expresses the view that parenthood is "a moral relationship with children, not a material or merely physical relationship[3]. According to traditional standards, Fletcher's notion of parenthood is overbroad and arbitrary. Traditionally parenthood is not merely a moral relationship; it is incarnate, incorporating the material and physical aspects. Motherhood and fatherhood integrate marriage, conjugal intimacy, genetic contribution, and custodial care. There are situations where it is impossible to integrate all these elements, as in parenthood through adoption. From a traditional perspective, however, such parents do not negate or avoid parenthood's biological dimension. In adopting a child they affirm the guardianship dimension that the biological parents are unable to fulfill (because of death or incompetence, for example).

Technology may be used to expand possibilities for adoption, such as embryo transfer from a dying woman to a host mother.[4] But in such cases technology is not used to negate one or another aspect of parenthood. Those who adopt children maintain a clear understanding of the distinction between adopting and biological parents. They are not under the illusion that they are parents in the complete sense merely because they have a good moral relationship with their adoptive child. The nature of a relationship and its intensity are different matters.

Technology helps bring about an attenuation of the very meaning and understanding of motherhood and fatherhood when it is deliberately employed in negating, avoiding, circumventing, or demeaning certain elements that are constitutive of full parenthood. A few contemporary examples well illustrate this point. Noel Keane, a Michigan lawyer who operates a fertility clinic, has agreed to find a surrogate mother for a university professor who wants a child but who does not want pregnancy to interfere with her chance of obtaining tenure. Keane is also willing to find a surrogate for a single man who would like a son but who does not want to raise him. This man intends to provide a $20,000 trust fund for the boy, who will be raised by the surrogate and her husband while he maintains an avuncular relationship with the child.[5] A 36-year-old woman has sued the Wayne State University Arti-

---

[3]Lori Andrews, *New Conceptions: A Consumer's Guide to the Newest Infertility Treatments, Including In Vitro Fertilization, Artificial Insemination, and Surrogate Motherhood* (New York: St. Martin's, 1984), p. 14.

[4]Bernard Häring, Ethics of Manipulation (New York: Seabury, 1975), p. 201. See also Bishop Walter Curtis, "Bishop Gives Church View on Surrogate Parenthood," Catholic Transcript 13 April 1984, pp. 1-2.

[5]Andrews, p. 210.

ficial Insemination Clinic because it restricted its services to married couples. With the American Civil Liberties Union representing her, she alleged that the clinic's policy violated her right to privacy.[6]

In such cases as these the parties involved are using technology to negate pregnancy, avoid custodial fatherhood, circumvent sexual intercourse, and demean marriage. The net effect of such uses of technology is the attenuation of motherhood and fatherhood. By allowing people to select specific aspects of parenthood that are to their liking and reject those they find inconvenient, a consumer mentality is fostered. Thus as technology subserves a consumer-oriented form of parenthood, motherhood and fatherhood suffer the dissolution of their distinctive integrities. Throughout the ensuing discussion, the expression "technologized parenthood" will refer to that particular use of reproductive technology which attenuates the meaning of motherhood and fatherhood while encouraging a consumer approach to parenthood.

By contrast, technology can be used to affirm motherhood and fatherhood without purposely negating any of its various dimensions. For example, a procedure known as "low tubal ovum transfer" (LTOT) relocates the egg so that it is in a position where *in vivo* (inside the body) fertilization can take place.[7] In such a procedure motherhood is affirmed while none of its dimensions are negated. The same can be said of conventional forms of medical intervention that have genuinely therapeutic objectives, such as laser surgery to repair a blocked oviduct or the use of ultrasound in monitoring the fetal heartbeat.

Technologized parenthood serves consumer demands. It does not defend the inviolable integrity of traditional motherhood and fatherhood. It is directed toward reducing complex functions to their component parts, rather than toward respecting the nature of the whole. It is more mechanized than organic, more impersonal than personal. The expression "technologized parenthood," therefore, represents a conjunction of essentially incompatible factors. The reality, however, re-

---

[6] *Ibid.*, p. 194.

[7] See David Q. Liptak, "Catholic Hospital Begins 'In Vivo' Ovum Transfers," *The Catholic Standard and Times* 22 September 1983, p. 14. See also David Q. Liptak, "New 'Infertility Bypass (LTOT)' Assessed," *Catholic Transcript* 6 January 1984. In these two articles the author offers a positive assessment of LTOT. For a discussion of other possibly licit forms of reproductive technology see Orville N. Griese's, "Promising Approaches to Human Infertility," *International Review of Natural Family Planning*, Fall 1986, pp. 243-255 where the author presents Gamete Intrafallopian Transfer (GIFT) and Sperm Intrafallopian Transfer (SIFT) as forms of "assisted insemination" (as opposed, following the distinction made by Pope Pius XII, to "artificial insemination").

veals a process in which technology seeks to gain control of parenthood. This process clearly illustrates the split between technological and moral imperatives.

In his book *Mechanization Takes Command*, cultural historian Siegfried Giedion details how modern processes of mechanization have brought about a comparable split between thought and feeling. He found this split to be particularly evident in biology, where it is commonplace to exclude feelings (especially those that carry moral implications) in order to bring everything under the reign of thought (for the purpose of rational control). By reducing the living organism to a mere assemblage of material parts, the entire dimension of feeling is thereby made irrelevant. According to Giedion, "in *biology* the animate being was considered simply as the sum of its separate parts assembled like those of a machine. Organic processes were regarded as purely physico-chemical in nature, as if an organism were a kind of chemical plant".[8]

Marshall McLuhan titled his first book *The Mechanical Bride* (1951) in order to jolt his readers into realizing that to the blind processes of mechanization and technologization nothing is sacred. Not even a bride, the quintessential image of unravished loveliness, would be spared. As a sequel to this work McLuhan wrote *Culture is Our Business* (1970) to show how technology has created modern culture itself.

McLuhan's claims are amply validated by the contemporary verbal hybrids that are the logical offspring of our age of the "Mechanical Bride." Thus we speak blandly of artificial flowers, astro-turf, synthetic food, and the bionic man. We watch movies such as *The Love Machine*, *Heartbeeps*, *Electric Dreams*, and *The Computer Wore Tennis Shoes*. And we casually incorporate into our daily life such glaring incongruities as artificial intelligence, electronic voice-prints, atomic cocktails, and computer dating. We have been conditioned to take verbal incongruities in stride, thereby preparing the way for the broad cultural acceptance of genetic engineering, test-tube babies, and technologized parenthood.

Surveying the threat that technology poses for life, McLuhan saw an antagonism between "technologized determinism" and "organic autonomy,"[9] between the total dominance over life by technology and the freedom human organisms need in order to live and reproduce according to personal moral norms.

---

[8]Siegfried Giedion, *Mechanization Takes Command* (New York: W.W. Norton & Co., 1969), p. 718.

[9]Wilbert E. Moore (ed.), *Technology and Social Change* (Chicago: Quadrangle Books, 1972), p. 97.

Contraception played a crucial historical role in clearing the ground for the employment of various reproductive technologies. It introduced technologized sexuality, a logical precursor to technologized parenthood. Contraception separates sex from procreation; technologized parenthood is merely the converse of this separation. Whereas contraception means sex without babies, technologized parenthood means babies without sex (or at least without the fullness of the conjugal union), a point that molecular biologist Leon R. Kass made in a celebrated article he wrote in 1972 for *The Public Interest* when he said that the new reproductive technologies "provide the corollary to the pill: babies without sex."[10]

Contraceptive sex violates the organic unity of sex and procreation. As a result it leaves both these factors isolated and unprotected. Organically united, sex and procreation function together as protective complementaries. Procreation protects sex from degenerating into an act that makes pleasure primary; bodified sex gives procreation a basis in personal intimacy, protecting it from exploitation by laboratory technicians and marketing managers.

The large-scale cultural approbation of contraception has made technologized parenthood unavoidable, even though most people did not realize that when they accepted the separation of sex from procreation they were inaugurating the separation of procreation from sex.

When organic, incarnate unities are separated into isolated parts, a host of separations on moral, spiritual, and psychological levels take place concomitantly. One separation in particular is the focus of this discussion. It is the separation, through various modes of technological interventions in human reproduction, of parenthood from either motherhood or fatherhood. The fullness of both motherhood and fatherhood demands the unification of procreation and bodified, conjugal love. As this unity is compromised or violated, the moral and spiritual meanings of motherhood and fatherhood are proportionally jeopardized. The separation of parenthood from its context in full motherhood and fatherhood also represents the attenuation of these larger realities. Technologized parenthood does not leave motherhood and fatherhood intact, but dilutes them so that they become indistinguishable from parenthood.

At the same time, the separation between parenthood and bodified motherhood and fatherhood is occasioned by the split between thought and feeling. In this context such a split is tantamount to separating the desire to control reproduction technologically from the will-

---

[10]Leon R. Kass, "Making Babies—The New Biology and the 'Old' Morality," *The Public Interest* Winter 1972, p. 22.

ingness to recognize and protect the qualities that are peculiar to motherhood and fatherhood. Parenthood in its most elementary form is achieved whenever there is the slenderest biological connection between progenitor and offspring. Parenthood is something humans share with all species of the animal and plant kingdoms. But motherhood and fatherhood possess moral and spiritual dimensions that mere parenthood lacks. It is precisely these dimensions that are at risk whenever there is an attempt to technologize parenthood.

We will examine five specific modes of technologized reproduction in order to illustrate the fundamental antagonism that exists between technologized parenthood and incarnate motherhood and fatherhood. These modes are: 1) artificial insemination; 2) *in vitro* fertilization; 3) embryo transfer; 4) extracorporeal gestation; 5) surrogate motherhood.

We turn first to *artificial insemination*. In 1884, a wealthy Philadelphia couple approached Dr. William Pancoast, a medical school professor. The couple had been trying to have a child but without success. The doctor offered help. Since the cause of the problem seemed to be with the husband, Pancoast looked for someone to donate semen to be injected into the wife's womb. He invited the best looking student in his class to be the artificial insemination donor (AID). The student complied and the doctor injected the semen into the woman, which resulted in pregnancy.

Pancoast performed the artificial insemination while the woman was under anesthesia, and had not told her or her husband exactly what he had done. But he saw fit to change his mind once the baby was born. The infant bore such a striking resemblance to its biological father that Pancoast felt obligated to explain to the husband what really transpired. The rich Philadelphian, happy to have a child, bore no grudge against the doctor. He asked only that his wife not be told how the child was conceived.[11]

We may ignore, in this instance, the factors of adultery, rape (involuntary intercourse), and gross deception. Our concerns here have to do with the effect of this technological procedure on the notion of fatherhood. While the Philadelphian was ignorant of the true paternity of the child, he believed that he was the father. After he was told he was not the father, his wife continued to believe that he was. Thus fatherhood is made so tenuous as to be classified information that may or may not be revealed. At best it is a mere belief. The husband believes he is not a father, the wife believes he is.

---

[11]Francoeur, pp. 1-3.

Dr. Pancoast's pioneer experiment in artificial insemination[12] has prepared the way for no end of deception and confusion with regard to fatherhood. Technologized parenthood which allows a third party into the marriage relationship has proved to be extremely troublesome, even from the legal point of view. In Germany, for example, a husband who consents to AID can disclaim his paternity anytime during the first two years of the child's life. In the United States, 15 states have laws which make a man who consents to the artificial insemination of his wife the legal father of the child. But in other states where no legal precedents exist, a husband who consents to AID and later changes his mind could conceivably charge his wife with adultery and refuse to support the AID child after a divorce.[13]

In order to avoid certain legal problems involving paternity, some doctors deliberately try to make the identity of the biological father impossible to determine. Dr. A. H. Ansari, an Atlanta gynecologist, purposely inseminates a woman with a number of different sperm samples. He writes:

> Even in the same cycle, I may use four different donors for that individual. I do this so that if the case comes to court and they ask who the father is, it might give the lawyer a hard time to determine which of the four donors should be sued. As for the patient, she is just receiving biological material. She never meets the guy; she doesn't care whose semen you use.[14]

Not only does technologized parenthood through artificial insemination make fatherhood tenuous, it creates situations in which its specific determination is undesirable. Most medical students who provide semen for the customary fee of $50 probably do not desire to know whether or not their "biological material" has made them fathers. For

---

[12]Pancoast's unusual experiment is likely the first medically documented case of human artificial insemination in North America. After Pancoast's death in 1898, a former student of his, Addison Davis Hard, brought the story to light with an article in *Medical World* in 1909. Dr. Hard urged the use of AID from respected and successful men who were free of the scourge of venereal disease, with the intent of improving the human race and protecting women. His article met with mixed reaction: one doctor identified Pancoast's questionable use of AID as "ethereal copulation," whereas another doctor condemned it as raping a patient under anesthesia. AID is not always a prophylactic against the transmission of venereal disease. As a result of using AID, some women have contracted AIDS (See "Artificial Insemination is Called AIDS Hazard," *St. Louis Post-Dispatch* 22 May 1986.

[13]Lori B. Andrews, "Embryo Technology," *Parents*, May 1981, p. 65.

[14]Quoted in *ibid*, p. 65.

them, such fatherhood places no moral or legal obligations whatsoever on them and is purely hypothetical. A sperm donor at the Tyler Medical Clinic in Los Angeles can contribute two or three times a week for $20 per "donation." Whether such a donor has sired tens or even hundreds of offspring is, as far as he is concerned, a mere abstraction.

A few legal cases in the United States show the extent to which the AID technology can erode the notion of fatherhood.

In a New York State case, *Adoption of Anonymous*,[15] a woman's second husband petitioned to adopt the child of his wife's first marriage. Her first husband refused consent to the adoption procedure, claiming that he is the father. Confronted by this legal impediment, the petitioner argued that his consent is not needed since he is not the father, the child having been conceived by an anonymous donor. In this case, the judge ruled that the wife's first husband (though not the biological father) is the "parent" of the child and that his consent is required for the adoption of the child by another.

It is instructive, however, to note that not all courts have ruled or reasoned in the same way in similar cases. In California (*People v. Sorenson*)[16] the Supreme Court reasoned that "a child conceived through AID does not have a 'natural' father, that the anonymous donor is not the 'natural' father." Another New York case (*Gursky v. Gursky*)[17] went further in its depreciation of biological fatherhood:

> An AID child is not "begotten" by a father who is not the husband; the donor is anonymous; the wife does not have sexual intercourse or commit adultery with him; if there is any "begetting" it is by the doctor who in this specialty is often a woman.

A child conceived through artificial insemination may have no natural father, may not be begotten by a father, or may be begotten by a "father" who is a woman! When fatherhood is reduced to the plane of the biological, it edges perilously close to oblivion. At the same time, the other dimensions of fatherhood—psychological, moral, spiritual, and legal—are subjects for the Court's sometimes arbitrary ruling.

In Pipersville, Pennsylvania, a man sued his former wife, contending that she used his sperm without his permission to conceive a

---

[15]"In the Matter of the Adoption of Anonymous, Surrogates' Court, Kings County, N.Y. (1973), 345 N.Y.S. 2d 430 in Mark Coppenger, *Bioethics: A Casebook* (Englewood Cliffs, N. J.: Prentice-Hall, 1985), p. 4.

[16]*People v. Sorenson*, 68 Cal 2d 280, 437 P 2d Cal Rptr 7 (1968).

[17]*Gursky v. Gursky*, 39 Misc. 2d 1083, 242 N.Y.S. 2d 406 (Kings County, New York, Supreme Court, 1963).

child through the University of Pennsylvania's fertility program. The man gave sperm samples to his wife believing that she was using them to take his sperm count. He is asking that he be freed from supporting their daughter. In this case, though allegedly the biological father, the man finds no moral grounds for his role as a provider. Unlike men whose wives conceived through AID and want to be considered fathers, this man, even if he were the biological father, wants to disclaim any relationship with fatherhood.[18]

Technologized fatherhood unravels the integrated totality of incarnate or unified fatherhood. The result is a divorce of full fatherhood from mere parenthood as well as a divorce of the spiritual from the material, which greatly weakens fatherhood, making it appear nebulous, arbitrary, and even hypothetical.

In artificial insemination, only the male gamete is isolated from the body. But, in *in vitro* fertilization, both the male and female gametes are isolated from the body. Because these gametes can effect conception in a dish, totally apart from the bodified husband and wife, the impression is created that in technical sense the gametes themselves are the parents.

This impression is not without its own biological analogues. Parenthood is conferred upon reproducing protozoans despite the fact that they are single-celled. Moreover, in ordinary mitosis, where somatic cells reproduce through replication, the resulting cells are called "daughter cells." Thus, parenthood is attributed to biological entities of a single cell; why not to gametes as well?

The form of technologized parenthood we find with IVF creates the bizarre impression that a married couple's own gametes are challenging their claim to parenthood. This, of course, is reductionism in its extreme form. In a holistic perspective it is the couple who become parents, not their gametes.

There is a time-honored axiom—*actiones sunt suppositorum*—which means that actions belong to the person.[19] We do not say that my eye sees or that my ear hears or that my feet walk. Rather we say that I see with my eyes, I hear with my ears, and I walk with my feet. Since the source of our actions is in our subjectivity as persons, we attribute our actions to ourselves and not to one or another isolated part of ourselves. It is I who love, not my heart; it is I who think, not my

---

[18]"Man Sues Former Wife Over Use of His Sperm," *New York Times* 6 July 1986, p. A-10.

[19]See Jacques Maritain, *Existence and the Existent* (Garden City, N.J.: Doubleday, 1956), p. 70; Fulton J. Sheen, *The Mystical Body of Christ* (New York: Sheed & Ward, 1935), p. 30.

brain.

Likewise, it is the person who becomes a parent—in a specific way as a mother or father—and not the gametes. Technologized parenthood drives a wedge between specific parenthood, which is predicated of the person, and technical or material parenthood, which is predicated of the gametes or parts of the person.

By separating the gametes from husband and wife and effecting new life in a Petri dish *in vitro* fertilization fractures and fractionalizes incarnate parenthood, thereby allowing parenthood to be equivocally assigned to a variety of impersonal factors and to persons on a limited basis. The very expression "test-tube baby," although a journalistic creation, nonetheless suggests that the parent is a test-tube. And since the newly formed embryo can be implanted in a woman other than the one who contributed the egg, the gestational woman as well as the genetic woman are both called parents, though neither is a parent in the whole sense. Thus *in vitro* fertilization creates the possibility of assigning parenthood to a variety of people in diverse ways and for different reasons.

On May 2, 1984, test-tube quadruplets were born in London to a Mrs. Janice Smale who, according to her account, was married to Mr. Denis Smale. Upon investigation, however, it was learned that despite the name by which she identified herself, Mr. Smale is not her husband, but her boyfriend. "Mrs. Smale" is twice married and living apart from her second husband, pending divorce. Nonetheless, the doctors at Hammersmith Hospital in London fertilized six of her ova with Mr. Smale's sperm and implanted them in her uterus. Of the six embryos implanted, four survived.[20]

All the parties involved in the Smale case accept the moral premise that one need not be a husband before he becomes a father. They also endorse the premise that a wife may bear as many as six children at one time who are fathered by a man other than her own husband. The senior consultant of the hospital, who had been accused of actions "bordering on the unethical," defended his position by stating that it was certainly more ethical than that displayed at Bourn Hall, where embryos were used merely as subjects for research.

By condoning such a procedure the hospital is significantly weakening parenthood. Approving the separation of fatherhood from husbandhood (Mr. Smale) and husbandhood from fatherhood ("Mrs. Smale's" second husband) is not in the interest of integrated parenthood. Moreover, it lends support to the separation of parenthood from marriage, and procreation from lovemaking. Such a sequence of dis-

---

[20]B. A. Santamaria, *Test Tube Babies?* (Melbourne: Australian Family Association, 1985), p. 27.

connections cannot but have a harmful effect on full motherhood and fatherhood.

Technologized parenthood can easily bypass a host of relevant moral concerns and bring about parenthood as a mere technological achievement. On the other hand, authentic parenthood, that is, full motherhood and fatherhood, is a personal realization that arises from a highly moral context of love, marriage and conjugal intimacy. Any true civilization must regard motherhood and fatherhood as personal and moral realizations, and not as mere technological achievements.

Separating procreation from loving sexual intercourse depreciates lovemaking, but it also weakens parenthood and the bond that love forms between parent and child. This point may be expressed in a variety of ways, from the shock expressed by one reporter who exclaimed: "People are conceiving not in clinches, but in clinics!" to sociologist George Gilder's more reflective assessment of the matter: "By circumventing the act of love, *in vitro* conception takes another step toward dislodging sexual intercourse from its pinnacle as both the paramount act of love and the only act of procreation. It thus promotes the trend toward regarding sex as just another means of pleasure, and weakens the male connection to the psychologically potent realm of procreation."[21]

Embryo transfer goes a step beyond what is logically implied by *in vitro* fertilization. With embryo transfer an embryo (whether or not formed through IVF) that has already implanted in the uterus is removed and transferred to the uterus of another woman. This technique is made available, fundamentally, for women who cannot conceive a child but are able to carry a child to term. A volunteer conceives the child (usually through artificial insemination) and the surrenders that child to the woman who will complete the period of gestation.

This technique effects the separation of pregnancy from motherhood and therefore assigns "motherhood" to various women on a limited basis. One woman supplies the egg, another the womb, yet a third might raise the child and supply the love and guidance. A child, therefore, may have three mothers: a genetic mother, a gestational mother, and an adopting mother. "We need to do a total rethinking of the notion of parenthood," writes Lori Andrews, a research attorney for the American Bar Foundation who teaches medical law at the University of Chicago Graduate School of Business. "We don't even have a word," she adds, "that describes the relationship between a woman donating

---

[21]George Gilder, "The Bioengineering Womb," *The American Spectator*, May 1986, p. 22.

an embryo and a woman who is carrying the child."[22]

Two parents who are related to each other by virtue of a common relationship to a child are usually called husband and wife, and their relationship with each other is a spousal one. But the genetic mother is not the spouse of the gestational mother. These women may not even know each other. In our fragmented world of technologized parenthood they may be regarded as partial parents, each contributing a part of what a traditional mother contributed by herself as a whole.

When the Harbor-U.C.L.A. Medical Center, the southern campus of the medical school of the University of California at Los Angeles, wanted to attract volunteers for its embryo-transplant project, it placed the following ad in several community and college newspapers covering the South Bay area of Los Angeles:

> HELP AN INFERTILE WOMAN HAVE A BABY. Fertile women, age 20-35 willing to donate an egg. Similar to artificial insemination. No surgery required. Reasonable compensation.[23]

Nearly 400 women responded to the ad, one of whom later became the genetic mother of the first child to come into the world as a result of the embryo-transfer procedure. The staff at the Medical Center referred to their program as the Ovum Transfer Project.

The ad and the project are willfully deceptive. A volunteer was not merely asked to donate an egg or an ovum. She was asked to become pregnant in a manner that implied adultery, to undergo an early-stage abortion, and give her child up for adoption. In addition she was asked to assume two rather serious risks in the event the lavage technique designed to remove her embryo failed. Either her child would be destroyed, or her pregnancy would persist. In the event the pregnancy persisted she would be faced with either choosing a conventional abortion or carrying an unwanted pregnancy to term. She was also asked, by calling the child she conceived an "egg," to deny her own motherhood in this instance. It was convenient, from a merchandising point of view, for the Ovum Transfer Project to emphasize as much as possible the motherhood of their clients who were to gestate the child by denying the "partial" motherhood of the genetic mother.

By involving human reproduction with reproductive middlemen, and linking it more and more with principles of business and marketing, parenthood becomes increasingly arbitrary and may be assigned and re-

---

[22]Harris Brotman, "Human Embryo Transplants," *New York Times Magazine*, January 8, 1984, p. 51.
[23]*Ibid.*, p. 42.

assigned virtually at will. Parenthood ceases to be an aspect of one's identity as a human being, and becomes a title that one is able to purchase for a price. When the ad asks for fertile women to donate an egg, it is trading on those altruistic sentiments that are evoked in human beings when they are asked to donate blood or to donate to the heart fund. But donating blood and donating one's own child are radically different from a moral standpoint. It is inhuman as well as unjust to treat a child as a donatable commodity. It is also unjust to mislead a woman into thinking that her embryo is only an egg. Human reproduction is becoming "commodified," warns Barbara Rothman, author of *The Tentative Pregnancy.*[24]

One gestational mother in the Ovum Transfer Project expressed elation that, as she put it, "someone else's egg has grown in my body."[25] She expressed a desire to thank the genetic mother, but the latter does not know she is the donor. In 1982 Doctors Alan Trounson and Carl Wood of Melbourne's Monash University pioneered a method of freezing the surplus ova that their IVF patients did not need. In cases where an egg is frozen before it is thawed and fertilized, a woman may never know whether she is a mother. She is the female counterpart of the anonymous sperm donor. To her, her own motherhood is made hypothetical.

Closely associated with embryo transfer is a procedure known as embryo adoption. The technology is the same, but with embryo adoption donor semen is used instead of the semen of the recipient's husband. As the name suggests, with embryo adoption, a couple has no genetic link to the embryo it adopts. Therefore, the child of embryo adoption has four parents: one who supplied the sperm, one who provided the egg, one who furnished the womb, and the male who raised the child as its father. What rights and status each of these parents has remains for the courts to decide. For example, do the parents who provided an adopted embryo's egg and sperm have visitation rights after that child is born? No doubt highly complex questions concerning intestate succession and will construction will have to be settled by the courts.

Extracorporeal gestation refers to the process by which the prenatal child is allowed to develop to term completely outside the mother's body in an artificial womb. No such womb has been developed to this point which could incubate a human being from conception to birth, but research continues. Scientists have predicted its arrival by the year

---

[24]Hartford College, p. 12.
[25]Brotman, p. 46.

2000.[26] Bernard Nathanson contends that an artificial womb will be perfected much sooner. "A feasible artificial placenta is on the horizon," he writes, which he believes will lead to a reliable life-support system for the pregnancy outside its original host womb.[27] Nathanson also believes that such artificial uteri will be produced in sufficiently large quantities to solve the abortion controversy by providing incubation for all those unwanted fetuses who are deprived of a mother's womb.

Joseph Fletcher welcomes the artificial womb because it makes pregnancy more accessible to the scrutiny of watchful scientists:

> The womb is a dark and dangerous place, a hazardous environment. We should want our potential children to be where they can be watched and protected as much as possible.[28]

Isaac Asimov concurs, arguing that an embryo developing outside the body can be more easily monitored for birth defects and, eventually, for desirable gene patterns. But he also endorses extracorporeal gestation because it would help women gain an important measure of equality with men. If a woman could "extrude the fertilized ovum for development outside the body," he writes, "she would then be no more the victim of pregnancy that a man is."[29]

Some observers predict that the time will come when natural pregnancy will become an anachronism and the uterus will shrink to appendixlike proportions. At such time girls can choose to be superovulated at the age of 20, have their eggs collected and frozen to be thawed and used whenever they decide the time has arrived to start the process of artificially fertilizing and incubating their progeny.[30]

The Italian embryologist Daniele Petrucci claims to have developed an artificial uterus in which he kept a female human embryo alive for as long as 59 days. Progress is being made all over the world in developing an artificial womb, yet replicating the give-and-take equilibrium that exists between mother and child poses immense difficulties. Given such problems, the suggestion has been put forward to use non-

---

[26]Tom Paskal, "Tampering With The Machinery of God," *Weekend Magazine* 18 September 1971, p. 7.

[27]Bernard Nathanson, *Aborting America* (Garden City, N.J.: Doubleday, 1979), p. 282.

[28]Joseph Fletcher, *The Ethics of Genetic Control* (Garden City, N.J.: Doubleday, 1979), p. 103.

[29]Isaac Asimov, "On Designing a Woman," *Viva* November 1973, p. 8.

[30]Edward Grossman, "The Obsolescent Mother: A Scenario," *Atlantic* May 1971, p. 49. See also Shulamith Firestone, *The Dialectic of Sex: The Case for Feminist Revolution* (New York: William Morrow, 1972, p. 238.

human animals as surrogate mothers. Recently cows have been suggested to serve as host "mothers." Emeritus professor of gynecology
Ian Donald at Glasgow University states: "I can foresee the day when a
human baby is born to a chimpanzee. That might happen within 20
years."[31] Edwards and Steptoe, who delivered the world's first IVF
baby, have proposed that human embryos be implanted in such animals
as sheep, rabbits, and pigs in order to study their development.[32]

The possible biological and psychological reaction of the fetus
must be considered. It is known that newborn lambs are psychologically
and bio-chemically conditioned or imprinted to respond to their natural
mother. An orphaned lamb will not feed from a substitute mother unless fleece from its dead mother is tied around her neck. Perhaps a human fetus that is gestated by an animal of another species would react
in a similar manner and reject its human mother.[33]

Current research on the subject of prenatal development indicates that the fetus is very much aware of his surrounding environment.
For example, a newborn infant is able to distinguish his mother's voice
from that of another woman, presumably from having heard it while
being in the womb. Boris Brott, conductor of Ontario's Hamilton Phil-
harmonic Orchestra, tells of an extraordinary musical experience he
had which very well may be connected with his pre-natal life in the
womb. While rehearsing a new musical score, Brott had a strong feeling
of *déjà vu*. Though he had never seen or heard the piece before,
somehow he already knew the cello part. Intrigued, he queried his
mother, who is also a musician, and discovered that she had been rehearsing the same score while pregnant with him.[34]

Psychiatrist Tom Verny has reported in his book, *The Secret Life
of the Unborn Child*, that babies in the womb can experience a startling
variety of sensations and emotions. To Verny, Boris Brott's story would
not be at all surprising. On the other hand, he fears that because a surrogate distances herself from the fetus she is carrying, the child later
may experience psychological problems of rejection. But how deprived
would a human fetus be if it developed in a metallic uterus, or one belonging to a member of the simian or bovine species? One embryologist
is most emphatic in his answer when he states that artificial wombs
"would produce nothing but psychological monsters."[35]

---

[31]"Creating Monsters," *TFP Newsletter* 4. 11 (1985), p. 10.
[32]*Ibid.*
[33]Francoeur, 1971, p. 106.
[34]Pablo Fenjves, "When Does Life Begin?" *Women's World* October 22,
1985, p. 6.
[35]"Man Into Superman: The Promise and the Peril of the New Genet-

George Gilder says that extracorporeal gestation on a large scale could ultimately make the womb obsolete.[36] If this came about, he reasons, women would lose their sexual appeal and cease to inspire men's love. By relegating procreation to science, the woman would forfeit her roles as wife as well as mother, and all the mystery and majesty that is inseparable from these roles. For similar reasons Norman Mailer, in *The Prisoner of Sex*, closed his critique of radical feminism (which he regarded as essentially technocratic) by appealing to women not to "quit the womb."[37]

Extracorporeal gestation separates motherhood from parenthood most graphically, creating the impression that motherhood is something external to a woman's parenthood. But so basic a function of motherhood as gestation cannot be apportioned to a machine or a nonhuman animal without seriously violating the integrity of motherhood. From the eminently realistic viewpoint of a woman's incarnate identity, extracorporeal gestation does not represent liberation but self-rejection.

Ethicist Paul Ramsey has criticized various modes of technologized parenthood for both depersonalizing and debiologizing human procreation.[38] These criticisms are perhaps nowhere more applicable than to extracorporeal gestation. To go a step further, extracorporeal gestation makes a woman's motherhood peculiarly discontinuous with her offspring to the point that she may inaugurate, abandon, and resume the motherly relationship with her child almost at will. She is initially a mother (genetically) but upon relegating the gestational phase of her motherhood to an artificial womb, she appears to discontinue her motherhood which she may later resume once the child is born.

Extracorporeal gestation makes parenthood the abiding relationship between mother and child and offers the woman opportunities for interrupting and resuming motherhood at her convenience. It also makes the profound biological tie with her child that is established during pregnancy an optional matter.

The designation *surrogate motherhood* is misleading because it denotes that the woman is a substitute mother and therefore not the real or original mother. The surrogate mother is indeed the mother of the child, both genetically and gestationally. She is called a "surrogate" merely for psychological and commercial reasons in order to help the infertile woman—on whose behalf the child is conceived and car-

---

ics," *Time* 19 April 1971, p. 49.

[36]Gilder, p. 23.

[37]Norman Mailer, *The Prisoner of Sex* (New York: The New American Library, 1971), p. 168.

[38]Paul Ramsey, *Fabricated Man* (New Haven: Yale, 1970) pp. 89, 135.

ried—feel that it is she who is the original mother. Such artful playing with language is a good indication of how easy it is to re-ascribe motherhood for reasons of convenience.

Most legal experts believe that in the event a surrogate mother should change her mind and decide to keep her child, she would have that right. The strength of her position lies in the fact that she is the natural mother of the child, a point that is often obscured by misleading language. The mother of Britain's first surrogate twins won her fight to keep them, despite that fact that the father and his wife offered a more stimulating intellectual environment, because, as Judge Sir John Arnold ruled, the strong maternal link between mother and child should be preserved.[39] It is well known that when surrogates do surrender their babies, they enter a period of grief and mourning which usually lasts four to six weeks. During this period they experience frequent crying and have difficulty sleeping. In the fiercely contested custody case in Hackensack, New Jersey, surrogate Mary Beth Whitehead, who sought to reclaim custody of her child, experienced intense bereavement, anxiety, and grief. A psychiatric social worker told the court that since Mrs. Whitehead defines herself as the mother, giving up her child constitutes an "assault on her identity."[40]

A disproportionately high ratio of women who offer to carry babies for childless couples have had abortions. Dr. Philip Parker, a Michigan psychiatrist, found that of the 125 women who took part in his study on surrogate motherhood, 26% had had abortions. Parker believes that many of these women want to have another baby and give it away as a way of compensating for the child they aborted.[41] On the other hand, applicants accepted for surrogate motherhood by Noel Keane, who has popularized surrogate motherhood in the United States, all agree to have abortions if tests show the child they are carrying is deformed or mentally retarded. Keane is the owner of the Infertility Center in New York, a profit-making agency which is involved in what one *Time* reporter describes as "the controversial business of matching *surrogate* mothers with infertile *parents*" (emphasis added).[42]

The association between surrogate motherhood and abortion also

---

[39]"British Judge Gives Twins to Surrogate Mother," *Kitchener-Waterloo Record* 13 March 1987, B-15.

[40]"Surrogate mother 'grieving'," *Kitchener-Waterloo Record* 26 February 1987, p. A-11.

[41]"Abortions frequent among candidates," *Toronto Globe and Mail* 6 September 1982.

[42]Claudia Wallis, "A Surrogate's Story," *Time*, September 10, 1984, p. 51.

raises the question of whether a woman who is carrying a child for another woman can exercise her prerogative to abort the child if her own health is threatened or even for personal reasons. Would a legal contract bind a surrogate mother to deliver the child she carries (apart from health considerations), whereas a marriage contract and a spousal relationship would be less binding? Should law regulate forms of technologized parenthood more rigorously than forms of natural motherhood and fatherhood? Should a woman be less free to abort the child of another man who is paying her a large sum of money to deliver his child, than she is to abort her husband's child? On the other hand, can a lawyer for surrogate mothers *require* them to abort when there are problems with the pregnancy, whereas a woman's own husband cannot exact such a requirement?

The problems and issues that surrogate motherhood generates seem to be endless. We observe an instance of the confusion in reading the following ad for surrogates that appeared in a California newspaper and drew 160 responses: "Childless couple with infertile wife wants female donor for artificial insemination."[43] A person might very well be led to believe that the advertiser is looking for a woman who will donate her ova for use in artificial insemination. The advertising couple was careful to avoid any reference to the word "mother," preferring to call a woman who conceives a child and carries it to term "a female donor for artificial insemination."

The desire to help an infertile couple to have a child is unassailable, even praiseworthy. But even the most laudable desires are not immune to the ill effects of sentimentality. The desire to help a couple to have a child does not justify adultery, kidnapping, or child-bartering. Sentimentality all too easily obscures reason, which must remain clear if we are to be assured that the means we choose are moral.

Robert Francoeur reports in his book *Eve's New Rib* an illuminating as well as amusing example of how a sentimental desire to help infertile couples can displace reason. At a convention of Catholic science-teachers, a nun suggested that we might "update the charitable work of some religious communities and perhaps even establish a new order, a type of 'Sisters of Charity (or Mercy)' for the Substitute Mother."[44] This enthusiastic and altruistic nun was proposing, in the name of Christian charity, that a religious order would come into being consisting of surrogate Sisters who would bear the children of infertile

---

[43]Elaine Markoutsas, "Women Who Have Babies for Other Women," *Good Housekeeping*, April 1981 p. 96.

[44]Robert Francoeur, *Eve's New Rib* (New York: Harcourt, Brace & Jovanovich, 1972), p. 20.

couples!

Some lawyers slight the embodied role the surrogate plays by arguing that *mental* conception (the desire to procreate a child) takes precedence over *physical* conception since the former is prior to the latter. Writing for the *Yale Law Journal*, Andrea Stumpf contends that "The psychological dimension of procreation precedes and transcends the biology of creation, "[45] and that "the childs existence begins in the minds of the desiring parents."[46] She has little regard for the more realistic and existentialposition that it is not an intention that brings new life into existence but an execution requiring the presence of certain corporeal entities. Only in God, we might add, are intention and execution inseparably united. To argue that an infertile couple should have legal claim to be parents of a child by virtue of having "mentally conceived" it,[47] is most dangerous because it presupposes that the couple has a power traditionally associated with the diety alone.

Finally, we note University of Texas law professor John Robertson's statement that current laws insufficiently protect what he terms "collaborative reproduction." His term is an interesting one because it implies neither motherhood, fatherhood, parenthood, marriage, or even procreation. It represents in two well chosen words the logical end-result of technologized parenthood. "Collaborative reproduction" does not describe human procreation or motherhood or fatherhood; it speaks of the tangled and impersonal world of our modern and highly commercialized techno-bureaucracy.

When we consider the various modes of technologized parenthood collectively, we discover that no feature of biological parenthood is considered indispensable for either motherhood or fatherhood. With artificial insemination by donor (AID), a husband becomes a father despite the absence of his sperm, while his wife consents to conceiving a child by a man to whom she is not married; with artificial insemination by the husband (AIH), a man becomes a father apart from the conjugal embrace. With IVF, husband and wife become parents independently of sexual intercourse. In embryo transfer, a woman is considered a mother even though she is not the genetic mother. In extracorporeal gestation, a woman is called a mother even though she does not gestate the child. The surrogate mother forsakes nursing and rearing her child, and the mother to whom she delivers the child is neither the genetic nor gestational mother.

---

[45] Andrea E. Stumpf, "Redefining Mother: A Legal Matrix for New Reproductive Technologies," *Yale Law Journal*, November 1986, p. 194.
[46] *Ibid.*, pp. 195-6.
[47] *Ibid.*, p. 205.

Collectively these forms of technologized parenthood exclude virtually all those features that are naturally and traditionally associated with motherhood and fatherhood: marriage, sexual intercourse the genetic contributions of husband and wife, gestation, nursing, and child rearing. It should be amply apparent that technologized parenthood not only produces attenuated forms of motherhood and fatherhood, but threatens their very meaning.

Combining different modes of technologized parenthood may make its threat to motherhood and fatherhood all the more salient. Lori Andrews speaks of "a busy career woman [who has] one of her eggs fertilized with her husband's sperm in a Petri dish and then implanted in another woman."[48] This same woman could arrange for her child to be reared by what some sociologists call "professional parents." And if this woman were single and had her egg fertilized by a donor's sperm, she would have avoided marriage, intercourse, conception, pregnancy, gestation, lactation, nursing, and child-rearing, and still have retained the name *mother*. But in such a case is the word "mother" anything more than an expression of will? Is this woman really a mother? Should not more be demanded of a mother than the donation of an egg?

To make matters even more confusing, some biotechnical revolutionaries would like to see men have children. At the George Washington University Medical School, Dr. Cecil Jacobsen has fertilized a chimpanzee egg *in vitro* with chimpanzee sperm, implanted it in the abdomen of a male of the same species, and later delivered a healthy baby chimp through a Caesarean section. Joseph Fletcher speaks enthusiastically about the prospect of a uterus being implanted in a human male's body and gestation achieved as a result of IVF and embryo transfer.[49] Fletcher also envisions hypogonadism being used to stimulate milk from the male's rudimentary breasts. The British magazine *New Society* claims that the technology to enable men to bear children is currently available and may eventually be utilized by homosexuals, transexuals, or men whose wives are infertile.[50]

Paul Ramsey has good reason to argue, then, that "when the transmission of life has been debiologized, human parenthood as a created covenant of life is placed under massive assault, and men and women will no longer be who they are."[51] By this Ramsey means that

---

[48]Andrews, 1981, p. 67.

[49]Fletcher, p. 45.

[50]"Just a matter of time until men give birth, scientist feels," *Kitchener-Waterloo Record* 9 May 1981, p. 1.

[51]Ramsey, p. 135.

human beings will not be able to live morally, that is, "be who they are," if they do not understand that they are embodied persons, inviolable and incarnate unities of spirit and flesh. Neither men nor women can "debiologize" themselves without denying and rejecting who they are as incarnate beings. Our modern scientific world has misled us into believing that matter is always something to be controlled, that thought is superior to flesh, that God's will is ever subject to technology's veto.

The various forms of technologized parenthood help people to have children, but they do not help them to become mothers and fathers in the full sense of these terms. Having a child does not make one a *father* or a *mother*; it only makes one a *parent*. Motherhood and fatherhood are fulfilling realizations of personal realities; they necessitate a continuity between incarnate being and moral act. In this regard the notion of *fruitfulness* is more inclusive than that of *fertility*.

Husband and wife are fruitful through a loving intercourse in which they affirm each other's distinctive personal reality as man and woman in a way that creatively directs them toward the realization of their motherhood and fatherhood. Fruitfulness, in contrast with fertility, is more than a mere exchange of gametes. One writer expresses this rich and elusive concept of fruitfulness between husband and wife in the following way:

> I not only affirm the unity of her person and nature as feminine but her integrity as an incarnate spirituality and its dynamism, that is, her possible maternity through which I, in turn, find my paternity as a self.[52]

As we have already stated, the processes by which boys become fathers and girls become mothers are by no means automatic; they demand include maturation, great personal effort, and the cooperation of other people and of culture in general. Technology, however, always plans to make things happen automatically. Its intervention in the area of human procreation clashes with the slow and arduous processes that prepare the emergence of motherhood and fatherhood. Nature always takes time. Technology is impatient. Nature is evolutionary. Technology wants to repeat the past. The clash, therefore, is between a rational plan and a natural process, between impersonal expediency and personal expression.

We do not help people to grow and fulfill their destinies by encouraging them to employ forms of technological parenthood which

---

[52]Terence P. Brinkman, "John Paul II's Theology of the Human Person and Technological Parenting," *Technological Powers and the Person*, ed. A. Moraczewski *et al.* (St. Louis: The Pope John Center, 1983), p. 377.

create the impression that there is no essential difference between fertility and fruitfulness, between pied parenthood and motherhood or fatherhood.

Technologized parenthood feeds on a philosophy of rational dualism that separates matter from morals and structure from activity. One does not behave as a mother or father simply because one is a parent in a legal or material way. It is not a legal document or a biological claim that makes one an authentic mother or father. Rather, the basis is in one's incarnate personhood and the willingness to embrace the moral responsibilities that motherhood and fatherhood entail. There should be a continuity between matter and morals, form and destiny. Motherhood and fatherhood should flow from their source in personhood as nature flows from the hand of the Creator.

When Gerard Manley Hopkins wrote, 'He fathers-forth whose beauty is past change",[53] he was drawing our attention to the fact that father and mother are verbs as well as nouns.

---

[53]G. M. Hopkins, 'Pied Beauty," Gerard Manley Hopkins (London: Unwin, 1953), p. 31.

Appendix

Instruction on Respect for Human Life in Its Origin and on the Dignity of Procreation: Replies to Certain Questions of the Day

FOREWORD

The Congregation for the Doctrine of the Faith has been approached by various episcopal conferences or individual bishops, by theologians, doctors and scientists, concerning biomedical techniques which make it possible to intervene in the initial phase of the life of a human being and in the very processes of procreation and their conformity with the principles of Catholic morality. The present instruction, which is the result of wide consultation and in particular of a careful evaluation of the declarations made by episcopates, does not intend to repeat all the church's teaching on the dignity of human life as it originates and on procreation, but to offer, in the light of the previous teaching of the magisterium, some specific replies to the main questions being asked in this regard.

The exposition is arranged as follows: An introduction will recall the fundamental principles of an anthropological and moral character which are necessary for a proper evaluation of the problems and for working out replies to those questions; the first part will have as its subject respect for the human being from the first moment of his or her existence; the second part will deal with the moral questions raised by technical interventions on human procreation; the third part will offer some orientations on the relationships between moral law and civil law in terms of the respect due to human embryos and fetuses* and as regards the legitimacy of techniques of artificial procreation.

---

*(The terms *zygote, pre-embryo* and *fetus* can indicate in the vocabulary of biology successive stages of the development of a human being. The present instruction makes free use of these terms, attributing to them an identical ethical relevance, in order to designate the result [whether visible or not] of human generation, from the first moment of its existence until birth. The reason for this usage is clarified by the text [cf. I, 1]).

INTRODUCTION

1. Biomedical Research and the Teaching of the Church

The gift of life which God the Creator and Father has entrusted to man calls him to appreciate the inestimable value of what he has been given and to take responsibility for it: This fundamental principle must be placed at the center of one's reflection in order to clarify and solve the moral problems raised by artificial interventions on life as it originates and on the processes of procreation.

Thanks to the progress of the biological and medical sciences, man has at his disposal ever more effective therapeutic resources; but he can also acquire new powers, with unforeseeable consequences, over human life at its very beginning and in its first stages. Various procedures now make it possible to intervene not only in order to assist, but also to dominate the processes of procreation. These techniques can enable man to "take in hand his own destiny," but they also expose him "to the temptation to go beyond the limits of a reasonable dominion over nature."[1] They might constitute progress in the service of man, but they also involve serious risks. Many people are therefore expressing an urgent appeal that in interventions on procreation the values and rights of the human person be safeguarded. Requests for clarification and guidance are coming not only from the faithful, but also from those who recognize the church as "an expert in humanity"[2] with a mission to serve the "civilization of love"[3] and of life.

The church's magisterium does not intervene on the basis of a particular competence in the area of the experimental sciences; but having taken account of the data of research and technology, it intends to put forward, by virtue of its evangelical mission and apostolic duty, the moral teaching corresponding to the dignity of the person and to his or her integral vocation. It intends to do so by expounding the criteria of moral judgment as regards the applications of scientific research and technology, especially in relation to human life and its beginnings. These criteria are the respect, defense and promotion of man, his "primary and fundamental right" to life,[4] his dignity as a person who is endowed with a spiritual soul and with moral responsibility[5] and who is called to beatific communion with God.

The church's intervention in this field is inspired also by the love which she owes to man, helping him to recognize and respect his rights and duties. This love draws from the fount of Christ's love: As she contemplates the mystery of the incarnate

---

[1]Pope John Paul II, Discourse to those taking part in the 81st Congress of the Italian Society of Internal Medicine and the 82nd Congress of the Italian Society of General Surgery, October 27, 1980: AAS 72 (1980) 1126.

[2]Pope Paul VI, discourse to the General Assembly of the United Nations, October 4, 1965: AAS 57 (1965) 878; encyclical *Populorum Progressio*, 13: AAS 59 (1967) 263.

[3]Ibid., Homily During the Mass Closing the Holy Year, December 25, 1975: AAS 68 (1976) 145; Pope John Paul II, encyclical *Dives in Misericordia*, 30: AAS 72 (1980) 1224.

[4]Pope John Paul II, Discourse to those taking part in the 35th General Assembly of the World Medical Association, October 29, 1983: AAS 76 (1984) 390.

[5]Cf. Declaration *Dignitatis Humanae*, 2.

word, the church also comes to understand the "mystery of man",[6] by proclaiming the Gospel of salvation, she reveals to man his dignity and invites him to discover fully the truth of his own being. Thus the church once more puts forward the divine law in order to accomplish the work of truth and liberation.

For it is out of goodness—in order to indicate the path of live—that God gives human beings his commandments and the grace to observe them; and it is likewise out of goodness—in order to help them persevere along the same path—that God always offers to everyone his forgiveness. Christ has compassion on our weaknesses: He is our Creator and Redeemer. May his Spirit open men's hearts to the gift of God's peace and to an understanding of his precepts.

2. Science and Technology at the Service of the Human Person

God created man in his own image and likeness: "Male and female he created them" (Gn. 1:27), entrusting to them the task of "having dominion over the earth" Gn. 1:28). Basic scientific research and applied research constitute a significant expression of this dominion of man over creation. Science and technology are valuable resources for man when placed at his service and when they promote his integral development for the benefit of all; but they cannot of themselves show the meaning of existence and of human progress. Being ordered to man, who initiates and develops them, they draw from the person and his moral values the indication of their purpose and the awareness of their limits.

It would on the one hand be illusory to claim that scientific research and its applications are morally neutral; on the other hand one cannot derive criteria for guidance from mere technical efficiency, from research's possible usefulness to some at the expense of others or, worse still, from prevailing ideologies. Thus science and technology require for their own intrinsic meaning an unconditional respect for the fundamental criteria of the moral law: That is to say, they must be at the service of the human person, of his inalienable rights and his true and integral good according to the design and will of God.[7]

The rapid development of technological discoveries gives greater urgency to this need to respect the criteria just mentioned: Science without conscience can only lead to man's ruin. "Our era needs such wisdom more than bygone ages if the discoveries made by man are to be further humanized. For the future of the world stands in peril unless wiser people are forthcoming."[8]

3. Anthropology and Procedures in the Biomedical Field

Which moral criteria must be applied in order to clarify the problems posed today in the field of biomedicine? The answer to this question presupposes a proper idea of the nature of the human person in his bodily dimension.

For it is only in keeping with his true nature that the human person can achieve

---

[6]Pastoral constitution *Gaudium et Spes*, 22; Pope John Paul II, encyclical *Redemptor Hominis*, 8: AAS 71 (1979) 270-272.

[7]Cf. *Gaudium et Spes*, 35.

[8]Ibid., 15; cf. also *Populorum Progressio*, 20: *Redemptor Hominis*, 15: Pope John Paul II, apostolic exhortation *Familiaris Consortio*, 8: AAS 74 (1982) 89.

self-realization as a "unified totality";[9] and this nature is at the same time corporal and spiritual. By virtue of its substantial union with a spiritual soul, the human body cannot be considered as a mere complex of tissues, organs and functions, nor can it be evaluated in the same way as the body of animals; rather it is a constitutive part of the person who manifests and expresses himself through it.

The natural moral law expresses and lays down the purposes, rights and duties which are based upon the bodily and spiritual nature of the human person. Therefore this law cannot be thought of as simply a set of norms on the biological level; rather it must be defined as the rational order whereby man is called by the Creator to direct and regulate his life and actions and in particular to make use of his own body.[10]

A first consequence can be deduced from these principles: An intervention on the human body affects not only the tissues, the organs and their functions, but also involves the person himself on different levels. It involves, therefore, perhaps in an implicit but nonetheless real way, a moral significance and responsibility. Pope John Paul II forcefully reaffirmed this to the World Medical Association when he said:

"Each human person, in his absolutely unique singularity, is constituted not only by his spirit, but by his body as well. Thus, in the body and through the body, one touches the person himself in his concrete reality. To respect the dignity of man consequently amounts to safeguarding this identity of the man *'corpore et anima unus,'* as the Second Vatican Council says (*Gaudium et Spes*, 14.1). It is on the basis of this anthropological vision that one is to find the fundamental criteria for decision making in the case of procedures which are not strictly therapeutic, as, for example, those aimed at the improvement of the human biological condition."[11]

Applied biology and medicine work together for the integral good of human life when they come to the aid of a person stricken by illness and infirmity and when they respect his or her dignity as a creature of God. No biologist or doctor can reasonably claim, by virtue of his scientific competence, to be able to decide on people's origin and destiny. This norm must be applied in a particular way in the field of sexuality and procreation, in which man and woman actualize the fundamental values of love and life.

God, who is love and life, has inscribed in man and woman the vocation to share in a special way in his mystery of personal communion and in his work as Creator and Father.[12] For this reason marriage possesses specific goods and values in its union and in procreation which cannot be likened to those existing in lower forms of life. Such values and meanings are of the personal order and determine from the moral point of view the meaning and limits of artificial interventions on procreation and on the origin of human life. These interventions are not to be rejected on the grounds that they are artificial. As such, they bear witness to the possibilities of the art of medicine. But they must be given a moral evaluation in reference to the dignity of the human person, who is called to realize his vocation from God to the gift of love and

---

[9]*Familiaris Consortio*, 11.

[10]Cf. Pope Paul VI, encyclical *Humanae Vitae*, 10: AAS 60 (1986) 487-488.

[11]Pope John Paul II, Discourse to the members of the 35th General Assembly of the World Medical Association, October 29, 1983: AAS 76 (1984) 393.

[12]Cf. *Familiaris Consortio*, 11, cf. also *Gaudium et Spes*, 50.

the gift of life.

4. Fundamental Criteria for a Moral Judgment

The fundamental values connected with the techniques of artificial human procreation are two: the life of the human being called into existence and the special nature of the transmission of human life in marriage. The moral judgment on such
methods of artificial procreation must therefore be formulated in reference to these
values.

Physical life, with which the course of human life in the world begins, certainly
does not itself contain the whole of a person's value nor does it represent the
supreme good of man, who is called to eternal life. However it does constitute in a
certain way the "fundamental" value of life precisely because upon this physical life
all the other values of the person are based and developed.[13] The inviolability of the
innocent human being's right to life "from the moment of conception until death"[14]
is a sign and requirement of the very inviolability of the person to whom the Creator
has given the gift of life.

By comparison with the transmission of other forms of life in the universe, the
transmission of human life has a special character of its own, which derives from the
special nature of the human person. "The transmission of human life is entrusted by
nature to a personal and conscious act and as such is subject to the all-holy laws of
God: immutable and inviolable laws which must be recognized and observed. For this
reason one cannot use means and follow methods which could be licit in the transmission of the life of plants and animals."[15]

Advances in technology have now made it possible to procreate apart from sexual relations through the meeting *in vitro* of the germ cells previously taken from the
man and the woman. But what is technically possible is not for that very reason
morally admissible. Rational reflection on the fundamental values of life and of human procreation is therefore indispensable for formulating a moral evaluation of
such technological interventions on a human being from the first stages of his development.

5. Teachings of the Magisterium

On its part, the magisterium of the church offers to human reason in this field
too the light of revelation: The doctrine concerning man taught by the magisterium
contains many elements which throw light on the problems being faced here.

From the moment of conception, the life of every human being is to be respected in an absolute way because man is the only creature on earth that God has
"wished for himself"[16] and the spiritual soul of each man is "immediately created" by

---

[13]Congregation for the Doctrine of the Faith, Declaration on Procured
Abortion, 9, AAS 66 (1974) 736-737.

[14]Pope John Paul II, Discourse to those taking part in the 35th General
Assembly of the World Medical Association, October 29, 1983: AAS 76 (1984)
390.

[15]Pope John XXIII, encyclical *Mater et Magistra*, III: AAS 53 (1961)
447.

[16]*Gaudium et Spes*, 24.

God;[17] his whole being bears the image of the Creator. Human life is sacred because from its beginning it involves the "creative action of God,"[18] and it remains forever in a special relationship with the Creator, who is its sole end.[19] God alone is the Lord of life from its beginning until its end: No one can in any circumstance claim for himself the right to destroy directly an innocent human being.[20]

Human procreation requires on the part of the spouses responsible collaboration with the fruitful love of God;[21] the gift of human life must be actualized in marriage through the specific and exclusive acts of husband and wife, in accordance with the laws inscribed in their persons and in their union.[22]

I
RESPECT FOR HUMAN EMBRYOS

Careful reflection on this teaching of the magisterium and on the evidence of reason, as mentioned above, enables us to respond to the numerous moral problems posed by technical interventions upon the human being in the first phases of his life and upon the processes of his conception.

1. What respect is due to the human embryo, taking into account his nature and identity?

The human being must be respected—as a person—from the very first instant of his existence.

The implementation of procedures of artificial fertilization has made possible various interventions upon embryos and human fetuses. The aims pursued are of various kinds: diagnostic and therapeutic, scientific and commercial. From all of this, serious problems arise. Can one speak of a right to experimentation upon human embryos for the purpose of scientific research? What norms or laws should be worked out with regard to this matter? The response to these problems presupposes a detailed reflection on the nature and specific identity—the word *status* is used—of the human embryo itself.

At the Second Vatican Council, the church for her part presented once again to

---

[17]Cf. Pope Pius XII, encyclical *Humani Generis*: AAS 42 (1950) 575; Pope Paul VI, *Professio Fidei*: AAS 60 (1968) 436.

[18]*Mater et Magistra*, III; cf. Pope John Paul II, Discourse to priests participating in a Seminar on "Responsible Procreation," Sept. 17, 1983, *Insegnamenti di Giovanni Paolo II*, VI, 2 (1983) 562: "At the origin of each human person there is a creative act of God: No man comes into existence by chance; he is always the result of the creative love of God."

[19]Cf. *Gaudium et Spes*, 24.

[20]Cf. Pope Pius XII, Discourse to the St. Luke Medical-Biological Union, Nov. 12, 1944: *Discorsi e Radiomessaggi* VI (1944-1945) 191-192.

[21]Cf. *Gaudium et Spes*, 50.

[22]Cf. ibid., 51: "When it is a question of harmonizing married love with the responsible transmission of life, the moral character of one's behavior does not depend only on the good intention and evaluation of the motives: The objective criteria must be used, criteria drawn from the nature of the human person and human acts, criteria which respect the total meaning of mutual self-giving and human procreation in the context of true love."

modern man her constant and certain doctrine according to which: "Life once conceived, must be protected with the utmost care; abortion and infanticide are abominable crimes."[23] More recently, the Charter of the Rights of the Family, published by the Holy See, confirmed that "human life must be absolutely respected and protected from the moment of conception."[24]

This congregation is aware of the current debates concerning the beginning of human life, concerning the individuality of the human being and concerning the identity of the human person. The congregation recalls the teachings found in the Declaration of Procured Abortion:

"From the time that the ovum is fertilized, a new life is begun which is neither that of the father nor of the mother; it is rather the life of a new human being with his own growth. It would never be made human if it were not human already. To this perpetual evidence . . . modern genetic science brings valuable confirmation. It has demonstrated that, from the first instant, the program is fixed as to what this living being will be: a man, this individual man with his characteristic aspects already well determined. Right from fertilization is begun the adventure of a human life, and each of its great capacities requires time . . . to find its place and to be in a position to act."[25]

This teaching remains valid and is further confirmed, if confirmation were needed, by recent findings of human biological science which recognize that in the zygote (the cell produced when the nuclei of the two gametes have fused) resulting from fertilization the biological identity of a new human individual is already constituted.

Certainly no experimental datum can be in itself sufficient to bring us to the recognition of a spiritual soul; nevertheless, the conclusions of science regarding the human embryo provide a valuable indication for discerning by the use of reason a personal presence at the moment of this first appearance of a human life: How could a human individual not be a human person? The magisterium has not expressly committed itself to an affirmation of a philosophical nature, but it constantly reaffirms the moral condemnation of any kind of procured abortion. This teaching has not been changed and is unchangeable.[26]

Thus the fruit of human generation from the first moment of its existence, that is to say, from the moment the zygote has formed, demands the unconditional respect that is morally due to the human being in his bodily and spiritual totality. The human being is to be respected and treated as a person from the moment of conception and therefore from that same moment his rights as a person must be recognized, among which in the first place is the inviolable right of every innocent human being to life.

This doctrinal reminder provides the fundamental criterion for the solution of the various problems posed by the development of the biomedical sciences in this field: Since the embryo must be treated as a person, it must also be defended in its integrity, tended and cared for, to the extent possible, in the same way as any other hu-

---

[23]*Gaudium et Spes*, 51.

[24]Holy See, Charter of the Rights of the Family, 4: L'Osservatore Romano, Nov. 25, 1983.

[25]Congregation for the Doctrine of the Faith, Declaration on Procured Abortion, 12-13.

[26]Cf. Pope Paul VI, Discourse to participants in the 23rd National Congress of Italian Catholic Jurists, Dec. 9, 1972 AAS 64 (1972) 777.

man being as far as medical assistance is concerned.

2. Is prenatal diagnosis morally licit?

If prenatal diagnosis respects the life and integrity of the embryo and the human fetus and is directed toward its safeguarding or healing as an individual, then the answer is affirmative.

For prenatal diagnosis makes it possible to know the condition of the embryo and of the fetus when still in the mother's womb. It permits or makes it possible to anticipate earlier and more effectively, certain therapeutic, medical or surgical procedures.

Such diagnosis is permissible, with the consent of the parents after they have been adequately informed, if the methods employed safeguard the life and integrity of the embryo and the mother, without subjecting them to disproportionate risks.[27] But this diagnosis is gravely opposed to the moral law when it is done with the thought of possibly inducing an abortion depending upon the results: A diagnosis which shows the existence of a malformation or hereditary illness must not be the equivalent of a death sentence. Thus a woman would be committing a gravely illicit act if she were to request such a diagnosis with the deliberate intention of having an abortion should the results confirm the existence of a malformation or abnormality. The spouse or relatives or anyone else would similarly be acting in a manner contrary to the moral law if they were to counsel or impose such a diagnostic procedure on the expectant mother with the same intention of possibly proceeding to an abortion. So too the specialist would be guilty of illicit collaboration if, in conducting the diagnosis and in communicating its results, he were deliberately to contribute to establishing or favoring a link between prenatal diagnosis and abortion.

In conclusion, any directive or program of the civil and health authorities or of scientific organizations which in any way were to favor a link between prenatal diagnosis and abortion, or which were to go as far as directly to induce expectant mothers to submit to prenatal diagnosis planned for the purpose of eliminating fetuses which are affected by malformations or which are carriers of hereditary illness, is to be condemned as a violation of the unborn child's right to life and as an abuse of the prior rights and duties of the spouses.

---

[27]The obligation to avoid disproportionate risks involves an authentic respect for human beings and the uprightness of therapeutic intentions. It implies that the doctor "above all . . . must carefully evaluate the possible negative consequences which the necessary use of a particular exploratory technique may have upon the unborn child and avoid recourse to diagnostic procedures which do not offer sufficient guarantees of their honest purpose and substantial harmlessness. And if, as often as happens in human choices, a degree of risk must be undertaken, he will take care to assure that it is justified by a truly urgent need for the diagnosis and by the importance of the results that can be achieved by it for the benefit of the unborn child himself." (Pope John Paul II, Discourse to participants in the Pro-Life Movement Congress, Dec. 3, 1982: *Insegnamenti di Giovanni Paolo II*, V, 3 (1982) 1512). This clarification concerning "proportionate risk" is also asked to be kept in mind in the following sections of the present instructions, whenever this term appears.

3. Are therapeutic procedures carried out on the human embryo licit?

As with all medical interventions on patients, *one must uphold as licit procedures carried out on the human embryo which respect the life and integrity of the embryo and do not involve disproportionate risks for it, but are directed toward its healing, the improvement of its condition of health or its individual survival.*

Whatever the type of medical, surgical or other therapy, the free and informed consent of the parents is required, according to the deontological rules followed in the case of children. The application of this moral principle may call for delicate and particular precautions in the case of embryonic or fetal life.

The legitimacy and criteria of such procedures have been clearly stated by Pope John Paul II: "a strictly therapeutic intervention whose explicit objective is the healing of various maladies such as those stemming from chromosomal defects will, in principle, be considered desirable, provided it is directed to the true promotion of the personal well-being of the individual without doing harm to his integrity or worsening his conditions of life. Such an intervention would indeed fall within the logic of the Christian moral tradition."[28]

4. How is one to evaluate morally research and experimentation* on human embryos and fetuses?

Medical research must refrain from operations on live embryos, unless there is a moral certainty of not causing harm to the life or integrity of the unborn child and the mother, and on condition that the parents have given their free and informed consent to the procedure. It follows that all research, even when limited to the simple observation of the embryo, would become illicit were it to involve risk to the embryo's physical integrity or life by reason of the methods used or the effects induced.

As regards experimentation, and presupposing the general distinction between experimentation for purposes which are not directly therapeutic and experimentation which is clearly therapeutic for the subject himself, in the case in point one must also distinguish between experimentation carried out on embryos which are still alive and experimentation carried out on embryos which are dead. *If the embryos are living, whether viable or not, they must be respected just like any other human person; experimentation on embryos which is not directly therapeutic is illicit.*[29]

---

[28]Pope John Paul II, Discourse to Participants in the 35th General Assembly of the World Medical Association, Oct. 29, 1983: AAS 76 (1984) 392.

*Since the terms *research* and *experimentation* are often used equivalently and ambiguously, it is deemed necessary to specify the exact meaning given to them in this document.

1)By *research* is meant any inductive-deductive process which aims at promoting the systematic observation of a given phenomenon in the human field or at verifying a hypothesis arising from previous observations.

2) By *experimentation* is meant any research in which the human being (in the various stages of his existence: embryo, fetus, child or adult) represents the object through which or upon which one intends to verify the effect, at present unknown or not sufficiently known, of a given treatment (e.g., pharmacological, teratogenic, surgical, etc.).

[29]Cf. Ibid., Address to a meeting of Pontifical Academy of Sciences, Oct.

No objective, even though noble in itself such as a foreseeable advantage to science, to other human beings or to society, can in any way justify experimentation on living human embryos or fetuses, whether viable or not, either inside or outside the mother's womb. The informed consent ordinarily required for clinical experimentation on adults cannot be granted by the parents, who may not freely dispose of the physical integrity or life of the unborn child. Moreover, experimentation on embryos and fetuses always involves risk, and indeed in most cases it involves the certain expectation of harm to their physical integrity or even their death.

To use human embryos or fetuses as the object or instrument of experimentation constitutes a crime against their dignity as human beings having a right to the same respect that is due to the child already born and to every human person.

The Charter of the Rights of the Family published by the Holy See affirms: "Respect for the dignity of the human being excludes all experimental manipulation or exploitation of the human embryo."[30] The practice of keeping alive human embryos *in vivo* or *in vitro* for experimental or commercial purposes is totally opposed to human dignity.

In the case of experimentation that is clearly therapeutic, namely, when it is a matter of experimental forms of therapy used for the benefit of the embryo itself in a final attempt to save its life and in the absence of other reliable forms of therapy, recourse to drugs or procedures not yet fully tested can be licit.[31]

The corpses of human embryos and fetuses, whether they have been deliberately aborted or not, must be respected just as the remains of other human beings. In particular, they cannot be subjected to mutilation or to autopsies if their death has not yet been verified and without the consent of the parents or of the mother. Furthermore, the moral requirements must be safeguarded that there be no complicity in deliberate abortion and that the risk of scandal be avoided. Also, in the case of dead fetuses, as for the corpses of adult persons, all commercial trafficking must be considered illicit and should be prohibited.

5. How is one to evaluate morally the use for research purposes of embryos obtained by fertilization "in vitro?"

Human embryos obtained *in vitro* are human beings and subjects with rights: Their dignity and right to life must be respected from the first moment of their existence. *It is immoral to produce human embryos destined to be exploited as disposable*

23, 1982: AAS 75 (1983) 37: "I condemn, in the most explicit and formal way, experimental manipulations of the human embryo, since the human being, from conception to death, cannot be exploited for any purpose whatsoever."

[30]Charter of the Rights of the Family, 4b.

[31]Cf. Pope John Paul II, Address to the participants in the Pro-Life Movement Congress, Dec. 3, 1982: *Insegnamenti di Giovanni Paolo II*, V, 3, (1982) 1511: "Any form of experimentation on the fetus that may damage its integrity or worsen its conditions is unacceptable, except in the case of a final effort to save it from death." Congregation for the Doctrine of the Faith, Declaration on Euthanasia, 4: AAS 72 (1980) 550: "In the absence of other sufficient remedies, it is permitted, with the patient's consent, to have recourse to the means provided by the most advanced medical techniques, even if these means are still at the experimental stage and are not without a certain risk."

"biological material."

In the usual practice of *in vitro* fertilization, not all of the embryos are transferred to the woman's body; some are destroyed. Just as the church condemns induced abortion, so she also forbids acts against the life of these human beings. *It is a duty to condemn the particular gravity of the voluntary destruction of human embryos obtained "in vitro" for the sole purpose of research, either by means of artificial insemination or by means of "twin fission."* By acting in this way the researcher usurps the place of God; and, even though he may be unaware of this, he sets himself up as the master of the destiny of others inasmuch as he arbitrarily chooses whom he will allow to live and whom he will send to death and kills defenseless human beings.

Methods of observation or experimentation which damage or impose grave and disproportionate risks upon embryos obtained *in vitro* are morally illicit for the same reasons. Every human being is to be respected for himself and cannot be reduced in worth to a pure and simple instrument for the advantage of others. *It is therefore not in conformity with the moral law deliberately to expose to death human embryos obtained "in vitro."* In consequence of the fact that they have been produced *in vitro*, those embryos which are not transferred into the body of the mother and are called "spare" are exposed to an absurd fate, with no possibility of their being offered safe means of survival which can be licitly pursued.

6. What judgment should be made on other procedures of manipulating embryos connected with the "techniques of human reproduction?"

Techniques of fertilization *in vitro* can open the way to other forms of biological and genetic manipulation of human embryos, such as attempts or plans for fertilization between human and animal gametes and the gestation of human embryos in the uterus of animals, or the hypothesis or project of constructing artificial uteruses for the human embryo. *These procedures are contrary to the human dignity proper to the embryo, and at the same time they are contrary to the right of every person to be conceived and to be born within marriage and from marriage.*[32] *Also, attempts or hypotheses for obtaining a human being without any connection with sexuality through "twin fission," cloning or parthenogenesis are to be considered contrary to the moral law, since they are in opposition to the dignity both of human procreation and of the conjugal union.*

The freezing of embryos, even when carried out in order to preserve the life of an embryo—cryopreservation—*constitutes an offense against the respect due to human beings* by exposing them to grave risks of death or harm to their physical integrity and depriving them, at least temporarily, of maternal shelter and gestation, thus placing them in a situation in which further offenses and manipulation are possible.

Certain attempts to influence chromosomic or genetic inheritance are not therapeutic, but are aimed at producing human beings selected according to sex or other predeter-

---

[32]No one, before coming into existence, can claim a subjective right to begin to exist; nevertheless, it is legitimate to affirm the right of the child to have a fully human origin through conception in conformity with the personal nature of the human being. Life is a gift that must be bestowed in a manner worthy both of the subject receiving it and of the subjects transmitting it. This statement is to be borne in mind also for what will be explained concerning artificial human procreation.

mined qualities. These manipulations are contrary to the personal dignity of the human being and his or her integrity and identity. Therefore in now way can they be justified on the grounds of possible beneficial consequences for future humanity.[33] Every person must be respected for himself: In this consists the dignity and right of every human being from his or her beginning.

II
INTERVENTIONS UPON
HUMAN PROCREATION

By *artificial procreation* or *artificial fertilization* are understood here the different technical procedures directed toward obtaining a human conception in a manner other than the sexual union of man and woman. This instruction deals with fertilization of an ovum in a test tube (*in vitro* fertilization) and artificial insemination through transfer into the woman's genital tracts of previously collected sperm.

A preliminary point for the moral evaluation of such technical procedures is constituted by the consideration of the circumstances and consequences which those procedures involve in relation to the respect due the human embryo. Development of the practice of *in vitro* fertilization has required innumerable fertilizations and destructions of human embryos. Even today, the usual practice presupposes a hyperovulaton on the part of the woman: A number of ova are withdrawn, fertilized and then cultivated *in vitro* for some days. Usually not all are transferred into the genital tracts of the woman; some embryos, generally called "spare," are destroyed or frozen. On occasion, some of the implanted embryos are sacrificed for various eugenic, economic or psychological reasons. Such deliberate destruction of human beings or their utilization for different purposes to the detriment of their integrity and life is contrary to the doctrine on procured abortion already recalled.

The connection between *in vitro* fertilization and the voluntary destruction of human embryos occurs too often. This is significant: Through these procedures, with apparently contrary purposes, life and death are subjected to the decision of man, who thus sets himself up as the giver of life and death by decree. This dynamic of violence and domination may remain unnoticed by those very individuals who, in wishing to utilize this procedure, become subject to it themselves. The facts recorded and the cold logic which links them must be taken into consideration for a moral judgment on *in vitro* fertilization and embryo transfer: The abortion mentality which has made this procedure possible thus leads, whether one wants it or not, to man's domination over the life and death of his fellow human beings and can lead to a system of radical eugenics.

Nevertheless, such abuses do not exempt one from a further and thorough ethical study of the techniques of artificial procreation considered in themselves, abstracting as far as possible from the destruction of embryos produced *in vitro*.

The present instruction will therefore take into consideration in the first place the problems posed by heterologous artificial fertilization (II, 1-3),* and subsequently those linked with homologous artificial fertilization (II, 4-6).**

Before formulating an ethical judgment on each of these procedures, the princi-

---

[33]Cf. Pope John Paul II, Discourse to those taking part in the 35th General Assembly of the World Medical Association, Oct. 29, 1983: AAS 76 (1984) 391.

ples and values which determine the moral evaluation of each of them will be considered.

A. Heterologous Artificial Fertilization

1. Why must human procreation take place in marriage?

Every human being is always to be accepted as a gift and blessing of God. However, from the moral point of view a truly responsible procreation vis-a-vis the unborn child must be the fruit of marriage.

For human procreation has specific characteristics by virtue of the personal dignity of the parents and of the children: The procreation of a new person, whereby the man and the woman collaborate with the power of the Creator, must be the fruit and the sign of the mutual self-giving of the spouses, of their love and of their fidelity.[34] *The fidelity of the spouses in the unity of marriage involves reciprocal respect of their right to become a father and a mother only through each other.*

The child has the right to be conceived, carried in the womb, brought into the world and brought up within marriage: It is through the secure and recognized relationship to his own parents that the child can discover his own identity and achieve his own proper human development.

The parents find in their child a confirmation and completion of their reciprocal self-giving: The child is the living image of their love, the permanent sign of their conjugal union, the living and indissoluble concrete expression of their paternity and maternity.[35]

---

*By the term *heterologous artificial fertilization* or *procreation*, the instruction means techniques used to obtain a human conception artificially by the use of gametes coming from at least one donor other than the spouses who are joined in marriage. Such techniques can be of two types:

a)*Heterologous "in vitro" fertilization and embryo transfer*: the technique used to obtain a human conception through the meeting *in vitro* of gametes taken from at least one donor other than the two spouses joined in marriage.

b)*Heterologous artificial insemination*: the technique used to obtain a human conception through the transfer into the genital tracts of the woman of the sperm previously collected from a donor other than the husband.

**By *artificial homologous fertilization* or *procreation*, the instruction means the technique used to obtain a human conception using the gametes of the two spouses joined in marriage. Homologous artificial fertilization can be carried out by two different methods:

a)*Homologous "in vitro" fertilization and embryo transfer*: the technique used to obtain a human conception through the meeting *in vitro* of the gametes of the spouses joined in marriage.

b)*Homologous artificial insemination*: the technique used to obtain a human conception through the transfer into the genital tracts of a married woman of the sperm previously collected from her husband.

[34]Cf. *Gaudium et Spes*, 50.

[35]Cf. *Familiaris Consortio*, 14

By reason of the vocation and social responsibilities of the person, the good of the children and of the parents contributes to the good of civil society; the vitality and stability of society require that children come into the world within a family and that the family be firmly based on marriage.

The tradition of the church and anthropological reflection recognize in marriage and in its indissoluble unity the only setting worthy of truly responsible procreation.

2. Does heterologous artificial fertilization conform to the dignity of the couple and to the truth of marriage?

Through *in vitro* fertilization and embryo transfer and heterologous artificial insemination, human conception is achieved through the fusion of gametes of at least one donor other than the spouses who are united in marriage. *Heterologous artificial fertilization is contrary to the unity of marriage, to the dignity of the spouses, to the vocation proper to parents, and to the child's right to be conceived and brought into the world in marriage and from marriage.*[36]

Respect for the unity of marriage and for conjugal fidelity demands that the child be conceived in marriage; the bond existing between husband and wife accords the spouses, in an objective and inalienable manner, the exclusive right to become father and mother solely through each other.[37] Recourse to the gametes of a third person in order to have sperm or ovum available constitutes a violation of the reciprocal commitment of the spouses and a grave lack in regard to that essential property of marriage which is its unity.

Heterologous artificial fertilization violates the rights of the child; it deprives him of his filial relationship with his parental origins and can hinder the maturing of his personal identity. Furthermore, it offends the common vocation of the spouses who are called to fatherhood and motherhood: It objectively deprives conjugal fruitfulness of its unity and integrity; it brings about and manifests a rupture between genetic parenthood, gestational parenthood and responsibility for upbringing. Such

---

[36]Cf. Pope Pius XII, Discourse to those taking part in the Fourth International Congress of Catholic Doctors, Sept. 29, 1949: AAS 41 (1949) 559. According to the plan of the Creator, "a man leaves his father and his mother and cleaves to his wife, and they become one flesh" (Gn. 2:24). The unity of marriage, bound to the order of creation, is a truth accessible to natural reason. The church's tradition and magisterium frequently make reference to the Book of Genesis, both directly and through the passages of the New Testament that refer to it: Mt. 19:4-6; Mk. 10:5-8; Eph. 5:31. Cf. Athenagoras, *Legatio pro christianis*, 33: PG 6, 965-967; St. Chrysostom, *In Matthaeum homiliae*, LXII, 19, 1: PG 58 597; St. Leo the Great, *Epist. ad Rusticum*, 4: PL 54, 1204; Innocent III, Epist. *Gaudemus in Domino*: DS 778; Council of Lyons II, IV Session: DS 860; Council of Trent, XXIV Session: DS 1798, 1802; Pope Leo XIII, encyclical *Arcanum Divinae Sapientiae*: AAS 12 (1879-1880) 388-391; Pope Pius XI, encyclical *Casti Connubii*: AAS 22 (1930) 546-547; *Gaudium et Spes*, 48; *Familiaris Consortio*, 19, Code of Canon Law, Canon 1056.

[37]Cf. Pope Pius XII, Discourse to those taking part in the Fourth International Congress of Catholic Doctors, Sept. 29, 1949: AAS 41 (1949) 560; Discourse to those taking part in the Congress of the Italian Catholic Union of Midwives, Oct. 29, 1951: AAS 43 (1951) 850; Code of Canon Law, Canon 1134.

damage to the personal relationships within the family has repercussions on civil society: What threatens the unity and stability of the family is a source of dissension, disorder and injustice in the whole of social life.

These reasons lead to a negative moral judgment concerning heterologous artificial fertilization: Consequently, fertilization of a married woman with the sperm of a donor different from her husband and fertilization with the husband's sperm of an ovum not coming from his wife are morally illicit. Furthermore, the artificial fertilization of a woman who is unmarried or a widow, whoever the donor may be, cannot be morally justified.

The desire to have a child and the love between spouses who long to obviate a sterility which cannot be overcome in any other way constitute understandable motivations; but subjectively good intentions do not render heterologous artificial fertilization conformable to the objective and inalienable properties of marriage or respectful of the rights of the child and of the spouses.

3. Is "surrogate"* motherhood morally licit?

No, for the same reasons which lead one to reject heterologous artificial fertilization: For it is contrary to the unity of marriage and to the dignity of the procreation of the human person..

Surrogate motherhood represents an objective failure to meet the obligations of maternal love, of conjugal fidelity and of responsible motherhood; it offends the dignity and the right of the child to be conceived, carried in the womb, brought into the world and brought up by his own parents; it sets up, to the detriment of families, a division between the physical, psychological and moral elements which constitute those families.

B. Homologous Artificial Fertilization

Since hetrologous artificial fertilization has been declared unacceptable, the question arises of how to evaluate morally the process of homologous artificial fertilization: *in vitro* fertilization and embryo transfer and artificial insemination between husband and wife. First a question of principle must be clarified.

4. What connection is required from the moral point of view between procreation and the conjugal act?

a) The church's teaching on marriage and human procreation affirms the "inseparable connection, willed by God and unable to be broken by man on his own initiative, between the two meanings of the conjugal act: the unitive meaning and the procreative meaning. Indeed, by its intimate structure the conjugal act, while most closely uniting husband and wife, capacitates them for the generation of new lives according to laws inscribed in the very being of man of woman."[38] This principle, which

---

*By *surrogate mother* the instruction means:

a) The woman who carries in pregnancy an embryo implanted in her uterus and who is genetically a stranger to the embryo because it has been obtained through the union of the gametes of "donors." She carries the pregnancy with a pledge to surrender the baby once it is born to the party who commissioned or made the agreement for the pregnancy.

is based upon the nature of marriage and the intimate connection of the goods of marriage, has well known consequences on the level of responsible fatherhood and motherhood. "By safeguarding both these essential aspects, the unitive and the procreative, the conjugal act preserves in its fullness the sense of true mutual love and its ordination toward man's exalted vocation to parenthood."[39]

The same doctrine concerning the link between the meanings of the conjugal act and between the goods of marriage throws light on the moral problem of homologous artificial fertilization, since "it is never permitted to separate these different aspects to such a degree as positively to exclude either the procreative intention or the conjugal relation."[40]

Contraception deliberately deprives the conjugal act of its openness to procreation and in this way brings about a voluntary dissociation of the ends of marriage. Homologous artificial fertilization, in seeking a procreation which is not the fruit of a specific act of conjugal union, objectively effects an analogous separation between the goods and the meanings of marriage.

Thus *fertilization is licitly sought when it is the result of a "conjugal act which is per se suitable for the generation of children, to which marriage is ordered by its nature and by which the spouses become one flesh."*[41] *But from the moral point of view procreation is deprived of its proper perfection when it is not desired as the fruit of the conjugal act, that is to say, of the specific act of the spouses' union.*

b) The moral value of the intimate link between the goods of marriage and between the meanings of the conjugal act is based upon the unity of the human being, a unity involving body and spiritual soul.[42] Spouses mutually express their personal love in the "language of the body," which clearly involves both "spousal meanings" and parental ones.[43] the conjugal act by which the couple mutually express their self-gift at the same time expresses openness to the gift of life. It is an act that is inseparably corporal and spiritual. It is in their bodies and through their bodies that the spouses consummate their marriage and are able to become father and mother. In order to respect the language of their bodies and their natural generosity, the conjugal union must take place with respect for its openness to procreation; and the procreation of a person must be the fruit and the result of married love. The origin of the

---

b) The woman who carries in pregnancy an embryo to whose procreation she has contributed the donation of her own ovum, fertilized through insemination with the sperm of a man other than her husband. She carries the pregnancy with a pledge to surrender the child once it is born to the party who commissioned or made the agreement for the pregnancy.

[38]*Humanae Vitae*, 12.

[39]Ibid.

[40]Pope Pius XII, Discourse to those taking part in the Second Naples World Congress on Fertility and Human Sterility, May 19, 1956: AAS 48 (1956) 470.

[41]Code of Canon Law, Canon 1061. According to this canon, the conjugal act is that by which the marriage is consummated if the couple "have performed (it) between themselves in a human manner."

[42]Cf. *Gaudium et Spes*, 14.

[43]Cf. Pope John Paul II, General Audience Jan. 16, 1980: *Insegnamenti di Giovanni Paolo II*, III, 1 (1980) 148-152.

human being thus follows from a procreation that is "linked to the union, not only biological but also spiritual, of the parents, made one by the bond of marriage."[44] Fertilization achieved outside the bodies of the couple remains by this very fact deprived of the meanings and the values which are expressed in the language of the body and in the union of human persons.

c) Only respect for the link between the meanings of the conjugal act and respect for the unity of the human being make possible procreation in conformity with the dignity of the person. In his unique and irrepeatable origin, the child must be respected and recognized as equal in personal dignity to those who give him life. The human person must be accepted in his parents' act of union and love; the generation of a child must therefore be the fruit of that mutual giving[45] which is realized in the conjugal act wherein the spouses cooperate as servants and not as masters in the work of the Creator, who is love.[46]

In reality, the origin of a human person is the result of an act of giving. The one conceived must be the fruit of his parents' love. He cannot be desired or conceived as the product of an intervention of medical or biological techniques; that would be equivalent to reducing him to an object of scientific technology. No one may subject the coming of a child into the world to conditions of technical efficiency which are to be evaluated according to standards of control and dominion.

The moral relevance of the link between the meanings of the conjugal act and between the goods of marriage, as well as the unity of the human being and the dignity of his origin, demand that the procreation of a human person be brought about as the fruit of the conjugal act specific to the love between spouses. The link between procreation and the conjugal act is thus shown to be of great importance on the anthropological and moral planes and it throws light on the positions of the magisterium with regard to homologous artificial fertilization.

5. Is homologous "in vitro" fertilization morally licit?

The answer to this question is strictly dependent on the principles just mentioned. Certainly one cannot ignore the legitimate aspirations of sterile couples. For some, recourse to homologous *in vitro* fertilization and embryo transfer appears to be the only way of fulfilling their sincere desire for a child. The question asked whether the totality of conjugal life in such situations is not sufficient to ensure the dignity proper to human procreation. It is acknowledged that *in vitro* fertilization and embryo transfer certainly cannot supply for the absence of sexual relations[47] and cannot be preferred to the specific acts of conjugal union, given the risks involved for the child and the difficulties of the procedure. But it is asked whether, when there is no other

---

[44]Ibid., Discourse to those taking part in the 35th General Assembly of the World Medical Association, Oct. 29, 1983: AAS 76 (1984) 393.

[45]Cf. *Gaudium et Spes*, 51.

[46]Ibid., 50.

[47]Cf. Pope Pius XII, Discourse to those taking part in the Fourth International Congress of Catholic Doctors, Sept. 29, 1949: AAS 41 (1949) 560: "It would be erroneous . . . to think that the possibility of resorting to this means (artificial fertilization) might render valid a marriage between persons unable to contract it because of the *impedimentum impotentiae*."

way of overcoming the sterility which is a source of suffering homologous *in vitro* fertilization may not constitute an aid, if not a form of therapy, whereby its moral licitness could be admitted.

The desire for a child—or at the very least an openness to the transmission of life—is a necessary prerequisite from the moral point of view for responsible human procreation. But this good intention is not sufficient for making a positive moral evaluation of *in vitro* fertilization between spouses. The process of *in vitro* fertilization and embryo transfer must be judged in itself and cannot borrow its definitive moral quality from the totality of conjugal life of which it becomes part nor from the conjugal acts which may precede or follow it.[48]

It has already been recalled that in the circumstances in which it is regularly practiced *in vitro* fertilization and embryo transfer involves the destruction of human beings, which is something contrary to the doctrine on the illicitness of abortion previously mentioned.[49] But even in a situation in which every precaution were taken to avoid the death of human embryos, homologous *in vitro* fertilization and embryo transfer dissociates from the conjugal act the actions which are directed to human fertilization. For this reason the very nature of homologous *in vitro* fertilization and embryo transfer also must be taken into account, even abstracting from the link with procured abortion.

Homologous *in vitro* fertilization and embryo transfer is brought about outside the bodies of the couple through actions of third parties whose competence and technical activity determine the success of the procedure. Such fertilization entrusts the life and identity of the embryo into the power of doctors and biologists and establishes the domination of technology over the origin and destiny of the human person. Such relationship of domination is in itself contrary to the dignity and equality that must be common to parents and children.

Conception *in vitro* is the result of the technical action which presides over fertilization. *Such fertilization is neither in fact achieved nor positively willed as the expression and fruit of a specific act of the conjugal union. In homologous "in vitro" fertilization and embryo transfer, therefore, even if it is considered in the context of de facto existing sexual relations, the generation of the human person is objectively deprived of its proper perfection: namely, that of being the result and fruit of a conjugal act* in which the spouses can become "cooperators with God for giving life to a new person."[50]

These reasons enable us to understand why the act of conjugal love is considered in the teaching of the church as the only setting worthy of human procreation. For the same reasons the so-called "simple case," i.e., a homologous *in vitro* fertilization and embryo transfer procedure that is free of any compromise with the abortive practice of destroying embryos and with masturbation, remains a technique which is morally illicit because it deprives human procreation of the dignity which is proper and connatural to it.

Certainly, homologous *in vitro* fertilization and embryo transfer fertilization is not marked by all that ethical negativity found in extraconjugal procreation; the family and marriage continue to constitute the setting for the birth and upbringing of the

---

[48]A similar question was dealt with by Pope Paul VI, *Humanae Vitae*, 14.

[49]Cf. *supra*: I, 1ff.

[50]*Familiaris Consortio*, 14: AAS 74 (1982) 96.

children. Nevertheless, in conformity with the traditional doctrine relating to the goods of marriage and the dignity of the person, *the church remains opposed from the moral point of view to homologous "in vitro" fertilization. Such fertilization is in itself illicit and in opposition to the dignity of procreation and of the conjugal union, even when everything is done to avoid the death of the human embryo.*

Although the manner in which human conception is achieved with *in vitro* fertilization and embryo transfer cannot be approved, every child which comes into the world must in any case be accepted as a living gift of the divine Goodness and must be brought up with love.

6. How is homologous artificial insemination to be evaluated from the moral point of view?

Homologous artificial insemination within marriage cannot be admitted except for those cases in which the technical means is not a substitute for the conjugal act but serves to facilitate and to help so that the act attains its natural purpose.

The teaching of the magisterium on this point has already been stated.[51] This teaching is not just an expression of particular historical circumstances, but is based on the church's doctrine concerning the connection between the conjugal union and procreation and on a consideration of the personal nature of the conjugal act and of human procreation. "In its natural structure, the conjugal act is a personal action, a simultaneous and immediate cooperation on the part of the husband and wife, which by the very nature of the agents and the proper nature of the act is the expression of the mutual gift which, according to the words of Scripture, brings about union 'in one flesh.'"[52] Thus moral conscience "does not necessarily proscribe the use of certain artificial means destined solely either to the facilitating of the natural act or to ensuring that the natural act normally performed achieves its proper end."[53] If the technical means facilitates the conjugal act or helps it to reach its natural objectives, it can be morally acceptable. If, on the other hand, the procedure were to replace the conjugal act, it is morally illicit.

Artificial insemination as a substitute for the conjugal act is prohibited by reason of the voluntarily achieved dissociation of the two meanings of the conjugal act. Masturbation, through which the sperm is normally obtained, is another sign of this dissociation: Even when it is done for the purpose of procreation the act remains deprived of its unitive meaning: "It lacks the sexual relationship called for by the moral

---

[51]Cf. Response of the Holy Office, March 17, 1897: DS 3323; Pope Pius XII, Discourse to those taking part in the Fourth International Congress of Catholic Doctors, Sept. 29, 1949: AAS 41 (1949) 560; Discourse to the Italian Catholic Union of Midwives, Oct. 29, 1951: AAS 43 (1951) 850; Discourse to those taking part in the Second Naples World Congress on Fertility and Human Sterility, May 19, 1956: AAS 48 (1956) 471-473; Discourse to those taking part in the Seventh International Congress of the International Society of Hematology, Sept. 12, 1958: AAS 50 (1958) 733; *Mater et Magistra*, III.

[52]Pope Pius XII, Discourse to the Italian Catholic Union of Midwives, Oct. 29, 1951: AAS 43 (1951) 850.

[53]Ibid., Discourse to those taking part in the Fourth International Congress of Catholic Doctors, Sept. 29, 1949: AAS 41 (1949) 560.

order, namely the relationship which realized 'the full sense of mutual self-giving and human procreation in the context of true love.'"[54]

7. What moral criterion can be proposed with regard to medical intervention in human procreation?

The medical act must be evaluated not only with reference to its technical dimension, but also and above all in relation to its goal, which is the good of persons and their bodily and psychological health. The moral criteria for medical intervention in procreation are deduced from the dignity of human persons, of their sexuality and of their origin.

Medicine which seeks to be ordered to the integral good of the person must respect the specifically human values of sexuality.[55] *The doctor is at the service of persons and of human procreation. He does not have the authority to dispose of them or to decide their fate.* A medical intervention respects the dignity of persons when it seeks to assist the conjugal act either in order to facilitate its performance or in order to enable it to achieve its objective once it has been normally performed.[56]

On the other hand, it sometimes happens that a medical procedure technologically replaces the conjugal act in order to obtain a procreation which is neither its result nor its fruit. In this case the medical act is not, as it should be, at the service of conjugal union, but rather appropriates to itself the procreative function and thus contradicts the dignity and the inalienable rights of the spouses and of the child to be born.

The humanization of medicine, which is insisted upon today by everyone, requires respect for the integral dignity of the human person first of all in the act and at the moment in which the spouses transmit life to a new person. It is only logical therefore to address an urgent appeal to Catholic doctors and scientists that they bear exemplary witness to the respect due to the human embryo and to the dignity of procreation. The medical and nursing staff of Catholic hospitals and clinics are in a special way urged to do justice to the moral obligations which they have assumed, frequently also, as part of their contract. Those who are in charge of Catholic hospitals and clinics and who are often religious will take special care to safeguard and promote a diligent observance of the moral norms recalled in the present instruction.

8. The suffering caused by infertility in marriage.

The suffering of spouses who cannot have children or who are afraid of bringing a handicapped child into the world is a suffering that everyone must understand and properly evaluate.

On the part of the spouses, the desire for a child is natural: It expresses the voca-

---

[54]Congregation for the Doctrine of the Faith, Declaration on Certain Questions Concerning Sexual Ethics, 9: AAS 68 (1976) 86, which quotes *Gaudium et Spes*, 51. Cf. Decree of the Holy Office, Aug. 2, 1929: AAS 21 (1929) 490; Pope Pius XII, Discourse to those taking part in the 26th Congress of the Italian Society of Urology, Oct. 8, 1953: AAS 45 (1953) 678.

[55]Cf. Pope John XXIII, *Mater et Magistra*, III.

[56]Cf. Pope Pius XII, Discourse to those taking part in the Fourth International Congress of Catholic Doctors, Sept. 29, 1949: AAS 41 (1949) 560.

tion to fatherhood and motherhood inscribed in conjugal love. This desire can be even stronger if the couple is affected by sterility which appears incurable. Nevertheless, marriage does not confer upon the spouses the right to have a child, but only the right to perform those natural acts which are per se ordered to procreation.[57]

A true and proper right to a child would be contrary to the child's dignity and nature. The child is not an object to which one has a right nor can he be considered as an object of ownership: Rather, a child is a gift, "the supreme gift"[58] and the most gratuitous gift of marriage, and is a living testimony of the mutual giving of his parents. For this reason, the child has the right as already mentioned, to be the fruit of the specific act of the conjugal love of his parents; and he also has the right to be respected as a person from the moment of his conception.

Nevertheless, whatever its cause or prognosis, sterility is certainly a difficult trial. The community of believers is called to shed light upon and support the suffering of those who are unable to fulfill their legitimate aspiration to motherhood and fatherhood. Spouses who find themselves in this sad situation are called to find in it an opportunity for sharing in a particular way in the Lord's cross, the source of spiritual fruitfulness. Sterile couples must not forget that "even when procreation is not possible, conjugal life does not for this reason lose its value. Physical sterility in fact can be for spouses the occasion for other important services to the life of the human person, for example, adoption, various forms of educational work and assistance to other families and to poor or handicapped children".[59]

Many researchers are engaged in the fight against sterility. While fully safeguarding the dignity of human procreation, some have achieved results which previously seemed unattainable. Scientists therefore are to be encouraged to continue their research with the aim of preventing the causes of sterility and of being able to remedy them so that sterile couples will be able to procreate in full respect for their own personal dignity and that of the child to be born.

III
MORAL AND CIVIL LAW

The Values and Moral Obligations That Civil Legislation Must Respect And Sanction in This Matter

The inviolable right to life of every innocent human individual and the rights of the family and of the institution of marriage constitute fundamental moral values because they concern the natural condition and integral vocation of the human person; at the same time they are constitutive elements of civil society and its order.

For this reason the new technological possibilities which have opened up in the field of biomedicine require the intervention of the political authorities and of the legislator, since an uncontrolled application of such techniques could lead to unforeseeable and damaging consequences for civil society. Recourse to the conscience of

---

[57]Cf. Ibid., Discourse to those taking part in the Second Naples World Congress on Fertility and Human Sterility, May 19, 1956: AAS 48 (1956) 471-473.

[58]*Gaudium et Spes*, 50.

[59]*Familiaris Consortio*, 14.

each individual and to the self-regulation of researchers cannot be sufficient for ensuring respect for personal rights and public order. If the legislator responsible for the common good were not watchful, he could be deprived of his prerogatives by researchers claiming to govern humanity in the name of the biological discoveries and the alleged "improvement" processes which they would draw from those discoveries. "Eugenism" and forms of discrimination between human beings could come to be legitimized: This would constitute an act of violence and a serious offense to the equality, dignity and fundamental rights of the human person.

The intervention of the public authority must be inspired by the rational principles which regulate the relationships between civil law and moral law. The task of the civil law is to ensure the common good of people through the recognition of and the defense of fundamental rights and through the promotion of peace and of public morality.[60] In no sphere of life can the civil law take the place of conscience or dictate norms concerning things which are outside its competence. It must sometimes tolerate, for the sake of public order, things which it cannot forbid without a greater evil resulting. However, the inalienable rights of the person must be recognized and respected by civil society and the political authority. These human rights depend neither on single individuals nor on parents; nor do they represent a concession made by society and the state: They pertain to human nature and are inherent in the person by virtue of the creative act from which the person took his or her origin.

Among such fundamental rights one should mention in this regard: a) every human being's right to life and physical integrity from the moment of conception until death; b) the rights of the family and of marriage as an institution and, in this area, the child's right to be conceived, brought into the world and brought up by his parents. To each of these two themes it is necessary here to give some further consideration.

In various states certain laws have authorized the direct suppression of innocents: The moment a positive law deprives a category of human beings of the protection which civil legislation must accord them, the state is denying the equality of all before the law. When the state does not place its power at the service of the rights of each citizen, and in particular of the more vulnerable, the very foundations of a state based on law are undermined. The political authority consequently cannot give approval to the calling of human beings into existence through procedures which would expose them to those very grave risks noted previously. The possible recognition by positive law and the political authorities of techniques of artificial transmission of life and the experimentation connected with it would widen the breach already opened by the legalization of abortion.

As a consequence of the respect and protection which must be ensured for the unborn child from the moment of his conception, the law must provide appropriate penal sanctions for every deliberate violation of the child's rights. The law cannot tolerate—indeed it must expressly forbid—that human beings, even at the embryonic state, should be treated as objects of experimentation, be mutilated or destroyed with the excuse that they are superfluous or incapable of developing normally.

The political authority is bound to guarantee to the institution of the family, upon which society is based, the juridical protection to which it has a right. From the very fact that it is at the service of people, the political authority must also be at the

---

[60]Cf. *Dignitatis Humanae*, 7.

service of the family. Civil law cannot grant approval to techniques of artificial pro-creation which, for the benefit of third parties (doctors, biologist, economic or gov-ernmental powers), take away what is a right inherent in the relationship between spouses; and therefore civil law cannot legalize the donation of gametes between per-sons who are not legitimately united in marriage.

Legislation must also prohibit, by virtue of the support which is due to the fam-ily, embryo banks, post-mortem insemination and "surrogate motherhood."

It is part of the duty of the public authority to ensure that the civil law is regulated according to the fundamental norms of the moral law in matters concerning human rights, human life and the institution of the family. Politicians must commit themselves, through their interventions upon public opinion, to securing in society the widest possible consensus on such essential points and to consolidating this consensus wherever it risks being weakened or is in danger of collapse.

In many countries the legalization of abortion and juridical tolerance of unmar-ried couples make it more difficult to secure respect for the fundamental rights re-called by this instruction. It is to be hoped that states will not become responsible for aggravating these socially damaging situations of injustice. It is rather to be hoped that nations and states will realize all the cultural, ideological and political implica-tions connected with the techniques of artificial procreation and will find the wisdom and courage necessary for issuing laws which are more just and more respectful of human life and the institution of the family.

The civil legislation of many states confers an undue legitimation upon certain practices in the eyes of many today; it is seen to be incapable of guaranteeing that moral-ity which is in conformity with the natural exigencies of the human person and with the "unwritten laws" etched by the Creator upon the human heart. All men of good will must commit themselves, particularly within their professional field and in the exercise of their civil rights, to ensuring the reform of morally unacceptable civil laws and the correction of illicit practices. In addition, "conscientious objection" vis-a-vis such laws must be sup-ported and recognized. A movement of passive resistance to the legitimation of practices contrary to human life and dignity is beginning to make an ever sharper impression upon the moral conscience of many, especially among specialists in the biomedical sciences.

CONCLUSION

The spread of technologies of intervention in the processes of human procre-ation raises very serious moral problems in relation to the respect due to the human being from the moment of conception, to the dignity of the person, of his or her sexu-ality and of the transmission of life.

With this instruction the Congregation for the Doctrine of the Faith, in fulfilling its responsibility to promote and defend the church's teaching in so serious a matter, addresses a new and heartfelt invitation to all those who, by reason of their role and their commitment, can exercise a positive influence and ensure that in the family and in society due respect is accorded to life and love. It addresses this invitation to those responsible for the formation of consciences and of public opinion, to scientists and medical professionals, to jurists and politicians. It hopes that all will understand the incompatibility between recognition of the dignity of the human person and contempt for life and love, between faith in the living god and the claim to decide arbitrarily the origin and fate of a human being.

In particular, the Congregation for the Doctrine of the Faith addresses an invitation with confidence and encouragement to theologians, and above all to moralists, that they study more deeply and make ever more accessible to the faithful the contents of the teaching of the church's magisterium in the light of a valid anthropology in the matter of sexuality and marriage and in the context of the necessary interdisciplinary approach. Thus they will make it possible to understand ever more clearly the reasons for and the validity of this teaching. By defending man against the excesses of his own power, the church of God reminds him of the reasons for his true nobility; only in this way can the possibility of living and loving with that dignity and liberty which derive from respect for the truth be ensured for the men and women of tomorrow. The precise indications which are offered in the present instruction therefore are not meant to halt the effort of reflection, but rather to give it a renewed impulse in unrenounceable fidelity to the teaching of the church.

In the light of the truth about the gift of human life and in the light of the moral principles which flow from that truth, everyone is invited to act in the area of responsibility proper to each and, like the Good Samaritan, to recognize as a neighbor even the littlest among the children of men (cf. Lk. 10:29-37). Here Christ's words find a new and particular echo: "What you do to one of the least of my brethren, you do unto me" (Mt. 25:40).

During an audience granted to the undersigned prefect after the plenary session of the Congregation for the Doctrine of the Faith, the supreme pontiff, John Paul II, approved this instruction and ordered it to be published.

Given at Rome, from the Congregation for the Doctrine of the Faith, Feb. 22, 1987, the feast of the chair of St. Peter, the apostle.

Cardinal Joseph Ratzinger
Prefect
Archbishop Alberto Bovone
Secretary

INDEX

abortifacients, 16, 72
abortion, impact on siblings, 64
abortion, 2, 3, 7, 8, 9, 10, 12, 13, 14, 15, 16, 17, 18,
    19, 20, 21, 22, 23, 24, 25, 26, 27, 28, 29, 30,
    31, 32, 33, 34, 35, 36, 37, 38, 39, 40, 41, 42,
    44, 45, 46, 48, 49, 50, 52, 53, 54, 55, 56, 57,
    58, 59, 60, 61, 62, 63, 64, 65, 66, 67, 68, 69,
    70, 71, 72, 73, 74, 75, 76, 77, 78, 79, 80, 81,
    82, 83, 84, 85, 86, 87, 88, 89, 90, 91, 92, 93,
    94, 95, 96, 97, 98, 99, 106, 131, 132, 133, 134,
    135, 136, 137, 138, 139, 140, 141, 142, 145,
    146, 148, 152, 153, 155, 156, 160, 164, 166,
    167, 168, 174, 175, 181, 194, 196, 199, 209,
    210, 211, 212, 214, 216, 222, 226, 227
        and bio-egineering, 82, 84, 86, 87, 88
        and Church teaching, 7, 8, 10, 12, 14, 16,
            18, 20, 22, 24
        and compassion, 89, 90, 92, 94, 96, 98
        and contraception, 67, 68, 70, 72, 74, 76,
            78, 80
        and language, 26, 28, 30, 32, 34, 36, 38,
            40, 42, 44
        and sterilization, 57, 77, 106, 145
        and the family, 55, 56, 58, 60, 62, 64, 66
        and the unborn, 46, 48, 50, 52, 54
        consent to, 57, 60, 62, 63, 84, 87, 124,
            133, 135, 139, 142, 159, 181, 189,
            190, 201, 212, 213, 214
        direct, 9, 17, 18, 19, 20
        indirect, 19
        objective perspective in, 46, 47, 50
        subjective perspective in, 46, 49, 50
actual sin, 24
Adoption of Anonymous, 190
Ambrose of Milan, St., 16
American Citizens for Life, 142
American Civil Lib. Union, 71, 73
Andrews, Lori, 176, 177, 184, 193, 202
Anglican Church of Canada, 67
Ansari, A. H., 189
Antoninus, Arbp. of Florence, 14, 19
Antonius de Corduba, 18
Aquinas, Thomas, St., 1, 17, 18, 24, 25, 94, 97,
    116, 117
Aristotle, 11, 12, 97, 98, 128
artificial insemination, 57, 87, 107, 110, 155, 160,
    162, 167, 176, 178, 179, 180, 184, 185, 188,
    189, 190, 191, 193, 194, 200, 201, 214, 216,
    217, 218, 219, 223
        heterologous, 217, 218
        homologous, 217, 223
Asimov, Isaac, 196
Athenagoras, 16, 218
Auden, W. H., 30, 81
Augenstein, Leroy, 125
Augustine, St., 12, 13, 16, 50, 117

Baby Thrane, 175
Badgley Report, 75
Baird, William, 40, 131
Ballina, Joseph, 150
baptism (of fetus), 16, 24
Baran, Annette, 175
Basil the Great, St., 12, 13

Becker, Ernest, 119
Beernink, Ferdinand, 168
Bellotti v. Baird, 60, 61
Berdyaev, Nikolai, 51
Bianchi, Eugene C., 22, 23
Bible, attitude toward life, 116, 117, 118, 120, 121
bio-engineering, 3, 82, 84, 85, 86, 87, 88, 115
bioethics, 103, 104, 105, 106, 107, 109, 110, 111,
    112, 113, 115, 117, 119, 121, 134, 154, 156,
    158, 190
        and Church Teaching, 103, 105, 107,
            109, 111
        and Theology, 112, 113, 115, 117, 119,
            121
Blackmun (Justice), 58
Blandau, Richard J., 154
Brown, Harold O. J., 21
Brown, Louise, 85, 86, 143, 144, 153
Buber, Martin, 50, 51

Caesarean section, 155, 202
Caesarius, Bishop of Arles, 16
Callahan, Daniel, 122, 150
Canadian Abort. Rights League, 59
Canavan, Francis, 58, 59
cancer, cervical, 77
Caramuel of Prague, 15
Cardenas, Juan, 15
Carrera, Michael, 24
Carter, Cardinal, 44
Catholics for a Free Choice, 65, 95
Catholic University, 3, 8, 150
Chandrasekhar, S., 20
Chart. of Rights of Family, 210, 214
Chesterton, G. K., 30, 90, 116
children, 2, 11, 24, 48, 50, 51, 53, 55, 56, 57, 60,
    61, 62, 64, 66, 68, 70, 73, 77, 82, 85, 107, 132,
    139, 142, 145, 146, 147, 148, 155, 156, 157,
    158, 163, 169, 170, 171, 172, 176, 178, 181,
    184, 192, 196, 200, 202, 203, 213, 217, 220,
    222, 224, 225, 228
Church, Catholic, 1, 2, 3, 4, 7, 8, 9, 10, 11, 12, 13,
    14, 15, 16, 17, 18, 19, 20, 21, 22, 23, 24, 25,
    27, 29, 31, 33, 35, 37, 39, 41, 43, 45, 47, 49,
    51, 53, 57, 59, 61, 63, 65, 67, 69, 71, 73, 75,
    77, 79, 81, 83, 85, 87, 91, 93, 94, 95, 97, 99,
    103, 104, 105, 106, 107, 108, 109, 110, 111,
    114, 116, 118, 120, 124, 126, 128, 130, 133,
    135, 137, 139, 141, 145, 147, 149, 151, 153,
    155, 157, 159, 161, 163, 165, 167, 169, 170,
    171, 175, 177, 179, 181, 184, 185, 187, 189,
    191, 193, 195, 197, 199, 201, 203, 205, 206,
    207, 209, 210, 211, 213, 214, 215, 217, 218,
    219, 221, 222, 223, 225, 227, 228
Clark, Tom, 78
Code of Canon Law, 15, 16, 218, 220
        canonical penalties, 8, 10
Comfort, Alex, 69
Cong. for Doctrine of Faith, 205, 209, 211, 214,
    223, 227, 228
conjugal act, 109, 110, 219, 220, 221, 222, 223,
    224
Connell, Elizabeth, 40
Connery, John, 9, 10, 21

contraception, 3, 42, 67, 68, 69, 70, 71, 72, 74, 75, 76, 77, 78, 79, 80, 106, 160, 187, 220
Corea, Gena, 174, 183
Court cases, 59
    Adoption of Anonymous, 190
    Bellotti v. Baird, 60, 61
    Doe v. Bolton, 141
    Gursky v. Gursky, 190
    People v. Sorenson, 190
    Pl. Prnthd. of Mo. v. Danforth, 57, 60
    Roe v. Wade, 73, 74, 84, 94, 95, 136
    Wom. Com. Hlth. Ctr. v. Cohen, 61
Cowell, Carol, 67
Cyprian, St., 16
Cyril of Alexandria, 12

Damian, Peter, 32
Danforth, John C., 57
Dannemeyer, William, 138
Davis, Kingsley, 68
Dawson, Christopher, 70
Denes, Magda, 37
Derrick, Christopher, 147, 170
Descartes, René, 47, 95
Developmental Biology, Soc.for, 141
Diamond, Eugene, 85, 135, 136, 141, 144
Dickens, Bernard M., 59
Didache (of 12 Apostles), 10, 16
DNA, 122, 123, 124, 126, 200
Dobzhansky, Theodosius, 127
Doe v. Bolton, 141
Donald, Ian, 197
Dorsen, Norman, 73
doublethink, 31, 41, 42, 43, 44
Douglas (Justice), 74
Down's Syndrome, 39, 42, 140

Edsall, John, 127
Edwards, R. G., 152, 165
Edwards and Steptoe, 85, 197
Ellis, Havelock, 72
embryos, freezing of, 157
embryo, 14, 16, 40, 85, 86, 87, 106, 107, 110, 132, 135, 136, 141, 144, 151, 152, 153, 154, 155, 157, 158, 165, 175, 184, 188, 189, 192, 193, 194, 195, 196, 197, 201, 202, 205, 210, 211, 212, 213, 214, 215, 216, 217, 218, 219, 221, 222, 224, 226
    transfer of, 86, 87, 152, 153, 154, 155, 175, 184, 188, 193, 195, 201, 202, 216, 217, 218, 219, 221, 222
Ericsson, Ronald, 162
euthanasia, 70, 214

Fallopian tubes, 150
family, 4, 27, 33, 36, 44, 47, 51, 53, 54, 55, 56, 57, 58, 60, 61, 62, 63, 64, 65, 66, 68, 70, 72, 75, 77, 78, 86, 92, 97, 132, 143, 151, 154, 157, 158, 163, 164, 166, 178, 181, 182, 185, 192, 210, 214, 217, 218, 222, 225, 226, 227
Farraris, Lucius, 8
fatherhood, 57, 58, 182, 183, 184, 185, 187, 188, 189, 190, 191, 192, 193, 200, 201, 202, 203, 204, 218, 219, 224, 225

Feinberg, Gerald, 115
feminism, 50, 73, 169, 198
fertilization, 3, 72, 85, 86, 87, 106, 107, 109, 110, 122, 143, 144, 146, 148, 150, 151, 152, 153, 154, 156, 158, 159, 160, 162, 165, 169, 176, 184, 185, 188, 191, 192, 193, 210, 211, 214, 215, 216, 217, 218, 219, 220, 221, 222
fetus, 3, 9, 10, 11, 12, 13, 14, 15, 17, 18, 19, 21, 22, 23, 24, 27, 28, 36, 37, 39, 40, 41, 42, 44, 52, 60, 66, 72, 91, 92, 97, 98, 99, 106, 131, 132, 133, 134, 135, 136, 137, 138, 139, 140, 142, 144, 175, 196, 197, 205, 210, 211, 212, 213, 214
    experimentation on, 3, 42, 131, 132, 133, 134, 135, 136, 138, 139, 140, 141, 142
    formed, 12, 13, 14, 17
    unformed (preformed), 12, 13, 14, 17
Feuerbach, 114
Fienus, Thomas, 14
Fitzgerald, Richard, 179
Fletcher, Joseph, 95, 115, 131, 150, 159, 184, 196, 202
Ford, James, 77
Fortier, Lise, 79
France, J., 162
Francke, Linda Bird, 21, 97
Francoeur, Robert, 126, 150, 183, 188, 197, 200
Frankl, Viktor, 48
freedom, 2, 27, 50, 52, 56, 85, 93, 95, 96, 98, 99, 105, 113, 119, 127, 128, 150, 159, 169, 180, 181, 182, 186
Freeman, Beverly, 149
Fromm, Erich, 96, 115, 116

gametes, 122, 162, 171, 180, 191, 192, 203, 211, 215, 217, 218, 219, 226
Garrigou-Lagrange, Reginald, 65
Gaylin, Wilfred, 140
genetic engineering, 106, 122, 123, 124, 125, 126, 127, 128, 129, 150, 186
gestation, extracorporeal, 87, 188, 195, 196, 198, 201
Giedion, Siegfried, 186
Gilder, George, 193, 198
Gilson, Etienne, 116, 117
God, 1, 4, 10, 12, 16, 23, 24, 25, 32, 39, 41, 54, 89, 93, 94, 95, 104, 105, 106, 107, 109, 110, 112, 113, 114, 115, 116, 117, 118, 119, 120, 121, 125, 126, 130, 146, 170, 171, 178, 196, 201, 203, 205, 206, 207, 208, 209, 210, 214, 216, 219, 222, 227
Gomel, Victor, 154
good of man, 103, 104, 105, 106, 159, 209
Gordon, Suzanne, 63
Granfield, David, 10
Gratian, 13
Greer, Germaine, 71
Gregory IX, Pope, 13
Gregory XIV, Pope, 8
Grisez, Germain, 10
Gursky v. Gursky, 190
Guttmacher, Alan, 31, 72
Gynec. Laser Surg., Int. Cong., 150

Häring, Bernard, 123, 153, 154, 184
Hammarskjöld, Dag, 30
Hardon, John A., S.J., 9, 10
Hellegers, André, 27, 134, 153
Hellman, Louise, 74
Hildebrand, Dietrich von, 1
Hippolytus, 16
Hirshhorn, Kurt, 134
Hitchcock, James, 73
Holbrook, David, 35
homicide, 12, 16, 17, 22, 24
Horkheimer, Max, 70
Humanae vitae, 109, 143, 208, 219, 222
husband, 53, 54, 55, 57, 58, 59, 63, 97, 132, 147,
    155, 159, 160, 161, 170, 171, 173, 174, 175,
    176, 178, 180, 181, 182, 183, 184, 188, 189,
    190, 191, 192, 194, 195, 200, 201, 202, 203,
    210, 217, 218, 219, 223
Huser, R. J., 8

illegitimacy, 68, 69, 77
infertility, 3, 145, 147, 149, 169, 176, 184, 185,
    199, 224
Innocent X, Pope, 9, 14, 15, 22
Innocent XI, Pope, 9, 14, 22
in vitro fertilization, 3, 85, 86, 87, 106, 110, 122,
    143, 144, 146, 148, 150, 152, 154, 156, 158,
    159, 160, 165, 169, 176, 184, 188, 191, 192,
    193, 214, 216, 218, 219, 221, 222
        heterologous, 217
        homologous, 217, 221, 222

Jacobsen, Cecil, 202
Jaffe, Frederick, 74
Jerome, St., 14, 16
Jesus Christ, 4, 11, 12, 13, 16, 17, 21, 43, 50, 52,
    54, 56, 65, 66, 70, 75, 90, 91, 93, 94, 113, 114,
    118, 126, 144, 147, 158, 169, 170, 172, 181,
    191, 200, 206, 207, 213, 218, 228
        Incarnation of, 88, 107, 159
John of Naples, 13, 14
John Paul II, Pope, 2, 47, 51, 104, 107, 108, 109,
    110, 111, 147, 156, 170, 171, 203, 206, 207,
    208, 209, 212, 213, 214, 215, 220, 228
Jonas, Hans, 140, 141
joy, 2, 24, 52, 53, 61, 66, 69, 85, 91, 118, 130, 153,
    172, 177
Juan de Lugo, 17

Kantner, John, 76
Kass, Leon, 119, 127, 147, 149, 150, 155, 156,
    157, 158
Keane, Noel, 176, 184, 199
Kerin, John, 163
Kirby (Justice), 132

Lappé, Marc, 140, 141
La Mettrie, 47
Lee, Philip, 75
Leibniz, Gottfried, 125, 126
LeShan, Eda, 63, 68
Lewis, C. S., 48, 156, 172
Leyland, Zoe, 158

Le Clézio, 38, 181
Liguori, Alphonsus, St., 17
Liley, William, 41, 82
Louisell, David, 136, 137, 141
love, 2, 4, 16, 18, 21, 23, 25, 30, 38, 41, 45, 51, 52,
    53, 54, 55, 61, 62, 64, 66, 70, 71, 72, 88, 94,
    96, 108, 109, 114, 117, 118, 121, 126, 146,
    147, 148, 151, 156, 157, 159, 168, 170, 171,
    172, 175, 181, 182, 186, 187, 191, 192, 193,
    198, 206, 208, 210, 217, 219, 220, 221, 222,
    223, 224, 225, 227
Lubac, Henri de, 114
Luker, Kristin, 74
Lukits, Ann, 23

MacIntyre, Alasdair, 128
Malahoff, Alexander, 179, 180
Malraux, André, 115, 118
Marcel, Gabriel, 51
Marcus, Joannis, 9
Maritain, Jacques, 51, 90, 95, 191
marriage, 18, 53, 57, 58, 63, 70, 73, 78, 86, 107,
    143, 144, 147, 169, 170, 171, 172, 179, 181,
    182, 184, 185, 189, 190, 192, 193, 200, 201,
    202, 208, 210, 215, 216, 217, 218, 219, 220,
    221, 222, 223, 224, 225, 226, 227
Marshner, William, 154
Martin of Braga, 16
Marx, Fr. Paul, 76
Marx, Karl
Mastroiani, Luigi, 154
Matheson (Justice), 84
May, William E.
May, William, 123, 124, 150, 156
McCarthy, Donald, 148
McCormick, Richard, 140, 153, 157
McLuhan, Marshall, 186
Mead, Margaret, 48
Mecklenburg, Marjory, 67
Medhurst, Alex, 59
Merton, Thomas, 118
Montgomery, Alastair, 144
Morgentaler, Henry, 40, 44
motherhood, 146, 173, 174, 175, 176, 177, 178,
    180, 181, 182, 183, 184, 185, 187, 188, 193,
    194, 195, 198, 199, 200, 201, 202, 203, 204,
    218, 219, 224, 225, 226
Muggeridge, Malcolm, 45, 53
murder, 9, 13, 23, 24, 37
Mystical Body of Christ, The*, 54, 65, 191

Nathanson, Bernard, 36, 41, 196
National Abortion Foundation, 75
National Institutes of Health, 134, 138
Nietzsche, Friedrich, 112, 114
Noonan, John, 17, 57, 60, 73, 77
Noyes, James and Bjorna, 175

Ontario Medical Association, 62
original sin, 24
Ovum Transfer Project, 194, 195

Packwood, Robert, 138
Pancoast, William, 188, 189

parenthood
consumerism in (toward children), 50,
69, 149, 172, 173, 176, 180, 184, 185
technological (in procreation), 183, 184,
185, 186, 187, 188, 189, 190, 191,
192, 193, 194, 196, 198, 200, 201,
202, 203, 204
Parker, Philip, 177, 199
Paul VI, Pope, 108, 109, 143, 206, 208, 209, 211,
222
Peck, Ellen, 68
Peel, John, 133
People v. Sorenson, 190
personalism, 51
Petrucci, Daniele, 196
Picard, Ellen, 44, 62
Pill, the (contraceptive), 69, 70, 71, 73, 74, 75, 76,
79, 187
Piux IX, Pope, 15, 23, 24
Pius XI, Pope, 19, 20, 65, 107, 108, 109, 110, 185,
209, 210, 218, 220, 221, 223, 224
Pius XII, Pope, 19, 65, 107, 108, 109, 110, 185,
209, 210, 218, 220, 221, 223, 224
Pl. Prnthd. of Mo. v. Danforth, 57, 60
Planned Parenthood, 31, 40, 57, 58, 60, 67, 68, 71,
72, 74, 79, 166
Poltawska, Wanda, 78
Popenoe, Paul, 70
Popes (on abortion), 17, 106
Gregory IX, 13
Gregory XIV, 8
Innocent XI, 9, 14, 22
Innocent X, 9, 14, 15, 22
John Paul II, 2, 47, 51, 104, 107, 108,
109, 110, 111, 147, 156, 170, 171,
203, 206, 207, 208, 209, 212, 213,
214, 215, 220, 228
Paul VI, 108, 109, 143, 206, 208, 209,
211, 222
Pius IX, 15, 23, 24
Pius XI, 19, 20, 65, 107, 108, 109, 110,
185, 209, 210, 218, 220, 221, 223,
224
Pius XII, 19, 65, 107, 108, 109, 110, 185,
209, 210, 218, 220, 221, 223, 224
Sixtus V, 8, 21
Pope J. XXIII Med-Mor Res Ctr, 147, 170
Potts, Malcolm, 79, 151
prenatal diagnosis, 211, 212
privacy, right to, 49, 55, 56, 74, 84, 141, 180, 185
pro-abortion position, 2, 7, 23, 26, 27, 29, 40, 72,
73, 92, 93, 175
pro-choice position, 27, 28, 29, 33, 36, 39, 41, 43,
44, 53, 92, 93, 94, 95, 97, 98, 175
pro-life position, 2, 26, 27, 29, 35, 39, 40, 41, 48,
62, 92, 98, 99, 212, 214
procreation, 27, 69, 70, 79, 80, 86, 106, 109, 147,
156, 159, 173, 176, 183, 187, 192, 193, 198,
201, 203, 205, 206, 208, 209, 210, 215, 216,
217, 219, 220, 221, 222, 223, 224, 225, 226,
227
Promethean perspective (abor.), 113, 115, 117,
118, 119, 120, 121
promiscuity, 77

Prot. of Human Subj., Nat. Com, 135, 137

Rahner, Karl, 113, 126
Ramsey, Paul, 42, 86, 87, 112, 120, 124, 125, 128,
134, 139, 140, 148, 149, 150, 152, 155, 156,
198, 202
Rankin, Catherine, 156
Ratzinger, Joseph Cardinal, 228
Raynaud, Theophile, 14
Reed, James, 71
Reid, Robert, 59
Resolve (organization), 2, 49, 59, 78, 84, 91, 92,
149
right (to have a child), 146, 159, 169, 224
Rios, Mario and Elsa, 158
Rock, John, 72
Roe v. Wade, 73, 74, 84, 94, 95, 136
Royal Commission on Population, 77

Safire, William, 35, 44
Sanchez, Thomas, 9, 14
Sanger, Margaret, 72
Sartre, Jean-Paul, 26, 114
Schwartz, Michael, 77
Semm, Kurt, 155
Septuagint (Scripture), 11, 12, 14, 15, 17
sex-preselection, 160, 161, 162, 163, 164, 165,
166, 167, 168, 169, 170, 171, 172
sexism, 168
Shumiatcher, Morris, 82
Siegal, Seymour, 139
Silander, Mark
Sixtus V, Pope, 8, 21
Smale, Janice, 192
Sobran, M. J., 28, 36
Solzhenitsyn, Alexander, 30
soul, 9, 10, 11, 12, 13, 14, 15, 17, 18, 21, 22, 24,
53, 66, 107, 116, 117, 172, 206, 207, 209, 211,
220
ensoulment, 9, 10, 11, 14, 17, 22
Soupart, Rene*, 152
sperm, 144, 146, 151, 152, 155, 158, 160, 161,
162, 168, 173, 174, 179, 180, 183, 185, 189,
190, 191, 192, 195, 201, 202, 216, 217, 218,
219, 223
Stein, Gertrude, 32
Steiner, George, 32
sterilization, 57, 77, 106, 145
Stern, William and Elizabeth, 178
Stiver, Judy, 179, 180
Stratton, Clifford, 143
Stumpf, Andrea, 201
Suenens, Leo Cardinal, 70, 71
Supreme Court of Ontario, 59
Supreme Court, 56, 57, 59, 62, 71, 73, 78, 82, 133,
136, 141, 190
surrogate motherhood, 173, 174, 175, 176, 178,
180, 181, 182, 184, 188, 198, 199, 200, 219,
226

Teresa of Calcutta, Mother
Tertullian, 12, 21
Theodore, Arbp. of Canterbury, 13
Theodoret, 12

Thrane, Baby, 175
Thrane, Denise, 175
Trounson, Alan, 157, 195
United Church of Canada, 93

Vatican Council II, 107
venereal disease, 41, 69, 77, 145, 166, 189
Verny, Tom, 197
viability, pre-, 135, 136

Warnock, Mary, 110, 152, 165
Watters, Wendell, 21
Waxman, Henry, 138
Weaver, Richard, 29
White, Byron (Justice), 58
Whitehead, Mary Beth, 178, 199
wife, 53, 54, 55, 57, 58, 59, 97, 132, 147, 159, 161,
    170, 171, 173, 174, 175, 179, 180, 181, 182,
    188, 189, 190, 191, 192, 194, 198, 199, 200,
    201, 202, 203, 210, 218, 219, 223
Will, George, 34, 122, 148
Wogaman, J. Philip, 93, 94
Wom. Com. Hlth. Ctr. v. Cohen, 61
Wood, Carl, 157, 195
Wylie, Philip, 131

Yassu, Thomas and Catherine, 61

Zelnik, Melvin, 76